Communications
in Computer and Information Science 362

Stefano Chessa   Stefan Knauth (Eds.)

Evaluating AAL Systems Through Competitive Benchmarking

International Competitions and Final Workshop
EvAAL 2012
July and September 2012
Revised Selected Papers

 Springer

Volume Editors

Stefano Chessa
Università di Pisa, Dipartimento di Informatica
Largo B. Pontecorvo 3, 56127 Pisa, Italy
and
CNR – Istituto di Scienza e Tecnologie dell'Informazione
Via Moruzzi 1, 56100 Pisa, Italy
E-mail: ste@di.unipi.it

Stefan Knauth
HFT – Stuttgart University of Applied Sciences
Schellingstr. 24, 70174 Stuttgart, Germany
E-mail: stefan.knauth@hft-stuttgart.de

ISSN 1865-0929   e-ISSN 1865-0937
ISBN 978-3-642-37418-0   e-ISBN 978-3-642-37419-7
DOI 10.1007/978-3-642-37419-7
Springer Heidelberg Dordrecht London New York

Library of Congress Control Number: 2013934554

CR Subject Classification (1998): C.4, C.3, K.4.2, I.2.10, I.4.8, C.2, C.5.3, H.4.2, J.3, J.2

Typesetting: Camera-ready by author, data conversion by Scientific Publishing Services, Chennai, India

Printed on acid-free paper

Springer is part of Springer Science+Business Media (www.springer.com)

Message from the Editors

We are pleased to present with this book the results of the 2012 edition of the EvAAL competition. Like the previous edition, the objective of this edition of EvAAL was to bring together different communities and research teams focusing on the problem of the evaluation and assessment of Ambient-Assisted Living (AAL) systems and services by means of a competition on selected themes related to AAL.

Following a consolidated approach, EvAAL 2012 adopted a bottom-up approach by focusing the competition on the evaluation of a simple component of AAL systems rather than on complex AAL systems, since this allows one to build gradually the evaluation methodologies, benchmarks, and tools in view of their application in the evaluation of more complex components and systems. In this respect, EvAAL represents an excellent opportunity to exploit the different expertise of the participants and organizers to refine and improve the evaluation methodologies and to consider new and open problems, evaluate alternative approaches, and, in general, to envision new research opportunities inherent to the evaluation of AAL systems.

This year's edition of EvAAL comprised two tracks: one on indoor localization and tracking, and one on activity recognition for AAL. Both tracks addressed relatively simple but yet significant problems for achieving context awareness in AAL systems. The track on indoor localization and tracking for AAL, which was already part of the previous edition of EvAAL, involved eight competitors representing of six countries (Canada, France, Germany, Spain, Switzerland, USA), while the activity recognition track, which was entirely new, involved four competing teams from Ireland, Japan, Spain, and USA. EvAAL almost doubled the number of participants with respect to the previous year.

The competition was organized as three major events: the competition on the track of indoor localization and tracking that was hosted by the living lab of the Polytechnic University of Madrid (Spain), on July 2–6, 2012; the competition on the activity recognition track that was hosted by the CIAmI Living Lab in Valencia (Spain), on July 9-13, 2012; and the concluding workshop held on September 24, 2012, in conjunction with the AAL Forum in Eindhoven (The Netherlands). The winners were announced at the final workshop.

This book contains, along with the introductions to the two tracks, the contributions of all the competitors that include a complete technical description of the competing artifacts and the report on the experience and the lessons learned by the teams during the competition.

We wish to conclude this preface with a special mention of all the organizers who contributed to a successful EvAAL 2012; the AALOA community (http://www.aaloa.org), the universAAL project (http://www.universAAL.org), the Giraff plus project (http://www.giraffplus.eu/), ASUS, and Texas Instruments for the support they gave to this initiative.

Above all, we wish to give a special word of thanks to the competitors, who were the prime actors of the competition and who, more than anybody else, made of EvAAL a fervid and lively event.

January 2013   Stefano Chessa
                                                                Stefan Knauth

Organization

Organizing Committee

General Chair

Stefano Chessa — University of Pisa and ISTI-CNR, Italy

Local Committee Co-chairs

Dario Salvi — Polytecnic University of Madrid, Spain
Juan Carlos Narajo
    Martinez — ITACA, Spain

Publication Co-chairs

Reiner Wichert — Fraunhofer IGD, Germany
Stefan Knauth — Stuttgart University of Applied Sciences,
    Germany

Publicity Co-chairs

Casper Dhal Marcussen — Region Syddanmark, Denmark
Francesco Potortì — ISTI-CNR, Italy

Dataset Management Chair

Juan Pablo Lazaro — TSB Soluciones Tecnologicas, Spain

Software Tools Chair

Dario Salvi — Polytecnic University of Madrid, Spain

Financial Chair

Francesco Furfari — ISTI-CNR, Italy

Track 1 on Indoor Localization for AAL Technical Program Committee

Chair

Paolo Barsocchi — ISTI-CNR, Italy

Members

Adriano Moreira	University of Minho, Portugal
Ivan Martinovic	University of Oxford, UK
Rainer Mautz	ETH, Switzerland
Binghao Li	University of New South Wales, Australia
Neal Patwari	University of Utah, USA
Cesar Benavente-Peces	Polytechnic University of Madrid, Spain
Dante I. Tapia	University of Salamanca, Spain
Hanke Sten	AIT Austrian Institute of Technology, Austria
Francesco Furfari	CNR-ISTI, Italy
Stefan Knauth	Stuttgart University, Germany
Tomás Ruiz-López	University of Granada, Spain
Andreas Braun	Fraunhofer Institute, Germany
Patricial Abril	Polytechnic University of Madrid, Spain
Francesco Potortì	CNR-ISTI, Italy
Ma Pilar Sala Soriano	Polytechnic University of Valencia, Spain
Michele Girolami	CNR-ISTI, Italy
Filipe Meneses	University of Minho, Portugal
Dario Salvi	Polytechnic University of Madrid, Spain

Track 2 on Activity Recognition for AAL Technical Program Committee

Chair

Juan Antonio Álvarez García	Universidad de Sevilla, Spain

Members

Alessio Micheli	University of Pisa, Italy
Alexander Kroener	DFKI, Germany
Arantxa Rentería	Tecnalia, Spain
Cecilio Angulo	Technical University of Catalonia, Spain
Daniel Roggen	ETHZ, Switzerland
Diane J. Cook	Washington State University, USA
Francesco Furfari	CNR, Italy
Francesco Potortì	CNR, Italy
Juan Carlos Augusto	University of Ulster, UK
Kazuya Murao	Kobe University, Japan
Mohammad-Reza (Saied) Tazari	Fraunhofer IGD, Germany
Reiner Wichert	Fraunhofer IGD, Germany
Roberta Giannantonio	Telecom Italia, Italy
Roozbeh Jafari	University of Texas at Dallas, USA
Stefano Chessa	University of Pisa, Italy

Table of Contents

Track 1

Indoor Localization and Tracking for AAL (Smart Home Living Lab, ETSIT UPM, Madrid, 2012)

Track 2

Activity Recognition for AAL (CIAMI Living Lab, Valencia, 2012)

Evaluating Indoor Localization Systems for AAL Environments

Paolo Barsocchi*

ISTI Institute of CNR, Pisa Research Area, via Moruzzi 1, I-56124, Pisa, Italy
`paolo.barsocchi@isti.cnr.it`

Abstract. EvAAL is an international competition aimed to evaluate and assess AAL systems components, services and platforms. Since at present the complexity of AAL systems makes their full comparison hardly possible, EvAAL adopts a gradual approach. This is done by dividing the problem into sub-problems. The full problem is deferred to a time when the knowledge on AAL systems evaluation is more developed. Specifically the second edition of EvAAL promotes competitions on specific AAL components such as indoor localization and activity recognition. This paper describes the technical aspect of the second edition of EvAAL on the special theme of Indoor Localization and Tracking for AAL.

Keywords: AAL, localization, tracking.

1 Motivation

Localization is a key component of many AAL systems, since the user position can be used for detecting user's activities, activating devices, opening doors, etc. While in outdoor scenarios Global Positioning System (GPS) constitute a reliable and easily available technology, in indoor scenarios GPS is largely unavailable.

Several systems have been proposed for indoor localization, which can be classified based on the signal types (infrared, ultrasound, ultra-wideband, and radio frequency), signal metrics (AOA - angle of arrival, TOA - time of arrival, TDOA - time difference of arrival, and RSS - received signal strength), and the metric processing methods (triangulation and scene profiling) [1]. Each solution has advantages and shortcomings, which, in most cases, can be summarized in a trade-off between precision and installation complexity (and thus costs).

In practice, although indoor localization has been a research topic for several decades, there is still not a de-facto standard. Moreover, localization in AAL applications has specific requirements due to the fact that AAL systems must be deployed in homes. In particular, localization system for AAL should be well hidden, easy to install and configure, and reliable. For these reasons EvAAL includes a track on indoor localization.

---

* This work was supported in part by the European Commission in the framework of the FP7 project universAAL under Contract 247950.

S. Chessa and S. Knauth (Eds.): EvAAL 2012, CCIS 362, pp. 1–5, 2013.

2   Benchmarks

The score for measurable criteria described in Section 3 for each competing artifact was evaluated by means of benchmark tests. We chose the Smart Home Living Lab at the Technical University of Madrid [2] in Spain as site of the competition because it is well suitable for a real-time competition, meaning that a real human user has to be localized in a real home scenario. During the benchmark test, a user wears the equipment the competitors require to carry (if any) and moves along a set of predefined paths (Figure 2). While moving, the localization data produced by the localization system of the competitor are collected in real time by the data collection tool that automatically evaluates the score. Each localization system is requested to produce localization data (in bi-dimensional coordinates) with a frequency of 2 Hz.

The competing systems have also access to the domotic equipment of the Living Lab, therefore the localization algorithms can exploit the information produced by these devices as consequence of the movements and actions of the user. For this reason the benchmarks also include actions such as turning on/off lights or opening doors that are detected by the domotic equipment of the Living Lab and provided to the localization systems in form of "contextual" events. The benchmarks are divided into three phases.

- Phase 1. In this scenario the localization systems have to locate a person inside an Area of Interest (AoI). AoIs represent areas that can have a specific meaning in an AAL application. Examples of AoI can be specific rooms (kitchen, bedroom, etc.) or areas where appliances are located (close to the fridge, on the bed etc.). Each system is requested to identify 6 big AoIs (representing rooms) and 4 small AoIs (representing points of interest for the user). The user moves along predefined paths and stops inside each AoI for at least 5 seconds (Figure 1).
- Phase 2. In this scenario, the user has to be located while moving in the living lab along pre-defined paths. During this phase only the person to be localized is inside the Living Lab. This benchmark uses two paths: one 54 steps long (path 1 in Figure 2), and one 94 steps long (path 2 in Figure 2). Each path includes 3 waiting points, where the user has to stay still in the same position for 5 seconds.
- Phase 3. This scenario is similar to the second phase, with the difference that another user (a disturber) moves in the living lab together with the primary user. In this scenario only the primary user has to be localized as in the previous scenario. The disturbing user follows different, predefined paths, also activating domotic equipment, but at least 2 meters away from the user. In this scenario the paths followed by the user are path 3 (80 steps long) and path 2, while the disturber paths are path 2 and path 1, respectively.

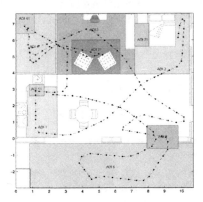 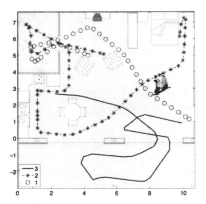

Fig. 1. The AoIs and the path of the user   **Fig. 2.** The three different paths

3   Evaluation Criteria

In order to evaluate the competing localization systems, the localization track uses a set of criteria weighted according to their relevance and importance for AAL applications. The localization track uses five criteria:

- Accuracy (weight: 25%). It expresses the degree to which the competing system is able to correctly localize the user. Accuracy is calculated by computing the error distance between each localization sample sent by the competitor and the reference position. Accuracy is evaluated in two different ways:
  - Phase 1: the accuracy is measured as the fraction of time in which the localization system provides the correct information about presence or not in a given AoI. The number of correctly guessed AoIs is averaged on the number of guessable AoIs.
  - Phases 2 and 3: the euclidean distance between the coordinates sent by the competitor and the reference position is computed at every sample, then the 75th percentile of the errors is computed.
- Availability (weight: 20%). Represents the fraction of time the localization system is active and responsive. The availability is measured as the ratio between the number of produced localization data and the number of expected data.
- Installation complexity (weight: 15%). It measures the effort required to install the AAL localization system in a home. It is measured as a function of the person-minutes of work needed to complete the installation.
- User acceptance (weight: 25%). It expresses how much the localization system is invasive in the user's daily life and thereby the impact perceived by the user. This parameter is estimated with a simple questionnaire that considers aspects of usability.

- Interoperability (weight: 15%). Measures the degree to which the system is easy to integrate with other systems. This parameter is fundamental in AAL scenarios, as localization can be exploited by other applications to offer advanced services. Also the interoperability is measured with a questionnaire that considers aspects of integrability.

All these metrics are then normalized to a common 0 to 10 scale and mixed with a weighted average.

4   Reference Localization System

The reference localization system was composed by predetermined coordinates of the paths followed by the user during the competition. As shown in Figure 3, the Living Lab's floor is covered with marks (with different colors to distinguish the right and left foot) that indicate each single step the user has to follow. In order to facilitate the installation and removal of the paths the marks are put on a wooden bar. The user is synchronized by a digital metronome that indicates the right cadence (one beep one step), guaranteeing that the user repeats the same paths at almost the same speed for every competitor.

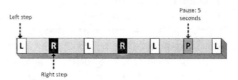

Fig. 3. The reference localization system: the black marks are related to the right foot while the white ones are related to the left foot. Marks denoted with "P" denote a stop of the user for a given time.

5   Contestants and Technologies

Seven teams were accepted to the indoor localization competition, namely CAR (from the Centre for Automation and Robotics, Spain), LOCOSmotion (from the University of Duisburg-Essen, Germany), OwlPS (from the Institute Femto-st, France), CPS Group @ Utah (from the University of Utah, USA), TAIS (from the University of Sevilla , Spain), iLoc+ (from Stuttgart University of Applied Sciences and iHomeLab at Lucerne University of Applied Sciences), and Smart-Condo (from the University of Alberta, Canada). Moreover, Lambda4 (from Hamburg, Germany) participates as guest team. A short description of these systems is as follows:

CAR, Spain -   *Gold Medal.* This system is based on the fusion of two complementary technologies; i.e. Inertial integration and RFID trilateration. The Inertial solution uses an IMU (Inertial Measurement Unit) mounted on the foot of the person while the IMU approach estimates the user's trajectory shape.

LOCOSmotion, Germany. It is an acceleration-assisted WLAN-based tracking system based on fingerprinting technique. In order to achieve high update rates and to capture movements, this system augments the fingerprinting information with acceleration measurements.

OwlPS, France - *Bronze Medal.* This system is WLAN-based localization system, that exploits the RSS to infer the user's position. OwlPS can be used as both fingerprinting-based system or trilateration-based system.

Lambda4, Germany - *Guest Team.* It is a system that use the measured phase between the transmitter and a receiver which has to be carried by the person to be localized.

CPS Group @ Utah, USA - *Silver Medal.* It is a device-free localization and tracking system, where people to be located do not carry any device. A static deployed wireless sensor network measures the received power on its links and locates people based on the variations caused by the movements of people.

TAIS, Spain. This system is based on RSS fingerprinting technique. The Manhattan distance metric is used to evaluate the user's position.

iLoc+, Germany/Switzerland. it is an ultrasound based system using a transmitter which has to be carried by the person to be localized, and about 25 reference nodes in the lab.

Smart-Condo, Canada. The knowledge of both the coordinates and the mounting angle of where the motion sensors have been placed is used by this system. In order to estimating the user's position the localization algorithm use a center-of-mass calculation and a tracking system.

6   Conclusions

Feedbacks from competitors and workshop audience were encouraging. For this reason we are currently planning EvAAL 2013, which will keep the tracks on indoor localization and on activity recognition. EvAAL 2013 will also add a new track on companion robots for AAK. Further reading about the organization aspects of the competition are available on the official EvAAL website [3].

References

1. Liu, H., Darabi, H., Banerjee, P., Liu, J.: Survey of wireless indoor positioning techniques and systems. IEEE Transactions on Systems, Man, and Cybernetics, Part C, 1067–1080 (2007)
2. Smart Home Living Lab web site, http://smarthouse.lst.tfo.upm.es
3. EvAAL web site, http://evaal.aaloa.org/

Indoor Position System Based on a Zigbee Network

A. Verónica Medina, José A. Gómez, José A. Ribeiro, and Enrique Dorronzoro

Grupo TAIS
Escuela Técnica Superior de Ingeniería Informática
Dpto. de Tecnología Electrónica
Universidad de Sevilla
Avda. Reina Mercedes s/n, 41014 Sevilla, Spain
{vmedina,jgomezdte,josriblim}@us.es, enriquedz@dte.us.es
http://matrix.dte.us.es/grupotais/

Abstract. TAIS group has developed an indoor position system prototype based on a fingerprint positioning algorithm. The prototype uses IEEE 802.15.4 mote and BitCloud Stack, a full-featured ZigBee Compliant, second generation embedded software stack from Atmel. The design requirements of the prototype were only to determine the actual position in a room of a user in a building, so the prototype accuracy is room accuracy. TAIS group decided to compete in the second edition of EvAAL Competition. This paper presents all the step made to adapt the prototype to the EvAAL environment, the found drawbacks and the obtained results. One of the most important drawback was that the Smart House Living Lab of the Polytechnic University of Madrid has only two rooms, the required accuracy was meters (error less than or equal to 0,5 meters the higher score, higher than 4 meters no score) and the room accuracy was substituted by areas of interest so the behavior of our prototype was going to work was an incognita.

Keywords: IEEE 802.15.4, RSSI, Centroid, Indoor position, ZigBee, WSN.

1 Introduction

Wireless Sensor Networks (WSNs) are present in many applications for solving data acquisition process in researching fields like Ambient Assisted Living [1][2][3][4] or Smart building [5][6][7][8][9]. Depending on its applications, ambient or user sensors and actuators can be used for making decisions. The knowledge of a subject's position is very useful in these kinds of systems because depending on it the decisions to be made are different.

As stated in [11][12], an amount of indoor location tracking systems have been proposed in the literature, based on Radio Frequency (RF) signals, ultrasound, infrared, or some combination of modalities. One of the most popular is using RF signal strength to determine the location of a mobile node applying different strategies. One of those is to use empirical measurements of received radio signals, known as RSSI, Receiver Signal Strength Indicator, to estimate location. By

S. Chessa and S. Knauth (Eds.): EvAAL 2012, CCIS 362, pp. 6–16, 2013.

recording a database of radio "signatures" along with their known locations, a mobile node position can be estimated by acquiring the actual signature and comparing it to the known signatures in the database, also known as fingerprints [10]. There is an intrinsic error in the use of RSS for localization purposes as stated in [16].

We have developed [13] a similar system to the one presented in [12], called MoteTrack, which localized a subject in a room of a building. The prototype uses different motes, Meshnetics´ ones, with other RCB (microcontroller and transceiver) and, also, different software, the BitCloud Stack[1] [15], a ZigBee PRO certified platform [14], an application layer stack, not a MAC (Medium Access Control) layer stack. This prototype was used in a research project[2] that tried to make an Intelligent Building. The Building had to adapt the environment to make it users feel comfortable by controlling air-conditioning, music, etc. The users of the building had to carry a mote (the mobile mote) and the decision maker software informed the actuator software to change the environments as user requirements using the output of our system (estimated position and sensors information) and other parameters they estimated. The focus of that research project was only an accuracy of room positioning.

In section 2 an overview of the prototype is introduced. Section 3 shows how the prototype is implemented and how the data are collected. The deployment and adaptation to EvAAL is presented in section 4. The results of the EvAAL test in the Living Lab in Madrid is shown in section 5. Finally conclusions are established in section 6.

2   Prototype Overview

In our prototype, a building or other area is populated with a number of Meshnetics´ motes acting as fixed nodes, one of them being the coordinator, C, and a set of mobile nodes, the ones whose position is going to be determined. Each fixed node sends to C periodic beacon messages, beacon 2, which consist of an n-tuple of the format {MobileID, RSSI}, where n is the number of mobile nodes, MobileID is a unique identifier of a mobile node, and RSSI is the signal strength which each fixed node received the last beacon message sent by MobileID node. The beacon message sent by a mobile node is different from the one sent by a fixed node, to differ one from others, the mobile node beacon messages are called beacon 1. Not all fixed motes receive beacon 1 messages, this depend on the coverage area. In this case they send a beacon 2 a zero value in RSSI.

The location estimation of the mobile nodes consists of a two-phase process: an offline collection of reference signatures followed by an online location estimation.

---

[1] Atmel acquires MeshNetics´ ZigBee Intellectual Properties
[2] Health Intelligent Technologies Oriented to Health and comfort in Interior Environments (TECNO-CAI) approved project at the fifth call of CENIT program by the Innovation Science Ministry of Spain (CDTI and Ingenio 2010 Program).

2.1   Offline Collection

As in other signature-based systems, the reference signature database is acquired manually by a user with a mobile node and a PC connected to C. Each reference signature, shown as black dots in Figure 1, consists of a set of signature tuples of the form {sourceID, meanRSSI}, where sourceID is the fixed node ID and meanRSSI is the mean RSSI of a set of beacon messages received over some time interval. Each signature is mapped to a known location by the user acquiring the signature database (P1-P5 in Figure 1).

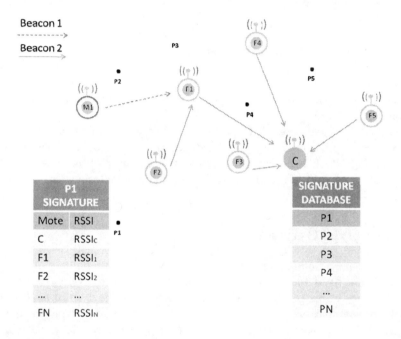

Fig. 1. System Overview. M1 is a mobile node, F1-F5 are fixed nodes, and C is the coordinator, also a fixed node. M1 periodically sends a beacon message, beacon 1, to inform the others nodes that is present. Each fixed node that receives beacon 1, saves the RSSI of that message in a table. Fixed node periodically sends a message to C, beacon 2, to inform about the RSSI that they have received from mobiles node, M1 in this case.

2.2   Location Estimation

Given a mobile node's received signature, s, received from the fixed nodes, and the reference signature set R, the mobile node's location can be estimated as follows. The first step is to compute the signature distances, from s to each reference signature $r_i \in R$. We employ the Manhattan distance metric,

$$M(r,s) = \sum_{t \in T} |\, RSSI(t)r - RSSI(t)s \,| \tag{1}$$

where T is the set of signatures tuples presented in both signature, $RSSI(i)r$ is the RSSI value in the signature appearing in signature r_i and $RSSI(i)s$ is the RSSI value in the signature appearing in signature s.

Given the set of signature distances, the location of a mobile node can be calculated in several ways. We consider the centroid of the set of signatures within some ratio of the nearest reference signature. Given a signature s, a set of reference signatures R, and the nearest signature $r^* = argmin_{r \,\in\, R} M(r, s)$, we select all reference signatures $r \in R$ that satisfy

$$\frac{M(r,s)}{M(r*,s)} < c \tag{2}$$

for some constant c, empirically-determined. The geographic centroid of the locations of this subset of reference signatures is then taken as the mobile node's position. Small values of c work well, generally between 1.1 and 1.2. If c=1 the position estimation is the position of the nearest signature saved in the signature database.

3   Implementation and Data Collection

Our system is implemented by using Meshnetics´ motes, Meshbean development board. We have used those motes because they have leds, buttons, additional sensors and other sensors can easily be connected to them for the purpose applications of this indoor position system, ambient living and smart buildings, so for prototyping works quite well. They also have a USART (Universal Synchronous/Asynchronous Receiver Transmitter) accessible by a USB connector, so a PC can be connected via a USB port, emulating a COM port, for both programming and receiving information, in our case beacons and sensor values.

A Meshnetics´mote is shown in Figure 2. This mote can have an integrated PCB or an external antenna. This affects only the range of coverage. In the prototype we use the one with external antenna. This mote has a MCU (MicroController Unit) wireless, called ZigBit, a compact 802.15.4/ZigBee module. It integrates both the ATmega1281 microcontroller and AT86RF212 transceiver of ATMEL so the AVR tools are necessary for programming purposes.

The BitCloud Stack has been used for software implementation. A full-featured, next generation embedded software stack from Atmel. BitCloud is fully compliant with ZigBee® PRO and ZigBee standards for wireless sensing and control. It provides an augmented set of APIs which, while maintaining compliance with the standard, offer extended functionality designed.

Fig. 2. Meshbean development board

In ZigBee, there are three kinds of devices, each one having its own purpose:

1. Coordinator (C): A full function device (FFD) that it is in charge of creating the PAN (Personal Area Network) and typically is the point of the WSN to acquire all sensors information from all the other motes to be shown in a computer. The icon used to represent this device is a filled circle, Figure 1 shows one.

2. Router (R): A FFD that it is in charge of routing when the range of coverage requires this capability, so it is possible to have dynamic topologies. The icon used to represent this device is a small filled circle inside a circle, Figure 1 shows six.

3. End device (ED): A reduced function device (RFD) that is always slept (to reduce consumption) and only wakes up to do a specific task, for instance, to send sensor information to the WSN, typically directed toward C. The icon used in Figure 1 is a not filled circle.

A ZigBee WSN is composed of one C, many EDs and many Rs. Each kind of devices can receive what the others transmit if they are in the same range of coverage, because the transmission media is shared by all of them. But not all the received information is processed (the explanation of why this is that way is out of the scope of this paper).

Atmel also provides a demo, called WSN demo, to help development tasks. The demo is prepared to create a dynamic ZigBee topology, controlled by the ZigBee´s Network layer. There is no positioning function in this demo so we have to modify the WSN Demo[3] source code to do so.

3.1   WSN Demo Modifications

As explained in section 2, to determinate the position, we require two kinds of beacons, beacon1 and beacon2. Beacon 1 is used to inform other devices that a

---

[3] This code was also supplied by Atmel.

mobile mote is present and beacon2 is used to inform C the RSSI value that a fixed mote receives from a mobile one for location estimation. To send both beacons in WSN the information saved in a table at the network layer called neighbor table has been used. This table registers all the FFD (motes that are C o R) that are in the range of coverage of a certain mote and for each one it registers the RSSI value of the received signal from that mote. Periodically, a FFD device sends a Zigbee Network layer message to inform others that it is in the WSN. This message is used by neighbor motes to measure the RSSI value of the received signal and to save it in their own neighbor table. So beacon 1 is automatically sent by the protocol stack. As only FFD can send this kind of message, the mobile motes have to be R, as shown in Figure 1.

The WSN demo code in motes has been changed to send periodically beacon 2 messages, for doing so, a search has to be done in the neighbor table to find out if the mobile mote is in its range of coverage, if so, the beacon 2 is sent to C with the required information as explained in section 3. As neighbor tables are only in FFDs, fixed motes have also to be R.

4   Deployment

The prototype was deployed over half floor of our Department Area, measuring roughly 225 m^2. The first step we did, was to test how the different kind of materials affect the RSSI value, taking into account those results, and that a mote can cover an area of 4-5 meters, we determined that with a number of 7 fixed motes is enough (Figure 3).

As shown in Figure 3, there are 11 rooms (room number G1.25 is the telecommunications room and doesn´t belong to our Department), being six of them double sized than the others and counting the halls as room, numbered from 1 to 3 (left to right). We determined that with two signature points for small rooms and four signature points for big rooms were enough. Halls had more troubles because signals propagated easily so we empirically determined to have a point every 3 meters. In total, we have 46 signature points placed as shown in Figure 3, crosses represent fixed motes, being C the mote called Mote 0, and black dots represent signature points. A similar determination have been done in Living Lab in Madrid, in this case the area is about 100 m^2 less than our Department Area. Because there were only one room and the bathroom, we estimate that with 5 fixed motes (they are shown in their approximate placement) and 27 signature points should be enough. Figure 4 shows the Living Lab area deployment taking the AOIs (Areas of Interest) into account.

Once all the signature points are determined, next step is to create the signature point database. It is an off-line process where the same Windows application for positioning is used to take signatures information for a period of time. The mean value of each received signature is calculated and saved in the signature database. All the received signatures in each signature points are also saved in a log file to be analyzed afterward in order to change later the signature database if it is necessary.

The required time for this phase depends on the number of samples used to calculate the RSSI mean value and the numbers of signature points to be determined, obviously the larger is the area, the more points are needed.

To separate positioning software application over the different deployment places, a floor plan is included, in charge of binding coordinates and rooms identifications.

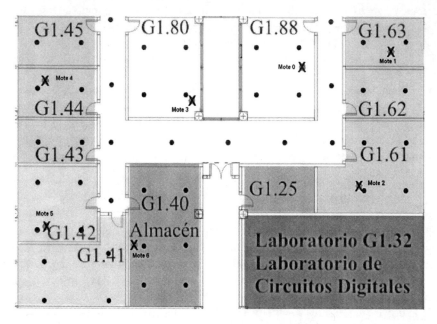

Fig. 3. Signature points. The six fixed motes, labeled as Mote 0 to 6, shown in their real placement.

Once the signature point database is created, the system is ready to determine the online position of a mobile mote. Figure 5 shows the computer software prototype used adapted to Living Lab. As it is shown, we not only determine the position of more than one mobile mote, number 1 to 4, but also the value of two of the sensors that those motes have, light in Figure 5, and temperature. In the online phase, simultaneously, all the acquired information by all the received signatures is saved in a log file in order to be able to make further analysis, and also information like time, the x , y estimated coordinates, battery charge and others extra values extracted through the integrated sensors; in this case light, temperature and battery. The adapted prototype also receives the domotic bus event that the Living Lab equipment generated but this information is not used in the positioning estimation due to time restrictions (the prototype was adapted to EvAAL in one month).

It is also possible to process the acquired information in order to make advices or send it via Internet, for instance to a hospital.

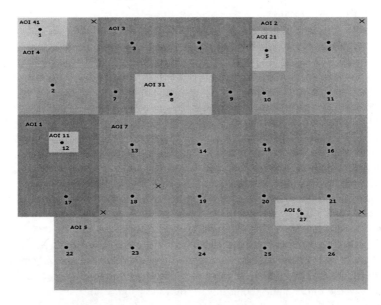

Fig. 4. Living Lab area deployment. AOIs are shown in different gray scales. Fixed motes are the cross dots.

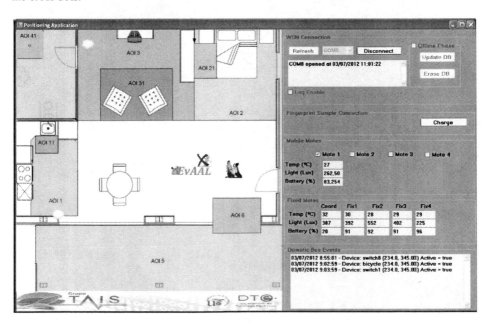

Fig. 5. Positioning User Interface adapted to the Living Lab plan view

5   Prototype Tests

Our prototype was tested in order to know if it is possible to determine if a mobile mote is placed in a room, i.e., it doesn´t matter exactly where it is inside de room, so the precision required was not very high. This has been this way, because, as mention before, the kind of applications for whom our indoor position solution was tested didn´t require more precision.

Based on empirical measurements, we determined that the precision of our system is about 77%, i.e., the right room was determined in that percentage being the accuracy among 0 meter to less than 1 meter from the real position. The rest were bad position determination, not the right room, but the accuracy was among 0,5 meters to less than 4 meters from the real position.

All the competitors knew the evaluation criteria before the test day in Living Lab, in our case, we didn´t pay attention because we were focused on adapting our prototype to the Living Lab. We didn´t even have time left to test correctly the adapted prototype prepared to the EvAAL. For a quick testing, we deployed the Living Lab in two of our Laboratories, marking on the floor the different AOIs as shown in Figure 6. The emulation was not quite good due to the fact that there were a wall between the kitchen and the living-room zone (Figure 7).

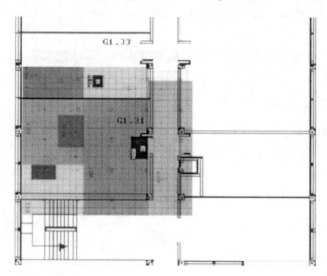

Fig. 6. Living Lab emulation in Electronic Technology Department Labs

The results weren´t very good but they were worse than we expected. In our test, the point to point accuracy was 3,1 meters in percentile 75, the result in Living Lab was 4,6 meters. The AOI accuracy result in our labs was 59% being 40% the right AOI and 19% not the right AOI but a subarea in that AOI. In Madrid we got a 20% in AOI accuracy which the right AOI score was 5,5%. So the wall in the labs we tested the adapted prototype made the emulation not as real as we thought. In addition, we forgot to save the log file during the test in Madrid, so we didn´t get any sample data to make further studies later on to compare with our test in Seville.

Fig. 7. Living Lab emulation photo

6   Conclusions

In this paper we have presented a prototype for an indoor position system based on BitCloud Stack over a WSN. The system requires to populate an area with a certain numbers of motes depending on the extension, to include the plant view (for instance Living lab one) in the PC application software where the position is going to be determined, and a calibration phase to fulfill the signature database. Once the system is calibrated, it is ready to be used.

As presented, the system could be easily applied to any applications of Assisted Ambient Living or Smart Building adding the specific sensors both to the mobile mote to acquire user information and the fixed mote to acquire environmental information, as all data gathered are received in a central point they should be processed for any purpose and send them via Internet if it is required. There is also a log file available both in the off-line and on-line phase for further analysis of data received.

The prototype has been adapted to the EvAAL competition environment and tested. The results weren´t very good but the experience has made us change our mind. Now we know how the goodness and badness of our prototype can be tested and all the things that have to be taken into account to design a system that real users have to use.

Acknowledgments. This work has been carried out within the framework of the research program: (P08-TIC-3631) – Multimodal Wireless interface (IMI) funded by the Regional Government of Andalusia.

References

1. Hristova, A., Bernardos, A.M., Casar, J.R.: Context-aware services for ambient assisted living: A case-study. First International Symposium on Applied Sciences on Biomedical and Communication Technologies. In: ISABEL 2008 (2008)
2. Figueiredo, C.P., Gama, O.S., Pereira, C.M., Mendes, P.M., Silva, S., Domingues, L., Hoffmann, K.-P.: Autonomy Suitability of Wireless Modules for Ambient Assisted Living Applications: WiFi, ZigBee, and Proprietary Devices. In: Sensor Technologies and Applications, SENSORCOMM (2010)

3. Hong, S., De Florio, V., Ning, G., Blondia, C.: Towards. 2008. Building Virtual Community for Ambient Assisted Living. In: 16th Euromicro Conference on Parallel, Distributed and Network-Based Processing (2008)
4. Sun, H., De Florio, V., Gui, N., Blondia, C.: PRomises and Challenges of Ambient Assisted Living Systems. In: Sixth International Conference on Information Technology: New Generations, ITNG 2009, pp. 1201–1207 (2009)
5. Martin, H., Bernardos, A.M., Bergesio, L., Tarrio, P.: Analysis of key aspects to manage wireless sensor networks in ambient assisted living environments. In: 2nd International Symposium on Applied Sciences in Biomedical and Communication Technologies, ISABEL 2009, pp. 1–8 (2009)
6. Dietrich, D., Bruckner, D., Zucker, G., Palensky, P.: Communication and Computation in Buildings: A Short Introduction and Overview. IEEE Transaction on Industrial Electronic 57(11) (2010)
7. Chen, P.-W., Ou, K.-S., Chen, K.-S.: IR indoor localization and wireless transmission for motion control in smart building applications based on Wiimote technology. In: SICE Annual Conference 2010 (2010)
8. Han, C., Chou, P., Duri, S., Hui, L., Reason, J.: The Design and Implementation of a Smart Building Control, pp. 255–262 (2009)
9. Snoonian, D.: Smart buildings. IEEE Spectrum 40(8), 18–23 (2003), doi:10.1109/MSPEC
10. Bahl, P., Padmanabhan, V.: RADAR: an in-building RF-based user location and tracking system. In: INFOCOM, pp. 775–784 (2000)
11. Lorincz, K., Welsh, M.: MoteTrack: A Robust, Decentralized Approach to RF-Based Location Tracking. In: Strang, T., Linnhoff-Popien, C. (eds.) LoCA 2005. LNCS, vol. 3479, pp. 63–82. Springer, Heidelberg (2005)
12. Konrad, L., Matt, W.: MoteTrack: A Robust, Decentralized Approach to RF-Based Location Tracking. To Appear in Springer Personal and Ubiquitous Computing, Special Issue on Location and Context-Awareness (2006) ISSN: 1617-4909, (Print) 1617-4917
13. Medina, A.V., Gómez, I., Romera, M., Gómez, J.A., Dorronzoro, E.: Indoor Position System based on BitCloud Stack for Ambient Living and Smart Buildings. In: 3rd International ICST Conference on IT Revolutions, Córdoba, Spain (2011)
14. ZigBee, 2009 RF4CE Specification. Version 1.00. ZigBee Document 094945r00ZB (March 17, 2009)
15. Medina, A.V., Gómez, J.A., Rivera, O., Dorronzoro, E., Merino, M.: Fingerprint Indoor Position System based on OpenMAC. In: International Conference on Wireless Information Networks and Systems, Sevilla, Spain (2011)
16. Potorti, F., Corucci, A., Nepa, P., Furfari, F., Barsocchi, P., Buffi, A.: Accuracy limits of in-room localisation using RSSI. Antennas and Propagation Society International Symposium, 2009. In: APSURSI 2009, June 1-5. IEEE (2009)

LOCOSmotion: An Acceleration-Assisted Person Tracking System Based on Wireless LAN

Ngewi Fet, Marcus Handte, Stephan Wagner, and Pedro José Marrón

Networked Embedded Systems,
University of Duisburg-Essen, Germany
{ngewi.fet,marcus.handte,stephan.j.wagner,pjmarron}@uni-due.de
http://www.nes.uni-due.de

Abstract. Pervasive computing envisions seamless and distraction-free support for tasks by means of context-aware applications. Location information is a key component in many context-aware applications. This article describes the design, implementation and evaluation of LOCOSmotion, an acceleration-assisted WLAN-based tracking system. The basis of localization in LOCOSmotion is WLAN fingerprinting as proposed in RADAR [2]. In order to achieve high location update rates, it augments fingerprinting with dead-reckoning using acceleration measurements to capture movement. To evaluate the performance of LOCOSmotion, this article presents the results of a set of laboratory experiments as well as results of the EvAAL 2012 competition in Madrid. Based on the lessons learned from deploying and using LOCOSmotion during EvAAL, we identify future directions for possible optimizations.

Keywords: Indoor Localization, Tracking, Pervasive Computing.

1 Introduction

Pervasive computing envisions seamless and distraction-free support for tasks by means of context-aware applications. In many of these applications, knowledge about the user's location is a key requirement. This holds especially true for applications in the area of Ambient Assisted Living where it is often necessary to track the user's location in order to detect dangerous situations, abnormal behavior or to issue location-dependent reminders. In outdoor scenarios, the global availability of GPS can provide a suitable basis for tracking. However, the lack of GPS signals in many indoor environments makes this approach ill-suited for precise tracking in indoor scenarios. Thus, in recent years, a lot of research has been focused on developing alternative localization solutions.

Rapid advances in wireless communication technologies and the miniaturization of consumer electronics have led to an increase in the deployment and accessibility of wireless local area networks (WLAN) and WLAN-capable devices. Smartphones – which are the fastest growing segment of computing devices [17] – are almost all capable of accessing WLAN. This presents a big opportunity to leverage and reuse the existing infrastructure for the development of localization systems without incurring extra costs for setup and maintenance. Also,

S. Chessa and S. Knauth (Eds.): EvAAL 2012, CCIS 362, pp. 17–31, 2013.
© Springer-Verlag Berlin Heidelberg 2013

most of the smartphones come packed with a plethora of other sensors such as accelerometer, magnetometer, gyroscope, lux sensors and more.

In this article, we describe the design, implementation and evaluation of LO-COSmotion, an acceleration-assisted WLAN-based tracking system. The basis of localization in LOCOSmotion is WLAN fingerprinting as proposed in RADAR [2]. In order to achieve high location update rates during tracking, it augments fingerprinting with dead-reckoning using acceleration measurements to capture movement. To evaluate the performance of LOCOSmotion, we present the results of a set of laboratory experiments as well as results of the EvAAL 2012 competition in Madrid. Based on the lessons learned from deploying and using LOCOSmotion during EvAAL, we identify future directions for possible optimizations.

The rest of this article is structured as follows; in the next section, we describe related work in the field of indoor localization. Section 3 describes the main design and development considerations, and thereafter the basic deployment and setup of LOCOSmotion. Section 4 presents an evaluation of the performance of the system both at our lab and at the EvAAL 2012 competition in Madrid. Based on these results, we present experiences and lessons learned in Section 5. Section 6 presents the next steps and future directions for improving LOCOSmotion and finally, we conclude the article with a short summary in Section 7.

2   Related Work

Many different systems have been developed for indoor localization and they employ different technologies to perform location estimation. There are vision-based systems [5], which make use of cameras and computer vision for location estimation. Other indoor localization systems have been developed on the basis of infrared light [19], ultrasound [20], or magnetic signals [8]. However, in this section, we will focus on RF-based systems since they are closest to our system in design.

2.1   WLAN

RADAR [2] is one of the earliest systems which uses WLAN signals for indoor localizaton. The system uses fingerprints where a fingerprint is a tuple of location coordinates and signal strengths of visible WLAN networks. In a training phase, WLAN fingerprints are collected at all locations in the target area to form a radio map. During localization, WLAN scans are matched against this radio map to estimate the location of the user. Conceptually, our system is an extension of RADAR with accelerometer-based enhancements for tracking.

Building a radio map by means of fingerprinting can be labor-intensive, hence there have been other systems which seek to reduce the mapping effort by performing simultaneous localization and mapping [13] or using signal propagation models[10][21]. ARIADNE [10] proposes to collect only a single measurement and together with a two-dimensional construction floor plan, generates a radio map for localization. Xiang et al in [21] use a signal distribution training scheme and achieve an accuracy of 5m with 90% probability for moving devices. The main limitations of indoor localization using propagation models are that due to the complexity of signal propagation in indoor environments, they either result in a high modelling effort or they only consider some of the variables affecting the signal distribution which reduces their precision.

2.2   RFID

There are also several indoor localization systems based on RFID technologies. RFID is a technology for automated identification of objects and people [11]. An RFID system typically comprises a tag and a reader. There are both active - where the tag has a battery - and passive - where the tag is induced by the reader - RFID based localization systems. LANDMARC [15] is an RFID-based localization system which uses reference tags. It uses multiple reference tags instead of multiple readers to mitigate cost. SpotOn [16] is another RFID based localization system which uses custom RFID readers to detect the tag and triangulate its position using signal strength measurements. RFID systems can produce sub-meter precision levels, but have the downside of requiring extra hardware and infrastructure to be acquired.

2.3   Others

Aside from WLAN and RFID, many other RF technologies have been used for indoor localization. For example, there are also IEEE802.15.4-based [4], Bluetooth-based indoor localization systems [1], Ultrawideband [9], and hybrid systems which use a combination of multiple RF technologies for indoor positioning. One such system is proposed by Baniukevic et al in [3]. It uses a combination of Bluetooth and WLAN signals for positioning. A good overview of possible approaches and technologies can be found in [14] and [6]. Most of these systems differ from our approach in that they require extra infrastructure to be purchased which can be sometimes expensive.

3   Design and Implementation

The primary goal in the development of LOCOSmotion is to be able to reuse existing WLAN infrastructure and low-cost off-the-shelf smartphones to enable tracking. In this section, we describe the key factors influencing our system design and how the resulting parts of the LOCOSmotion system fit together.

3.1   Design

The evaluation criteria for the EvAAL competition informed to a greater extent the design decisions made for LOCOSmotion. As described by the EvAAL competition guidelines, there are 5 main design goals that should be considered.

– *High Accuracy* – To be broadly applicable for various ambient assisted living applications, the accuracy provided by an indoor tracking system must be high. Consequently, LOCOSmotion uses WLAN fingerprinting as basis for localization since this approach is known to exhibit better performance than systems which use simple forms of signal propagation modelling [6]. More complex signal propagation models would require the consideration of additional variables such as the building materials, floor plan or access point locations – which may be hard to model accurately.

– *Low Installation Complexity* – To be cost efficient with respect to setup and maintenance, the installation complexity of an indoor tracking system should be low. This is especially true for tracking systems that target ambient assisted living applications since these must be often installed in the homes of the users. The users' homes may differ considerably with respect to size, room layout, materials, wiring of powerlines or available network connections, etc. Regarding the installation complexity, the use of fingerprinting is simultaneously beneficial and limiting. On the positive side, the use of fingerprinting solely requires a sufficiently dense deployment of WLAN access points. On the downside, it requires an on-site training phase where fingerprints are manually collected at several locations. In order to mitigate this, we decided to include a graphical user interface to speed up training.

– *High User Acceptance* – To be applicable for a broad range of users, the user acceptance of an indoor tracking system must be high. Especially, when considering that many users may not be technically inclined, the system should be easy to integrate in their daily activities. Furthermore, the total cost of ownership should be low. For this reason, we decided to use Android smartphones and off-the-shelf WLAN access points since they are broadly available, unobtrusive, and relatively affordable.

– *High Availability* – To be usable, a tracking system should provide high availability. This means that it quickly and reliably determines and provides the user location. This is especially beneficial for tracking moving targets. Due to measurement imprecisions, WLAN fingerprinting usually requires several measurements to accurately determine the location of the user. Thus, to meet the goal of achieving a location update rate of 2 Hz, we decided to combine fingerprinting with acceleration-based dead reckoning.

– *Interoperability* – To ease the integration with existing and future applications, a tracking system should be interoperable with respect to hardware and protocols. Towards this end, the decision to rely on unmodified off-the-shelf components simplifies the maintenance and upgradability of LOCOSmotion. In addition, in order to facilitate extensibility and to ease software integration, we decided to build LOCOSmotion using the NARF component system [7] developed by members of our research group. The NARF component system is a generic framework for personal context recognition which facilitates modularity and software reuse. It allows the replacement of different software components while maintaining the interfaces to the other parts of a system.

3.2   Implementation

The LOCOSmotion tracking system comprises two parts: the mapper application and the localization subsystem. The mapper is an Android application which is used for collecting fingerprints to build a radio map during the training phase. The localization subsystem handles the tracking duties during the localization phase. It consists of a set of components that are built using the NARF component system. The overall software architecture of LOCOSmotion is illustrated in Figure 1. In the following, we discuss the functionality and implementation of both subsystems in more detail.

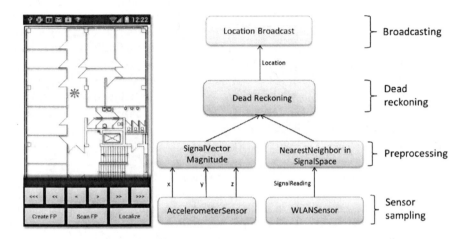

Fig. 1. LOCOSmotion Mapper and Localization Architecture

Training. The training starts by setting up the application for a particular environment. This is done by loading a graphical 2D representation of the environment which is overlaid with a configurable Cartesian grid. The Cartesian coordinates defined by the grid are used internally to capture the location of fingerprints during training and they are also used as the output during the localization phase. Higher levels of abstraction such as areas of interest or rooms can be defined by combining multiple coordinates into a single output[1]. After this setup, the person performing the training can cycle through the different points of the grid in order to capture fingerprints with the device. At each point, the person must capture four fingerprints thereby facing four different directions (i.e. North, East, South, West). For each fingerprint, the mapper application memorizes the position as well as the received signal strength (RSS) of all access points that can be received there. The result is stored as a vector $V_{training} = (X, Y, O, RSS(AP_1), RSS(AP_2), ..., RSS(AP_N))$ whereby X, Y and, O are determining the position and orientation and $RSS(AP_1)$ to $RSS(AP_N)$

---

[1] Note that these steps can be done offline given a map of the environment and a definition of the areas.

are capturing the signal strength of the corresponding access points. In order to cycle quickly through the different locations and orientations, the mapper application provides a graphical user interface that shows the next location and controls the capturing process.

Localization. The localization phase starts by starting a localization application on the smartphone. The application consists of a simple user interface to start and stop the localization subsystem that continuously computes and broadcasts the current user location using the set of components depicted in Figure 1.

To compute the current location, the smartphone continuously performs WLAN scans using a WLANSensor component. The component produces a new vector $V_{localization} = (RSS(AP_1), RSS(AP_2), ..., RSS(AP_N))$ roughly every 1.4 seconds. Once a new vector is produced, the NearestNeighborInSignalSpace component matches it against the corresponding parts of all vectors $V_{training}$ captured during the training phase. The output is a distance d between $V_{localization}$ and all instances of $V_{training}$ that is computed as the Euclidean distance $d = \sqrt{\sum (RSS(AP_{training}) - RSS(AP_{localization}))^2}$. When computing the distance, special care is taken to handle the fact that not all access points are visible at all locations. Thereby, the vectors are dynamically extended with adequate values to handle the non-visible access points. The resulting distances are then used as an input into a k-nearest-neighbor classifier which eventually outputs the location in terms of X and Y coordinates of the nearest vectors of $V_{training}$.

Given such a fingerprinting, it is possible to compute a new location update roughly every 1.5 seconds. Furthermore, due to possible measurement and aggregation errors in $V_{localization}$, consecutive location updates might exhibit high physical distances. To mitigate both issues, LOCOSmotion includes a AccelerometerSensor component that also captures measurements using the built-in accelerometer of the smartphone. The measurements are used to compute the force in the SignalVectorMagnitude component which is then forwarded to the DeadReckoning component. Using the force, the DeadReckoning component computes an approximate movement speed of the user by estimating the footstep frequency as described in [12]. The resulting speed is then used for dead reckoning and scoping. Dead reckoning estimates intermediate location updates by computing the trajectory between the last two updates and extrapolating the next location using distance estimates from the footstep frequency. Scoping corrects location updates by reducing the set of possible consecutive locations to those locations that exhibit a sufficiently close proximity to the last known location. Together, this results in a higher update rate as well as fewer false positives.

Once a new location has been computed, the LocationBroadcast component sends it out over WLAN such that the location can be received and used by other applications.

4   Evaluation

To evaluate LOCOSmotion, we present the results of a number of laboratory experiments as well as the results of the EvAAL 2012 competition in the following. In the lab, the evaluation was performed offline - meaning a set of fingerprints were collected and used for testing the performance - rather than online which would be time consuming. The EvAAL competition performed the evaluation online by having a person actively using the system.

4.1   Lab

For evaluating the performance of the LOCOSmotion system, we set it up on the 5th floor of our research building. The floor was logically divided into 2×2 meter cells with one coordinate in each cell. Using a smartphone, multiple training fingerprints were collected for 8 different orientations at each cell. After the completion of the training, a second set of fingerprints were collected with to perform the offline evaluation of the performance of the system.

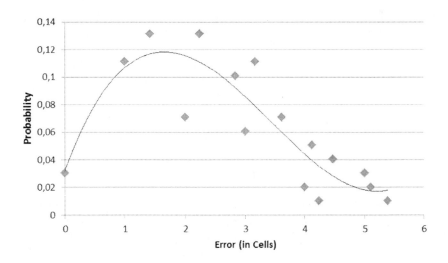

Fig. 2. Localization error probability distribution in the lab

For the evaluation, we compute the location of each individual fingerprint in the evaluation set by comparing it to all fingerprints in the training set. Figure 2 shows the resulting probability distribution for the error of the system over the whole evaluation set. The diamond points represent the actual values whereas the line represents the best polynomial fit of them.

The error with the highest probability is between 0 and 3 neighboring cells with an average distance error of 2.6 cells. The system can locate the user correctly within 2 neighboring cells 34% of the time and 4 neighboring cells 83.8% of the time. The maximum error recorded is 5.3 cells. For most office environments, this places the subject in the worst case scenario in a neighboring office.

For tracking, we set out to build a pedometer whose outputs are used to augment the location update frequency. In order to achieve this, we studied the movement pattern of several users in order to determine the patterns in the accelerometer data generated by someone who is walking. We placed the phone in the pocket of multiple test subjects and had them walk around at different speeds while the phones collected accelerometer readings for all the three axes. Later on, the three data points from each axis were combined to give the magnitude and the data was then analyzed. Figure 3 shows an example from one of the participants.

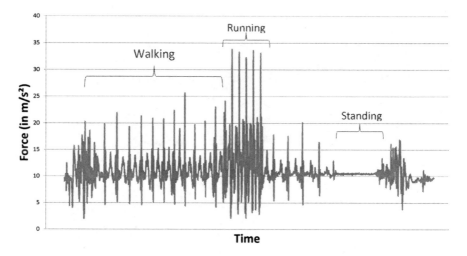

Fig. 3. Movement pattern example

The base reading of the signal magnitude of the accelerometer when the phone is held still is 1g (approximately $9.8\,\mathrm{m/s^2}$). When the person starts moving, it can be observed that the value jumps to about 2g. The exact value of the magnitude varied from person to person depending on the gait, weight, height and force of movement. However, the values were all above 1.6g when the person was in motion. Thus, we selected this value as the threshold for when to consider the person as moving. Once the person is considered as being in motion, the number of measurements exceeding the threshold were counted. Looking closely at the values for each step, it is recognizable that there are approximately three peaks for each step. Hence the number of peaks is divided 3 for each step and then multiplied by a constant factor to account for the distance. This simple approach worked well across all participants in the laboratory setting.

4.2   EvAAL

For the EvAAL 2012 competition held at the Living Lab of the Polytechnic University of Madrid in Spain, we used our own equipment to setup LOCOSmotion. We deployed 8 access points (Netgear WNR-3500L) to enable localization using WLAN fingerprinting. Furthermore, we used a smartphone (Nexus S) for training and localization. The access points were placed at different locations in the Living Lab, with at least one access point per room. In rooms with multiple access points, one access point was placed toward the center of the room in order to provide a more characteristic fingerprint. The layout of the Living Lab as well as the exact placement of the access points is depicted in Figure 4.

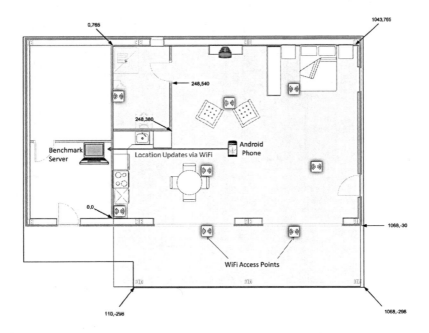

Fig. 4. Basic Deployment

To perform training, we overlaid a 2×2 meter grid on the floor plan of the Living Lab. For each of the cells in the grid, we collected several fingerprints for 4 different orientations. Deploying the access points and performing all the measurements for the complete environment took a single person 51 minutes which was within the 60 minutes threshold defined by the competition.

During the competition, the smartphone was put in the trousers pocket of the person performing the evaluation. The person then proceeded to move along several predefined paths while LOCOSmotion continuously computed and broadcast the person's location. The broadcast were then picked up by a benchmarking PC which used the values to compute performance scores. In the following, we describe the results:

Accuracy. The system's accuracy is measured as the error distance between each computed localization sample and the reference position. It accounts for 15% of the overall performance score. During the competition, the person follows a pace-setting sound so that the speed of movement is the same for all the contestants. However, for our system, we noticed that this caused the pedometer to miscalculate the distance covered by the person. Due to the long slow steps, the location was over-projected leading to rather low accuracy scores. The aggregate results of the paths walked during the EvAAL competition is shown in Figure 5.

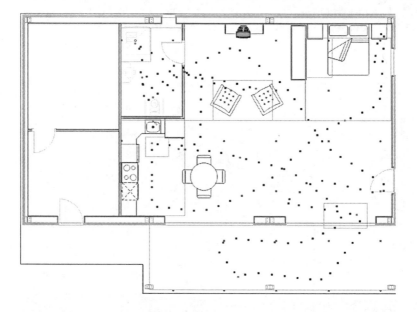

Fig. 5. Aggregate path localization results

The green lines represent the logical partitions of the space, which are the areas of interest. The black dots represent the ground truth location of the person and the blue dots are the corresponding location estimates by our system during the online evaluation. It can be observed that the using the WLAN location results, the location is predicted within the path of the person, then over-projected before being corrected again. This happens repeatedly, driving the overall accuracy score down to 8%.

Installation Complexity. Installation complexity represents a measure of the effort required to install the localization system in the Living Lab and makes up 15% of the total score. LOCOSmotion relies only on the presence of WLAN access points and the availability of a radio map. We were able to setup the access points and map the entire floor within 51 minutes with just one person resulting in an installation complexity score of 13.25%.

User Acceptance. User acceptance expresses how much the localization system is invasive in the users daily life and thereby the impact perceived by the user. In the EvAAL 2012 competition, user acceptance make up 25% of the total score. LOCOSmotion relies solely on off-the-shelf consumer electronics, and works with Android phones which are the fastest growing phone category as of today. This means that the chances that the user of the system already has one are high. WLAN access points are also common in most homes. Given that the localization system runs on a smartphone which fits in a user's pocket, the user acceptance of LOCOSmotion was rather high, coming it at 90.35%.

Availability. Availability is the fraction of time the localization system was active and responsive. Availability comprises 20% of the total score. LOCOSmotion uses WLAN to connect to the benchmarking PC and broadcast location updates. Thereby, the dead-reckoning keeps the location updates coming in at rates of at least 2Hz. As a result, the system had a 100% score on availability which is critical for tracking applications.

Integrability in AAL. Integrability in AAL evaluates the degree of interoperability of the solution in terms of openness of the software, adoption of standards for both software and hardware, replaceability of parts of the solution with other ones. It makes up 15% of the total competition score. LOCOSmotion makes use of off-the-shelf hardware components that can be easily upgraded or replaced. Furthermore, it uses the NARF component system in order to be easy to maintain and extend. With respect to this evaluation criterion, LOCOSmotion achieved a score of 50%.

Overall, LOCOSmotion got a score of 5.23 out of 10 at the EvAAL competition. It performed really well in most of the metrics, except for localization accuracy due to unanticipated movement patterns of the person and the installation complexity. In the next section, we describe the lessons learned from the laboratory experiments and the participation in the EvAAL competition.

5   Lessons Learned

Based on the results of our laboratory experiments and the results of the experiments performed during the EvAAL competition, there are several interesting lessons to be learned with respect to the suitability, the calibration as well as the performance of the system. In the following, we discuss each of them in more detail.

5.1   Suitability

With respect to the suitability of LOCOSmotion in an AAL context, both, our initial laboratory experiments as well as the results of the EvAAL competition indicate that the system is applicable to a broad range of scenarios. Due to the use of off-the-shelf hardware such as smartphones and access points, it is very cost efficient when compared to other alternatives that employ specialized hardware. With an average cost of approximately € 60 for an access point and roughly € 300 for a smartphone, the cost for a typical deployment stays well below € 1000. Moreover, in cases where the user already owns an Android-based smartphone or is using WLAN at home, the cost even drops further. In addition, due to the use of a single smartphone to perform all measurements and computations, LOCOSmotion is very convenient to set up and use. With a weight of approximately 130g and a size of $63 \times 123, 9 \times 10, 88$ mm, the smartphone running the localization system can be easily placed in a trouser pocket, thus, allowing the user to freely pursue his normal daily routine.

5.2   Calibration

With respect to the calibration procedure and effort, we found that LOCOS-motion's reliance on signal strength fingerprinting can be both, an advantage as well as a limitation. On the positive side, fingerprinting does not require a special wiring or placement of WLAN access points, thus, allowing us to easily adapt the deployment to any typical home environment that exhibits a sufficient number of power outlets. Furthermore, there is no need to manually generate a precise map of the deployment which minimizes the off-site preparation effort. On the negative side, however, WLAN fingerprinting requires an on-site training phase during which we collect a number of fingerprints for different locations. Ideally, this number should be large and the collection procedure should closely reflect the usage scenario. With LOCOSmotion's user interface collecting a large number of fingerprints can be done quickly. However, since the user interface is visual, it requires the person performing the calibration to hold the smartphone in the hand. Consequently, the location of the phone differs during calibration - where the phone is held in the hand - and usage - where the phone is placed in the pocket - which can introduce inaccuracy.

5.3   Performance

Due to the combination of WLAN-based localization as well as acceleration-based dead reckoning, LOCOSmotion is able to score high with respect to availability, meaning that it is able to produce localization results quickly. In addition, during laboratory testing, we found that it can also increase the accuracy. Unfortunately, with our current implementation of LOCOSmotion, we were not able to replicate the positive results of our laboratory measurements during the EvAAL competition. In fact, in many cases the acceleration-based dead reckoning even reduced the overall accuracy of the localization. This issue can be attributed primarily to the simplicity of our dead reckoning algorithm. Instead of trying to determine the distance that a person was actually walking, our prediction of upcoming locations were solely based on the number of steps taken by the person. In our laboratory setup, we then experimentally determined the typical distance of a step and integrated the resulting constant into the code. However, during the EvAAL competition, the person performing the evaluation was following a pace setter which resulted in an atypical movement pattern. Consequently, our dead reckoning algorithm frequently overestimated the person's speed which dramatically worsened the system's performance.

6 Next Steps

Based on our experiences with LOCOSmotion, we are currently improving the system regarding both, the calibration procedure as well as the accelerometer-based dead reckoning.

With respect to calibration, we are integrating two optimizations. First, to closely mimic the localization procedure - where the phone is placed in the user's pocket, we are using Android's headset APIs to enable the remote triggering of calibration measurements using the volume keys. Second, in order to further speed up the calibration process, we have extended LOCOSmotion to use multiple phones - placed in different pockets. The phones are set to continuously capture measurements. To combine their fingerprints with the locations provided via the headset triggers, we ensure that they are time-synchronized. This, in turn, allows us to perform a simple time-based aggregation. Clearly, the use of multiple phones slightly increases the hardware cost during calibration. However, it also significantly reduces the time required at the target site and thus, reduces the personnel cost. Given that mobile phones are comparatively inexpensive we believe that this trade-off will likely reduce the overall system cost even further.

With respect to the accelerometer-based dead reckoning, we are currently extending the simple pedometer with a more realistic model for movements. As indicated by the performance of LOCOSmotion during the EvAAL competition, the walking mode has a significant impact on the length of individual steps. For example, when looking at the left side of Table 1 – which shows the number of steps that different persons require for walking a certain (fixed) distance in different modes – it becomes apparent that the step length can more than double when comparing slow walking with fast running.

Table 1. Step count and frequency for different persons and walking modes when walking the same distance

| | Number of Steps | | | | Frequency in Hz | | | |
| | Walking | | Running | | Walking | | Running | |
	Slow	Fast	Slow	Fast	Slow	Fast	Slow	Fast
Person 1	276	255	159	135	1,60	1,96	2,58	2,61
Person 2	289	249	183	159	1,67	2,04	2,74	2,87
Person 3	319	299	174	150	1,70	2,21	2,64	2,73

As hinted in Figure 3 and on the right side of Table 1, both, the force as well as the step frequency can provide a good indication for the walking mode. Thus, instead of solely considering the number of steps, we also consider the actual frequency as well as the force per step in order to determine the walking mode which we then use to estimate a step length. Or initial experiments show that this approach allows us to predict the walking distance with an 80 percent accuracy. This can be further increased to 88 percent when considering the height of the person. Given these initial results, we are convinced that the improved version of LOCOSmotion will exhibit a considerably higher localization performance during the next EvAAL competition.

7 Conclusion

Pervasive computing envisions seamless and distraction-free support for tasks by means of context-aware applications. Location information is a key component in many of them. LOCOSmotion enables indoor localization by combining WLAN fingerprinting with speed estimations gathered from acceleration measurements. Given the fact that LOCOSmotion relies solely on standard off-the-shelf hardware, it is very cost efficient and a typical installation will be well below € 1000. Consequently, we are convinced that it is a suitable candidate for supporting the development of many pervasive computing applications that require person tracking in indoor scenarios.

Our experiences during the EvAAL competition provide a clear indication for the high applicability of LOCOSmotion to AAL scenarios. However, they also show that accelerometer-based dead reckoning requires a more sophisticated model for movement prediction in order to work well outside the laboratory environment. Based on our initial experiments, we assume that by considering the step frequency as well as actual acceleration force we will be able to improve the results presented in this article significantly.

At the present time, we are working on the improvements to the calibration procedure and the accelerometer-based dead reckoning. Thereafter, we are planning to investigate how to effectively integrate other sources of signals such as GSM [18] in order to improve the resulting localization accuracy and to reduce the training effort.

References

1. Akeila, E., Salcic, Z.: a Swain, a Croft, and J Stott. Bluetooth-based indoor positioning with fuzzy based dynamic calibration. In: IEEE Region 10 Conference on TENCON 2010, pp. 1415–1420 (November 2010)
2. Bahl, P., Padmanabhan, V.N.: Radar: an in-building rf-based user location and tracking system. In: Proceedings of the IEEE Nineteenth Annual Joint Conference of the IEEE Computer and Communications Societies, INFOCOM 2000, vol. 2, pp. 775–784 (2000)
3. Baniukevic, A., Sabonis, D., Jensen, C.S., Lu, H.: Improving Wi-Fi Based Indoor Positioning Using Bluetooth Add-Ons. In: 2011 IEEE 12th International Conference on Mobile Data Management, pp. 246–255 (June 2011)
4. Barsocchi, P., Lenzi, S., Chessa, S., Furfari, F.: Automatic virtual calibration of range-based indoor localization systems. Wirel. Commun. Mob. Comput. (12), 1546–1557 (2012)

5. Focken, D., Stiefelhagen, R.: Towards vision-based 3-D people tracking in a smart room. In: Proceedings of the Fourth IEEE International Conference on Multimodal Interfaces, pp. 400–405 (2002)
6. Gu, Y., Lo, A., Niemegeers, I.: A survey of indoor positioning systems for wireless personal networks. Communications Surveys & ... 11(1), 13–32 (2009)
7. Handte, M., Iqbal, U., Apolinarski, W., Wagner, S., Marrón, P.J.: The narf architecture for generic personal context recognition. In: 2010 IEEE International Conference on Sensor Networks, Ubiquitous, and Trustworthy Computing (SUTC), pp. 123–130 (June 2010)
8. Haverinen, J., Kemppainen, A.: A global self-localization technique utilizing local anomalies of the ambient magnetic field. In: 2009 IEEE International Conference on Robotics and Automation, pp. 3142–3147 (May 2009)
9. Ingram, S.J., Harmer, D., Quinlan, M.: UltraWideBand Indoor Positioning Systems and their Use in Emergencies (1803)
10. Ji, Y., Biaz, S., Pandey, S., Agrawal, P.: Ariadne: a dynamic indoor signal map construction and localization system. In: Proceedings of the 4th International Conference on Mobile Systems, Applications and Services, MobiSys 2006, pp. 151–164. ACM, New York (2006)
11. Juels, A.: RFID security and privacy: a research survey. IEEE Journal on Selected Areas in Communications 24(2), 381–394 (2006)
12. Libby, R.: A simple method for reliable footstep detection in embedded sensor platforms (2008),
    http://ubicomp.cs.washington.edu/uwar/libby_peak_detection.pdf
13. Lim, H., Kung, L.-C., Hou, J.C., Luo, H.: Zero-configuration indoor localization over ieee 802.11 wireless infrastructure. Wirel. Netw. 16(2), 405–420 (2010)
14. Liu, H., Darabi, H., Banerjee, P., Liu, J.: Survey of wireless indoor positioning techniques and systems. IEEE Transactions on Systems, Man, and Cybernetics, Part C: Applications and Reviews 37(6), 1067–1080 (2007)
15. Ni, L.M., Liu, Y., Lau, Y.C., Patil, A.P.: Landmarc: Indoor location sensing using active rfid. Wireless Networks 10, 701–710 (2004),
    10.1023/B:WINE.0000044029.06344.dd
16. Ni, L.M., Liu, Y., Lau, Y.C., Patil, A.P.: Landmarc: Indoor location sensing using active rfid. Wireless Networks 10, 701–710 (2004),
    10.1023/B:WINE.0000044029.06344.dd
17. NielsenWire. Nielsen wire blog,
    http://blog.nielsen.com/nielsenwire/online_mobile/smartphones-account-for-half-of-all-mobile-phones-dominate-.new-phone-purchases-in-the-us/
    (accessed: November 11, 2012)
18. Otsason, V., Varshavsky, A., LaMarca, A., de Lara, E.: Accurate GSM Indoor Localization. In: Beigl, M., Intille, S.S., Rekimoto, J., Tokuda, H. (eds.) UbiComp 2005. LNCS, vol. 3660, pp. 141–158. Springer, Heidelberg (2005)
19. Want, R., Hopper, A., Falcão, V., Gibbons, J.: The active badge location system. ACM Transactions on Information Systems 10(1), 91–102 (1992)
20. Ward, A., Jones, A., Hopper, A.: A new location technique for the active office. IEEE Personal Communications, 42–47 (1997)
21. Xiang, Z., Song, S., Chen, J., Wang, H., Huang, J., Gao, X.: A wireless lan-based indoor positioning technology. IBM Journal of Research and Development 48(5.6), 617–626 (2004)

Indoor Localization of Persons in AAL Scenarios Using an Inertial Measurement Unit (IMU) and the Signal Strength (SS) from RFID Tags

Antonio R. Jiménez, Fernando Seco, Francisco Zampella, Jose C. Prieto, and Jorge Guevara

Centre for Automation and Robotics (CAR)
Consejo Superior de Investigaciones Científicas (CSIC)-UPM,
Ctra., Campo Real km 0.2, 28500 La Poveda, Arganda del Rey (Madrid), Spain
{antonio.jimenez,fernando.seco,francisco.zampella}@csic.es
http://www.car.upm-csic.es/lopsi

Abstract. This paper presents an indoor localization system that is based on the fusion of two complementary technologies: 1) Inertial integration and 2) RFID-based trilateration. The Inertial subsystem uses an IMU (Inertial Measurement Unit) mounted on the foot of the person. The IMU approach generates a very accurate estimate of the user's trajectory shape (limited by the drift in yaw). However, being a dead-reckoning method, it requires an initialization in position and orientation to provide absolute positioning. The IMU-based solution is updated at 100 Hz and is always available. On the other hand, the RFID-based localization subsystem provides the absolute position using the Received Signal Strength (RSS) from several long-range active tags installed in the building. Since the transmitted RF signals are subject to many propagation artifacts (reflections, absorption,...), we use a probabilistic RSS-to-Range model and a Kalman filter to estimate the position. The output of both IMU- and RFID-based subsystems are fused into one final position estimation by adaptively fitting the IMU and RFID trajectories. The integrated solution provides: absolute positioning information, a static accuracy of less than 2.3 m (in 75% of the cases) for persons at fixed positions, a smooth trajectory for moving persons with a dynamic positioning accuracy of 1.1 m (75%), a full 100% availability, and a real-time update rate of up to 100 Hz. This approach is valid for indoor navigation and particularly for Ambient Assisted Living (AAL) applications. We presented this system to the 2nd EvAAL competition ("Evaluating AAL Systems through Competitive Benchmarking": http://evaal.aaloa.org/) and our CAR-CSIC system was awarded with the first prize. A detailed analysis of the experiments during the competition is presented at the end of this paper.

Keywords: Inertial Navigation, RFID Positioning, Indoor Localization, Fusion Algorithms, Ambient Assisted Living, EvAAL competition.

S. Chessa and S. Knauth (Eds.): EvAAL 2012, CCIS 362, pp. 32–51, 2013.
© Springer-Verlag Berlin Heidelberg 2013

1   Introduction

Two main research approaches are used in the indoor positioning problem: 1) solutions that rely on the existence of a network of receivers or emitters, some of them placed at known locations (beacon-based solutions), and 2) solutions that mainly rely on dead-reckoning methods with sensors installed on the person to be located (beacon-free solutions).

In the first approach (beacon-based), the positions are estimated by trilateration or triangulation from a set of measured ranges or angles, respectively. These methods are usually termed as Local Positioning Systems (LPS), or Wireless Sensor Networks (WSN), depending on the sensor configuration and processing approach. They use technologies such as ultrasound, short-range radio (WiFi, UWB, RFID, Zigbee, etc.) or vision [1].

The second approach (beacon-free or dead-reckoning) uses Inertial Measuring Units (IMU) to estimate the position of persons [2]. These IMU-based methodologies, often called Pedestrian Dead-Reckoning (PDR) solutions, can integrate the user step lengths and heading angles at each detected step, to estimate the user's position [3,4,5]; or, alternatively, integrate accelerometer and gyroscope readings of a foot-attached IMU (by strapdown INS mechanization [6]) to compute the position and attitude of the person [7,8,9].

IMU-based PDR solutions have the inconvenient of accumulating errors that grow with the path length (drift), while beacon-based solutions have limited absolute accuracy and coverage. The fusion of IMU-based PDR solutions with indoor absolute positioning has the potential to provide an accurate drift-free positioning solution. In this paper we propose an integrated IMU+RFID-based localization system. Section 2 presents the localization methodology, section 3 its evaluation at our site (CAR-CSIC) , and in section 4 we analyze in detail our experiences during the EvAAL competition.

2   The Localization System

The block diagram of the proposed indoor localization system is presented in Fig. 1. Two complementary but independent positioning methods are implemented: 1) IMU-based Positioning, and 2) RFID-based Positioning. The outputs of both systems Pos_{IMU} and Pos_{RFID}, which contains the two-dimensional positioning coordinates of both approaches, are fused to generate the final position estimation: Pos_{Fused}. The next three subsections give details on each method.

2.1   The IMU-Based Dead-Reckoning Localization Method

Our method assumes that an IMU is installed on the foot of a person (the most reliable PDR method). The IMU contains 3 accelerometers and 3 gyroscopes, and provides the sensor acceleration (m/s^2) and the angular rate (rad/s). An inertial navigation system (INS) algorithm is executed to integrate the accelerometer

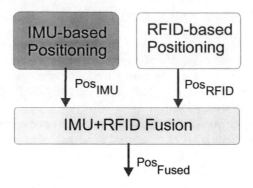

Fig. 1. Proposed positioning systems with "loose" IMU and RFID integration

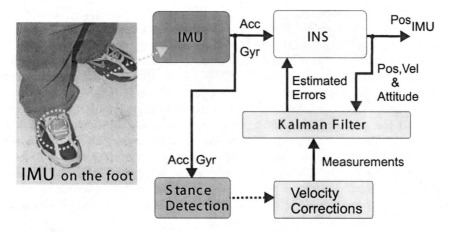

Fig. 2. Block diagram of the IMU-based dead-reckoning PDR method

readings into velocity and then into position, also the gyroscope angular rate readings are integrated to obtain the attitude of the IMU (i.e. Roll, Pitch and Yaw). See Fig. 2 for a simplified diagram of this approach.

The output of the INS needs to be corrected periodically or it will diverge quickly due to sensor drift. A very effective technique is the Zero Velocity Update (ZUPT), used every time that the foot is motion-less (stance phase), and consisting in updating the INS-estimated velocity with the "known" velocity of the foot at stance (zero velocity). This is a very effective way to reset the error in velocity of the INS.

A complementary Extended Kalman Filter (EKF), working with a 15-element error state vector [7,9], compensates position, velocity and attitude errors of the INS solution, as well as the IMU biases. Our methodology is valid for any kind of motion (forward, lateral or backward walk), and does not require a specific off-line calibration of the user gait.

2.2   The RFID RSS-Based Absolute Localization Method

It is assumed that an RFID reader is carried by a person and several active tags are fixed at known locations in the building. The RFID reader provides the Received Signal Strength (RSS) of each tag. A RSS-to-range model is used to estimate the expected range between the reader and a particular tag (also its uncertainty). Then, an EKF integrates all range measurements into a position fix (dynamic trilateration). See Fig. 3 for a simplified diagram of the RFID-based location method.

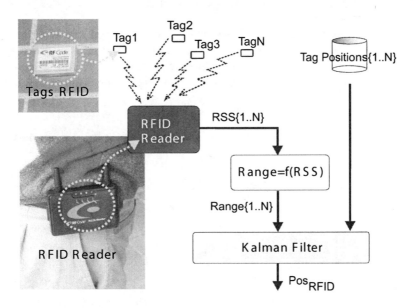

Fig. 3. Block diagram of the active RFID-based absolute positioning system

The path-loss model that we use to transform from RSS to distance, d, (maximum likelihood estimate) is given by

$$d = d_0 \cdot 10^{\frac{\text{RSS}_0 - \text{RSS}}{10 \cdot p}}, \tag{1}$$

where RSS_0 is a mean RSS value obtained at a reference distance d_0, and p is the path loss exponent (we experimentally found these values: $\text{RSS}_0 = 60$, $d_0 = 1$ m and $p = -2.3$).

The standard deviation of the estimated distance, σ_d, is needed by the Kalman filter as an indication of the belief we have on the modeled range value. It is

$$\sigma_d = \sigma_{\text{RSS}} \cdot \frac{\ln(10) \cdot d}{-10 \cdot p}, \tag{2}$$

where σ_{RSS} is the RSS standard deviation in dB. This sigma model is proportional to distance, giving low standard deviation values at short ranges (low uncertainty) and viceversa.

The Kalman filter uses a 4-component state vector (X) that contains the 2-D position and velocity, i.e. $X = [\text{Pos}_{\text{RFID}}(x), \text{Pos}_{\text{RFID}}(y), \text{Vel}_{\text{RFID}}(x), \text{Vel}_{\text{RFID}}(y)]$. In order to predict the next state, X^-, we use a movement model that relates the current state with its predicted state as $X^- = A \cdot X$, which uses a constant velocity model as detailed in matrix A:

$$A = \begin{bmatrix} I_{2x2} & \Delta T \cdot I_{2x2} \\ 0_{2x2} & I_{2x2} \end{bmatrix}, \tag{3}$$

being ΔT the sampling interval, I_{2x2} a 2 by 2 diagonal matrix, and O_{2x2} a 2 by 2 matrix of zeros.

We use a difference-in-range measurement model to feed our Kalman filter. This measurement is $\Delta d_i = d_i - d_i^-$, being Δd_i the differences between the measured range, d_i, to the i-th tag obtained with equation 1, and being d_i^- the computed range between the current estimation and the position of i-th tag, i.e.

$$d_i^- = [(\text{tag}_i(x) - \text{Pos}_{\text{RFID}}^-(x))^2 + (\text{tag}_i(y) - \text{Pos}_{\text{RFID}}^-(y))^2]^{0.5}. \tag{4}$$

After a first order linearization of the measurement equation, we obtain matrix H,

$$H = \begin{bmatrix} \frac{\text{tag}_1(x) - \text{Pos}_{\text{RFID}}^-(x)}{d_1^-} & \frac{\text{tag}_1(y) - \text{Pos}_{\text{RFID}}^-(y)}{d_1^-} & 0 & 0 \\ \frac{\text{tag}_2(x) - \text{Pos}_{\text{RFID}}^-(x)}{d_2^-} & \frac{\text{tag}_2(y) - \text{Pos}_{\text{RFID}}^-(y)}{d_2^-} & 0 & 0 \\ \cdots & \cdots & \cdots \\ \frac{\text{tag}_N(x) - \text{Pos}_{\text{RFID}}^-(x)}{d_N^-} & \frac{\text{tag}_N(y) - \text{Pos}_{\text{RFID}}^-(y)}{d_N^-} & 0 & 0 \end{bmatrix}, \tag{5}$$

that is used to compute the Kalman gain $K = P^- \cdot H^T \cdot (HP^-H^T + R)$, and this to update the state estimation of the EKF with $X = X^- + K \cdot \Delta d_i$, being R the system model covariance matrix and P^- the covariance of the predicted state estimation that is a 4 by 4 matrix. Finally, the covariance of the estimation after the measurement update is $P = (I_{4x4} - K \cdot H) \cdot P^-$.

This subsection has presented a long-range RFID strategy for localization. Alternatively we could have implemented a passive short-range RFID strategy based on cell-based or proximity positioning algorithms. However we prefer our long-range RFID solution since it is a general purpose approach. It can be easily adapted to provide location-awareness in large buildings simply by putting the tags apart from each other (lowering the tag density).

In the implementation presented in this paper, we use long-range RFID technology for a quite small space (approx. 100 m^2). Consequently it is expected that almost all tags will be detectable from any position in the AAL scenario. In order to obtain enough accuracy a high tag density guaranties that the person to be located is always close to some of the tags. We use all distances or RSS data available for positioning, however our algorithm (see eq. 4) weights short distances (strong RSS) much more than large distances (weak RSS). If the person is close enough to a tag (less than 1 m), the system performs a kind of cell-based positioning (the information from 1 tag is predominant over the others). This way, the positioning accuracy is expected to be about 1 m, which is better than the typical accuracy (2-3 meters) using distant or a low density of tags.

2.3   The Integrated IMU+RFID Positioning Method

The fusion method that we propose is based on the superposition of the smooth but not well-oriented IMU trajectory (Pos^i_{IMU}) over the noisy but well-aligned RFID-based trajectory (Pos^i_{RFID}). This superposition is made basically by iteratively fitting long sections of the IMU trajectory with the same temporal section of the RFID-based trajectory. The fitting process is stated as a least square minimization problem (Downhill Simplex method), where 3 variables are optimized: the offsets along X and Y axis (ΔX, ΔY), and the orientation mismatch between the IMU and RFID trajectories (θ). These parameters represent the misalignment of the IMU trajectory with respect the RFID trajectory.

Once we have a first estimation of the misalignment between the IMU and RFID trajectories (ΔX, ΔY, θ), the output of the fused solution is just a reoriented version, according to the misalignment parameters, of the IMU-based positioning solution. In this way we can provide a real-time positioning solution at a rate up to 100 Hz. Since the IMU suffers from drift we can not rely the fused solution on the initial misalignment parameters, then the fit is repeated once in a while at a low rate.

The rate at which we update the misalignment parameters (ΔX, ΔY, θ) is not critical. For example a fit can be performed at a fixed time interval, e.g. every 60 s, or when enough person's movement is detected. For example, the minimum amount of movement required to perform a new fit can be traveling a distance of at least 4 times the accuracy of the RFID-based positioning system (we use 10 meters as threshold).

Note that at the very beginning, when no fitting is still done and no misalignment parameters are known, the fused solution only uses the RFID data (Pos_{RFID}).

3   Evaluation at CAR-CSIC

We have tested the system in an indoor area (Research Lab) of 80 square meters, at the Center of Automation and Robotics (CAR-CSIC) (see Fig. 4). This area was selected since it is similar in size to an apartment in Ambient Assisting Living (AAL) applications.

3.1   Complexity of the Installation

Infrastructure in the Building. The building has to be equipped with several active RFID tags placed on the walls or the furniture. A total of 24 tags were installed. The installation process is very fast, but the position of the tags must be annotated in an existing floor plan which provides the coordinate

Fig. 4. Lab used for tests (CAR-CSIC)

reference frame for the localization. The used tags are model M100 from RFCode (www.rfcode.com), which are battery-powered RF transmitters operating in the 433 MHz radio band. Every tag broadcasts its unique ID and a status message at a periodic rate (1 Hz).

Sensors Installed on the Person. The user must carry an IMU on the foot and an RFID reader on its waist. We use a commercially available IMU, model MTi from Xsens Technologies (www.xsens.com), which weights 50 grams. It is configured to provide inertial data at 100 Hz. The RFID reader is model M220 from RFCode, which is a light-weight (160 g) portable battery-powered device. This RFID reader is able to detect the active tags at long distances; the typical maximum detection range is about 25 meters, and in our indoor experiments the reader detects tags at a distance of 12 meters in 75% of the cases.

Computation Platform. We use a netbook computer to execute the location algorithms and to make a graphical representation in real-time. The computer in our current prototype is carried by the user, and sensors are connected to it by USB. In the near future, we plan to use a more wearable platform (tablet or smartphone) to read the internal sensors (Accelerometers, Gyroscopes and WiFi) or any additional wireless external sensors (IMU or RFID reader). The tablet/smartphone could also perform the data processing to estimate the localization of the person.

3.2 Tracking with the IMU Subsystem

The estimation of the shape of the trajectory with an IMU is very reliable at short-term and it is always available. It accumulates an error of about 1% of the Total Travelled Distance (TTD), i.e. if we start at a given position and end at the same place after 100 meters of walk, the expected positioning error will be about 1 m. However, the main inconvenient is that the absolute position and orientation of the trajectory remain unknown unless they are provided at initialization. The path at the top of Fig. 5 is a typical IMU-based estimation, where small dots represent the detected foot stances (notice the error in the orientation of the trajectory).

3.3   Tracking with the RFID Subsystem

This absolute positioning method has typical positioning errors of about 2.3 m (75th percentile). This limitation, common to most RSS-based positioning methods (fingerprinting can obtain better results but at a cost of a systematic calibration), makes difficult to give accurate tracking results at apartment-size scale. However, the use of a higher density of tags helps in the accuracy that can be obtained, specially if tags are placed close to the site where the person is prone to pass by. At shorter reader-to-tag distances the uncertainty on the range is lower (eq. 4) so position estimations are more accurate. See the middle trajectory in Fig. 5 to get an idea of the tracking performance obtained.

3.4   Tracking with the Fused IMU-RFID System

The availability of the fused solution is 100% because the IMU is always providing inertial data and also the RFID system in apartment-size spaces is always available. The static positioning accuracy for a person at a fixed location is similar to the RFID alone system (2.3 meters, 75%). However, if the person moves from time to time to a different area, the generated trajectory and the fusion process helps to improve the accuracy in positioning (down to 1.1 m, 75%). The histograms in Fig. 6 show the distribution of the measured positioning errors for the RFID and fused estimations. This improvement is specially effective with long paths and diversified routes because in that case the systematic positioning errors that appear at certain areas with the RSS-based method are averaged. In the bottom of Fig. 5 it can be seen that the fused trajectory is smooth and well-positioned over the ground-truth path.

3.5   Regions of Interest Detection

Sometimes symbolic positioning provides more meaning than coordinate positioning. The detection of particular Regions of Interest (RoI) where the user can be located is very important in AAL (e.g. to be in the Kitchen, bathroom or bedroom).

In our symbolic location tests we use a polygon to define each particular RoI. Whenever the physical location estimate Pos_{Fused} is inside the area defined by the polygon, the system indicates that the person is located in that RoI. We have defined 6 RoI as depicted in Fig. 7a. The success in the identification of the correct RoI is shown in Fig. 7b, in which 7 RoI are visited sequentially, stopping 30 s in

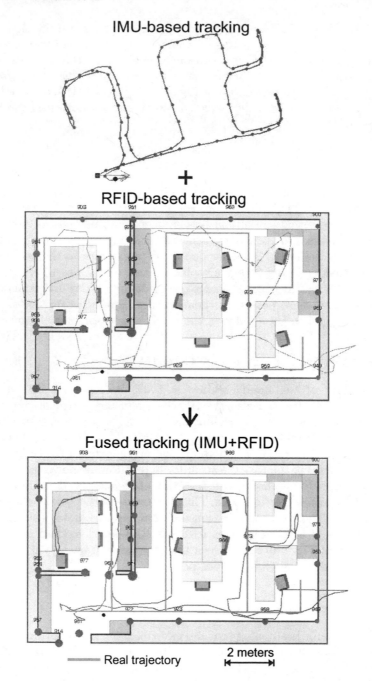

Fig. 5. Tracking with the IMU-based method (top), with the RFID-based method (middle), and with the Fused IMU+RFID method (bottom). Red circles represent the RFID tags positions with their sizes proportional to the RSS received from them at a given instant. The ground truth is marked in the middle and bottom plot with orange straight lines.

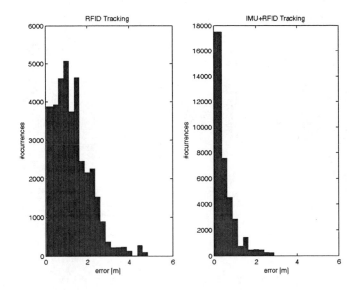

Fig. 6. Positioning error Histograms for the RFID and fused estimations

each area, with 10 s transition time employed to move from one RoI to the next. We did two different tests (plotted in Fig. 7b), and concluded that the system does not have a perfect detection rate, but detects many of the regions of interests.

The detailed performance statistics indicate that when the user is in any of the six RoIs, the system estimates the correct region in 65% of the cases. The system did not generated any region detection, when it actually was in one of them, in 33.8% of the cases. However only in 1.2% of the cases the systems indicates a wrong region. On the other hand, when the user was not in any of the regions of interest, the system correctly detected that state in 44.5% of the cases, so in 55.5% of the cases a false alarm is generated indicating that the user is in a region when actually is not.

4   Performance at EvAAL

We presented this system to the 2nd 2012 EvAAL competition ("Evaluating AAL Systems through Competitive Benchmarking": http://evaal.aaloa.org/), which is a competition to test AAL solutions in two different specialities: 1) tracking a person inside an apartment and 2) doing action recognition. We participated in the tracking and localization section, which had a total of eight competitors from countries all around the world.

The evaluation of our system was performed in the morning of the 3th of July 2012, between 8:30 and 11:30, in the Living Lab of the Polytechnic University of Madrid, Spain. This system was the first one to be evaluated in the localization track. Next subsections will give some details about this evaluation.

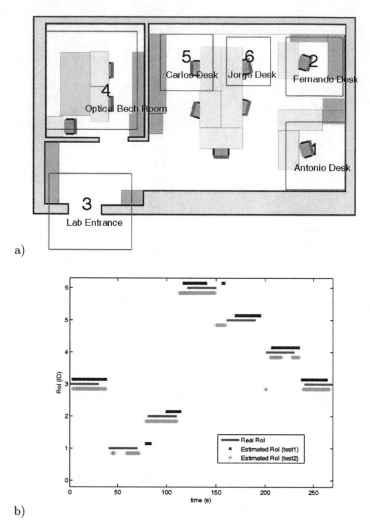

Fig. 7. RoI detection tests. a) Six selected RoIs, b) Identification results for two different tests (ground truth in red).

4.1   Installation of RFID Tags and Sensors

We installed 30 RFID tags in the Living Lab. The CAR team had previously defined where to locate each tag using the map information available for competitors. One person stuck the 30 tags using BlueTack® sticky gum in 6 minutes and 39 seconds. The distribution of the tags can be seen in figure 8, the vertical position of all tags was approximately the same (about 1 meter). The exact position of the tags once installed was not measured by any measuring device, they were just placed by hand approximately at the locations previously defined (red circles in the map in figure 8). A probable positioning error of about 20 cm is not significant neither important for our system's accuracy.

The installation of the sensors on the actor was simple but somehow tricky. The RFID reader was placed on the actor's waist easily, but the IMU sensor was a bit more complicated since the actor used sandals with a very reduced surface to attach the sensor. Finally we fixed it with double-side sticky foil and secured it with some electrical tape. See figure 9 for details. The user has also to carry with him the netbook computer where the localization algorithms are executed. In order to facilitate the transportation we initially put the computer inside a back pack. Finally, in order to avoid a lower processing power mode of the computer when folded in the bag, the actor carried the computer close to his hip keeping the arm straight to diminish muscle stress due to computer's weight.

It is important to mention that after installing the sensors in this Living Lab, we did not perform any calibration of the RFID subsystem. In principle the RSS-to-distance model presented in section 2.2 was calibrated for the CAR-CSIC building, but this model is a general purpose one that should not be significantly affected by operating in different buildings made using typical construction methods. We do not need a very precise and particular calibration, as opposite to other methods such as fingerprinting. So all the test at EvAAL were performed using the same model as explained in section 2.2 (i.e. $RSS_0 = 60$, $d_0 = 1$ m and $p = -2.3$).

4.2   Generated Data

Our localization algorithm generated, as required for the competition, the position information and the detected areas of interest at a 2 Hz update frequency. The method used to transfer the information to the EvAAL server was to create a TCP/IP socket using port 4444 and transmitting the information to the local IP address '127.0.0.1'. The computer had installed a socket receiver (provided by the EvAAL team) that finally retransmits it to the EvAAL server. The format used to transmit the information consists of a header indicating the competitors identification name followed by the 2D position, the time stamp and a variable field with none, one or several areas of interest, i.e.:

<Competitors ID> <X position in meters> <Y position in meters> <Posix time in milliseconds> <AOI-Areas of Interest (1 o several integers)>.

See Fig. 10 for an example of real data transmitted during the competition. Note in this example that at the begining the user is close to the lab's table and no region of interest (RoI) is transmitted, but after that it detects to be on RoI 31 that is a subregion contained in RoI number 3. In figure 11 it can be seen all the RoIs that had to be detected, as defined by the EvAAL team.

Apart from the information previously described which is transmitted in real-time, the CAR system also generates some log files (saved in real-time during each session test) containing much more data of interest. At the end of the evaluation we made available to the EvAAL team two files: 'logfile_2012.7.3_11.15.57.511.mat' and 'logfile_2012.7.3_10.19.25.904.mat' (*.mat

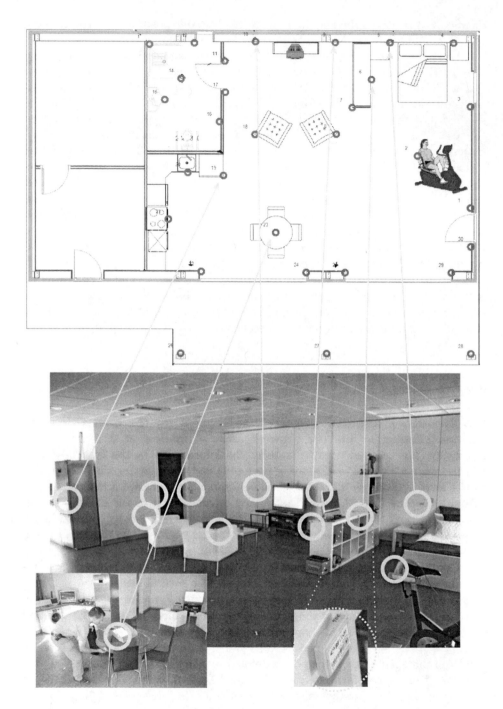

Fig. 8. Installation of 30 RFID tags in the Living Lab of the Polytechnic University of Madrid, Spain

Fig. 9. Installation of the sensors on the actor. The IMU on one of the sandal's strips and the RFID reader on the waist belt.

```
CAR-CSIC 5.043 3.192 1341313375147
CAR-CSIC 5.043 3.192 1341313375647
CAR-CSIC 4.832 2.63 1341313376147
CAR-CSIC 4.832 2.63 1341313376647
CAR-CSIC 3.761 3.71 1341313377147
CAR-CSIC 3.761 3.71 1341313377647
CAR-CSIC 4.072 5.097 1341313378147 3   31
CAR-CSIC 4.072 5.097 1341313378647 3   31
CAR-CSIC 4.969 4.149 1341313379147 3   31
CAR-CSIC 4.969 4.149 1341313379647 3   31
CAR-CSIC 5.326 4.94 1341313380147 3   31
CAR-CSIC 5.326 4.94 1341313380647 3   31
CAR-CSIC 5.663 4.533 1341313381147 3   31
CAR-CSIC 5.663 4.533 1341313381647 3   31
CAR-CSIC 6.623 4.194 1341313382147 3
CAR-CSIC 6.623 4.194 1341313382647 3
CAR-CSIC 6.239 5.858 1341313383147 3
CAR-CSIC 6.239 5.858 1341313383647 3
```

Fig. 10. Example of data transmitted from the CAR-CSIC system to the EvAAL server

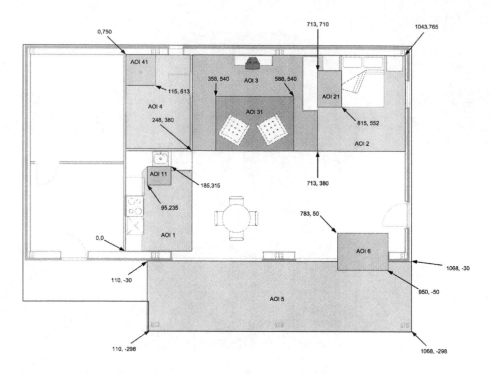

Fig. 11. Regions of Interes (RoI) defined to be detected al the Living Lab

is a Matlab file format) that can be post processed to evaluate other algorithms or approaches. These files contain, among other information, the following data:

1. The 3D (X-Y-Z) position coordinates of the fused RFID+IMU estimation.
2. The 3D (X-Y-Z) position coordinates of the IMU alone estimation.
3. The 2D (X-Y) position coordinates of the RFID alone estimation.
4. The Orientation of the person (Yaw angle with respect to the North).
5. Region-of-Interest (RoI) Identity in which the user is believed to be located.
6. User's foot activity (Walking or Still) and Step length (SL).
7. Raw Sensor data:
    - The sensor acceleration (m/s^2) provided by the 3 accelerometers.
    - The angular rate (rad/s) provided by the 3 gyroscopes.
    - Magnetic field (a.u.) provided by 3 magnetometers.
    - The Received Signal Strength (RSS) of tags provided by the RFID reader.

4.3   The Different Tests and the Obtained Results

There were three different parts during the evaluation period: 1) System installation in the Lab, 2) Tracking and Localization tests, and 3) Removing the installation. For each of the three parts a maximum time-slot of one hour was allowed. Our system was installed and uninstalled in just a few minutes (less than 10 minutes in total), so we obtained the maximum score in the 'Installation Complexity' metric. The second part ('Tracking and Localization tests') consisted of three different phases: a) Location of a moving person inside the lab, b) Similar to the latter but with another disturbing person walking around, and c) detection of areas of interest. Each of these phases was repeated twice, and the best of the two tests was used to compute the final score.

The tracking accuracy was measured as the 75% percentile error of the Euclidean distance between the estimated position and the ground-truth reference, as computed in section 3. Errors below 0.5 m are scored 10 points; scores are given between 10 and 4 for errors from 0.5 m to 2 m; and finally scores goes linearly down from 4 to 0 for errors between 2 and 4 meters. Our system obtained and average localization accuracy of 7.9 which corresponds with a 75% error of 1.1 meters. This performance is exactly the same that we obtained in our own tests at CAR-CSIC Lab as presented before. Some of the estimated trajectories can be seen in figure 12.

The RoI test obtained a 6.3 score which is again similar to the score we obtained in our premises.

The total computed metrics are shown in Table 1, where it can be seen that the availability of the system was 82.1%, the user acceptance received a 6.56 score, and the interoperability of the system obtained a 6.81 score. The total score of the system was **7.70**, which was the maximum of the eight competitors at EvAAL, so the CAR-CSIC system was the winner of this second EvAAL competition.

Note that we did not obtain a 100% availability, even when our system is by definition a 100% available (the IMU always provides data at a 100 Hz rate and the RFID tags are always visible in this small localization area). After the competition we analyzed, looking into the log files, any kind of problems during the data transmission. We verified that we correctly transmitted data packets every 500 ms (2Hz), although the clock that we used to decide when to transmit the next package was the IMU clock. The IMU clock accumulated 8.71 seconds of delay with respect to the PC clock in a test that lasted for 839.7 seconds. So the IMU's clock was 1.1% slower than the PC's clock. Nevertheless this was not the cause of the 81% availability since a 1.1% slower clock would have cause a 98.9% availability. We finally found that the wireless transmission from the CAR PC to the server suffered some random delays that caused some time jitter (significantly larger than 0.25 s), causing the server to ignore approximately one data packet of five intents (80%). In figure 13 we can clearly see that instead of receiving each packet with a 500 ms separation, we get significant undesirable delays around a mean value of 500 ms.

4.4   Lessons Learned and Future Improvements

Although our system was a research prototype, and we already knew that it was not very wearable (the need to carry a netbook computer and a tethered IMU), it did not receive a bad score in user acceptance metric. The reason of

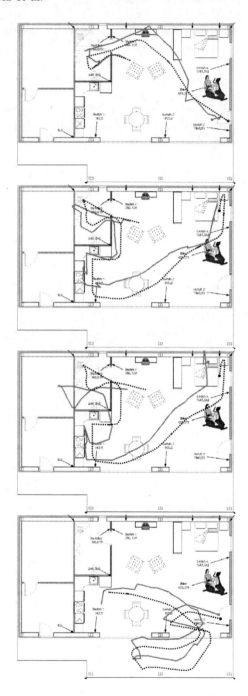

Fig. 12. Some of the individual path estimations during the tracking tests at the EvAAL Living Lab. The discontinuous line is the reference and the solid line is our estimation. A big dot on those trajectories represents the starting point. The scores for these tests were: 8.9, 8.02, 5.89 and 8.68 from top to bottom, respectively.

Table 1. Detailed score of CAR system

Metric	Weight	Score
Accuracy	0.25	7.57
- Tracking Location		8.8
- RoI detection		6.3
Availability	0.2	8.21
Installation Complexity	0.15	10.0
User Acceptance	0.25	6.56
Interoperability	0.15	6.81
Final score		**7.70**

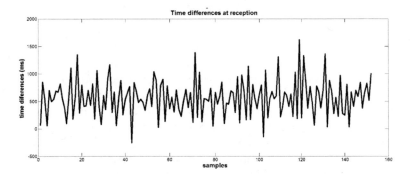

Fig. 13. Detected jitter at the reception of each data packet. This is the cause of the 81% availability of the system.

this, we believe, is that the localization concept proposed by us is in reality quite wearable. In fact we plan for a near future to have the system implemented on a smartphone, making use of its internal sensors (accelerometer and gyroscopes), as well as, their capacity to read RFID/WiFi/Bluetooth signals. With this hardware we can create a similar hybrid localization solution (IMU+RF) that only requires the use of a smartphone carried by a person, and some small RFID/WiFi/Bluetooth tags stuck on the walls of the smart home. A challenge will be to process the IMU signals coming from the smartphone, since in that case a Zero Velocity Update (ZUPT) can not be done.

Our system, as described before, is able to read the Earth magnetic field since our IMU has three magnetometers. With this information we could have better estimated the orientation of the person, but we decided not to use that information because in general magnetic information is not reliable in indoor environments (due to the presence of metallic objects, magnets, motors, and some other magnetic field disturbers). So it is commonly admitted that magnetic information can be beneficial outdoors, but indoors it could be detrimental [10]. When we analyzed, after the competition, the orientation estimated with the magnetic compass and compared it to the actual orientation, we saw that the orientation errors were frequent in the Living Lab, so we took a good decision not making use of it.

Our system could have also been improved if the map information (position of doors, walls, and so on) of the living Lab had been used. Map information could have avoided the generation of localization points outside the living lab space, and also it would have improved the RoI correct detection rate. Additionally, our system was able to read the switch messages provided by the building when the user switch on or off a lamp, but we finally decided not to use it since the correction methodology was not well studied and debugged at the time of the competition. So, in conclusion, we get satisfied by the results that we obtained at this competition, but we think that there is room to improve our results a little bit more with a future prototype that would use a more wearable device, as well as the information from a floor map and the user's actions.

5 Conclusion

We have presented one localization system integrating two independent but complementary positioning methods: 1) IMU-based Positioning, and 2) RFID-based Positioning. The output of both systems Pos_{IMU} and Pos_{RFID}, which contains the two-dimensional positioning coordinates of both approaches, are fused to generate the final position estimation, Pos_{Fused}. This estimate gathers together the benefits of each individual solution: absolute estimation, quite smooth tracking, full availability and real-time update rate. A complete evaluation is performed in two labs: CAR-CSIC and the Living Lab of UPM. Over an area of 100 square meters we obtained an accuracy of 1.1 m in %75 of the cases, and a capability to detect RoI of 65%. the system also had excellent installation times and good user acceptance. The described system was the winner of the second edition of the 2012 international EvAAL competition.

References

1. Hightower, J., Borriello, G.: Location Systems for Ubiquitous Computing. Computer 34(8), 57–66 (2001)
2. Collin, J.: Investigations of Self-Contained Sensors for Personal Navigation. PhD thesis (2006)
3. Stirling, R.: Development of a Pedestrian Navigation System Using Shoe Mounted Sensors. PhD thesis, University of Alberta (2004)
4. Ladetto, Q.: J Van Seeters, S Sokolowski, Z Sagan, and B. Merminod: Digital Magnetic Compass and Gyroscope for Dismounted Soldier Position and Navigation. Sensors & Electronics Technology Panel, NATO Research and Technology Agency Sensors, pp. 1–15 (2002)
5. Jiménez, A.R., Seco, F., Prieto, J.C., Guevara, J.: A comparison of Pedestrian Dead-Reckoning algorithms using a low-cost MEMS IMU. In: 2009 IEEE International Symposium on Intelligent Signal Processing, pp. 37–42. IEEE (August 2009)

6. Chatfield, A.: Fundamentals of High Accuracy Inertial Navigation. AIAA, American Institute of of Aeronautics and Astronautics (1997)
7. Foxlin, E.: Pedestrian tracking with shoe-mounted inertial sensors. IEEE Computer Graphics and Applications, 38–46 (December 2005)
8. Feliz, R., Zalama, E., García-Bermejo, J.G.: Pedestrian tracking using inertial sensors. Journal of Physical Agents 3(1), 35–43 (2009)
9. Jiménez, A.R., Seco, F., Prieto, J.C., Guevara, J.: Indoor Pedestrian Navigation using an INS/EKF framework for Yaw Drift Reduction and a Foot-mounted IMU. In: WPNC 2010: 7th Workshop on Positioning, Navigation and Communication, vol. 10, pp. 135–143 (2010)
10. Jiménez, A.R., Seco, F., Zampella, F., Prieto, J.C., Guevara, J.: Improved heuristic drift elimination with magnetically-aided dominant directions (MiHDE) for pedestrian navigation in complex buildings. Journal of Location Based Services 6(3), 186–210 (2012)

Locating Technology for AAL Applications with Direction Finding and Distance Measurement by Narrow Bandwidth Phase Analysis

Rönne Reimann, Arne Bestmann, and Mirjam Ernst

Lambda:4 Entwicklungen GmbH, Hamburg, Germany
{reimann,bestmann,ernst}@lambda4.com

Abstract. Localization within buildings is a demanding task. The principles of a radio technology are described, which allow to determine direction and distance between a transponder and a receiver. Such information can be determined by performing phase measurements based on mathematical methods such as MUSIC for example. Results from field tests conducted with several prototypes have demonstrated the efficiency of this technology indoors as well as outdoors. The demo-application "ArgusNetViewer" shows the localization results in a position plan in a graphical representation and provides an exhaustive protocol. For AAL, such information can be used in the localization process.

Keywords: Real Time Locating System, indoor navigation, indoor localization, phase analysis, narrow bandwidth, Ambient Assisted Living.

1   Introduction

In the recent years, GPS technology is offering an excellent solution for most out-door-localization tasks, however, for localization applications inside buildings, no comparable solution has yet been provided.

Many different types of application require indoor localization as the basic principle. For indoor-navigation applications in larger buildings such as shopping centers and airports, as well for location based services, or monitoring tasks in certain security sensitive areas, indoor-operable localization technology can be used.

Unlike the solution presented here, in most cases, preliminary measures have to be taken, such as for example WiFi fingerprinting. For localization tasks indoors, radio waves can be used, however, here the multipath propagation of radio waves constitutes a major challenge. The technology as presented here provides a viable solution for such cases.

For the AAL area, by means of localization technology, a person's whereabouts, unusual movement patterns and special events can be detected. In order to be able to use an indoor-localization technology for AAL, the equipment has to work very reliably and relatively accurately. The recognition of a person's whereabouts requires a different kind of accuracy than the recognition of movement patterns. For the recognition of special incidents, such as a fall for example, sensors can be used in the transponders.

S. Chessa and S. Knauth (Eds.): EvAAL 2012, CCIS 362, pp. 52–62, 2013.

The transponders should be small, lightweight and easy to wear. Power consumption should allow for use over several days (preferably several months) without requiring recharging or battery change. The localization units should be cost-efficient and easy to install.

The technology presented here, already provides many of the required AAL-properties in the prototype-phase. The combination with inertial systems is promising an impressive level of performance if needed.

2 Technology

2.1 Direction Finding (DF)

Common Principles of DF with Antenna Arrays. Typically, linear antenna systems are used [1]. A linear antenna system is composed of N (for example 8, 16 or 100) antennas, which all provide the same construction and which are all arranged in one line in relation to each other, with a constant distance D. Sufficient distance between the antennas reduces or avoids coupling effects.

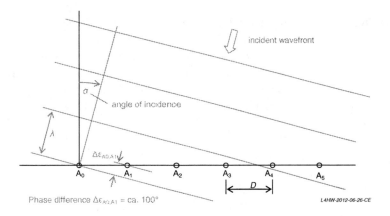

Fig. 1. Linear antenna array in the wave field

Phase difference between two adjacent antennas:

$$\Delta\varepsilon_{A_{n-1}A_n} = \frac{2 \cdot \pi \cdot D}{\lambda} \cdot \sin(\alpha) \tag{1}$$

D the distance between two adjacent antennas,
l the wavelength,
α the angle of incidence of the wave front.

In a construction of uniform circles, coupling effects can easily be compensated. Such antenna systems (Fig. 2) are often used in aeronautics.

The time difference detected for when the wave front arrives at the different antennas, allows to measure a phase difference depending on the angle of incidence α. On the basis of the phase difference between the antennas, the angle of incidence can be reconstructed.

Fig. 2. Direction Finder [2]

Multipathing. The signal will reach the antenna system through many different paths by way of reflection, diffraction, etc. The measured result represents the sum of all individual signal portions. Nevertheless, a resolution of the different signal portions is possible. The phases and amplitudes measured are summarized as complex number to provide one vector which represents one measurement (as performed on all antennas simultaneously). Several measurements which are de-correlated from each other have to be carried out.

Individual measurements can be performed on different frequencies (frequency hopping), or the measurement position can also be slightly changed in space (spatial smoothing). Such vectors are evaluated by means of different classical beam-forming methods. Preferred are super-resolution methods such as „Capon's Method" and „MUSIC" [3], by means of which the auto-correlation matrix of the measurement vectors is analyzed, and 'compared' to the theoretical measurement images of all the directions of incidence to be considered (spectral analysis). The significant signal portions are to be expected in the areas of maximum conformity.

2.2   Direction Finding Improvements by Lambda:4

Use of Arbitrary Antenna Arrays. In practice, for indoor applications, linear antenna systems often cannot be used. The solution as developed by Lambda:4, with a patent application pending, constitutes the application of any arbitrary, complex antenna system with an arbitrary polarization of the antennas and with arbitrary distances between the individual antennas (arbitrary antenna array).

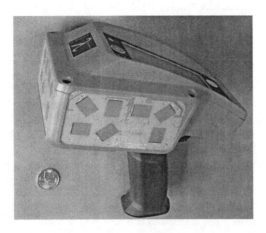

Fig. 3. Handheld locating device, antenna array

An analysis of the direction of incidence of the radio wave in all <u>three dimensions</u> (typically as alpha & phi), <u>and additionally</u> of the polarization is performed. The process constitutes a further development of MUSIC, where – in rather simplified terms – the subspace, extended by the additional dimensions, undergoes a spectral analysis.

Depending on the number of significant signal portions to be resolved, with said signal portions coming from different directions or with different paths, the number of antennas should be chosen to be double, and the number of measurements (frequencies) at least equal. A system with 28 antennas can easily resolve 14 significant signal portions, in practice this will suffice even in worse complex indoor environments.

Qualification of Signal Portions. The four-dimensional spectral analysis provides the significant signal portions in alpha=direction, phi=angle of height and polarization angle. Each measurement vector (on each frequency) has to consist, if applicable, in a different parametrization, of a sum of these signal portions.

By resolving the linear equation system, the composition of each measurement vector can be determined and compared individually from these signal portions in phase and amplitude. Herein, the change of the measurement frequency leads to phase shifts between the individual signal portions.

The signal portions all come from the same source, even though they provide a different run time, due to the different respective distance in the multipathing process. The longer the running distance of a signal portion, the bigger the phase shift will be in the frequency change. Thus, the signal portion with the shortest running distance can be assumed to be the most direct direction to the signal source.

2.3   Distance Measurement (DM)

Basic Principle of DM by Narrow Bandwidth Phase Analysis. The distance measurement can be performed between two transponders or between one station S1 and one transponder T1.

A set of individual phase measurements is provided on different successive discrete frequencies. The individual phase measurements then constitute the basis for calculating the distance by means of mathematical methods. Each individual measurement sets up a simulated (functional equivalent) 'standing wave' between station S1 and the low-cost transponder T1, see Fig. 5.

The patent protected method achieves the same result (see functional equivalent, Fig. 4) as if:

1. the unmodulated carrier of station S1 were transmitted to transponder T1,
2. there were an active (amplified) reflection in T1 and
3. the reflected signal were mixed with the emitted signal in station S1 and measured as a complex I/Q value.

The phase as measured (I/Q) is then constant (in a constant frequency and an unmoved system). The phase as measured (I/Q), however, changes upon variation of the frequency (wave length) in direct proportion to the distance (ideal case without multipathing).

Example
Supposing, (at c=300,000km/s), the following 10 frequencies are used:
f_0=2401MHz, f_1=2402MHz ... f_9=2410MHz.

Wave lengths:
$\lambda_0 = 0.124948$m, $\lambda_1 = 0.124896$m ...

Distance to be determined:
10m for one way, 20m for both ways

For f_0 (20m / 0.124948m) = 160.067 waves (measured I/Q phase = 0.067 = 24°) are obtained
For f_1 (20m / 0.124896m) = 160.133 waves (measured I/Q phase = 0.133 = 48°) are obtained
Etc.

Thus (in an ideal case), per 1MHz of frequency change, a phase shift between the measurements of ca. 24° can be observed respectively. Twice the distance leads to a double phase shift. So much concerning the ideal case without multipathing - with multipathing included, everything becomes much more complex.

However, methods such as Fourier analysis and high resolution methods are applicable (except small restrictions), because this is a linear system.

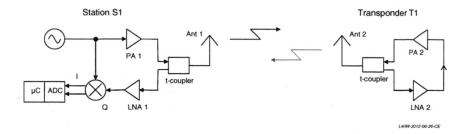

Fig. 4. Functional equivalent with station S1 and transponder T1

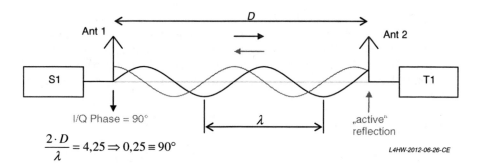

$$\frac{2 \cdot D}{\lambda} = 4{,}25 \Rightarrow 0{,}25 \equiv 90°$$

Fig. 5. "Standing wave" between station S1 and transponder T1

In Practice: Simulating the Standing Wave with Low Cost Parts. In practice, the "simulating standing wave" is realized by a sequence of single frames of clean carriers which are exchanged between the two partners S1 and T1. Only one partner is transmitting at a time [4].

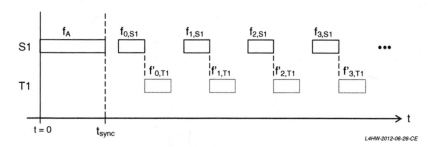

Fig. 6. Frame diagram for distance measurement

f_A: carrier to adjust frequency, transmitted by station S1;

f_n,S_1, $f'_n,T1$: transmitted carrier from station S1 und transponder T1 for phase measurement for distance determination;

typical: $|f_n,S1 - f'_n,T1| < 800 Hz$

The sequence is initiated by regular packet data communication. One first longer frame f_A is used for time synchronisation and to approximate frequency in the second partner. In the following, for each frequency, each partner sends one frame of e.g. 2ms, consisting of a clean carrier (f_n,S1, f'_n,T1). The partner receives such frame and measures its frequency and phase difference in comparison to his own local oscillator.

The transmission frequencies of both partners can be different, but should be similar (e.g. difference < 800Hz). The system used in the prototypes is a little more complex because gain-control mechanisms are necessary and multiple antennas are used in the station.

The results of this technology are substantially improved due to the use of multiple antennas.

Complex Technology, Low-Cost Realization Possible. The complete system of a transponder can be realized by a low cost radio chip, in this case a TI CC2500 (costs 1.4$ / 1k) and a very small FPGA A3PN030 with 30k system gates by Microsemi (formerly Actel) (costs 3.4$ / 1k) for data acquisition together with a small Microcontroller TI MSP430F2272 (costs 2.0$ / 1k). The future will offer low-cost single chip solutions.

3   Implementation

The present prototype system of localization technology is composed of a localization device and a trans-ponder. It is not optimized for an AAL application, but it demonstrates the efficiency of this technology. Several transponders can be localized, a combination of several localization devices is possible. The current software status is optimized for the use of one localization device plus four transponders. The frequency band 2.4 – 2.5 GHz is used, others, such as 868/915 MHz or 5.8 GHz are also possible and have partially been tested. The optimum frequency range depends of the exact type of application.

In order to be localized by means of a localization device, a transponder needs to be carried. The transponder prototypes differ in their output performance, power supply, built-in sensors and size. The smallest (Fig. 7) transponders provide the following dimensions and respectively weight, including power supply:

- Yankee 7 conductor board   77 * 45 * 2.5mm, ~ 9g
- Zulu conductor board   70 * 43 * 8.5mm, ~40g

Fig. 7. Transponder prototypes "Yankee 7" and "Zulu"

The transponders do not provide any operating elements, they are permanently working, are equipped with an acceleration sensor and only have a relevant power consumption, when the localization device requires them to transmit.

An antenna array providing 28 antennas is built into the localization devices (Fig 3). For localization tasks in rescue applications (buried or missing persons or team members), a prototype of a handheld localization device (ca. 1.2 kg) with a colour display has been developed. The handheld localization device allows to search for transponders, without providing any infrastructure whatsoever.

The localization device provides distance measurements, angles of incidence (3D), transponder information, sensor information and indications relating to accuracy. The current prototypes carry out one measurement approximately once per second.

For the determination or respectively visualization of a position in an apartment, Lambda:4 demo-software 'ArgusNetViewer' is used. This software contains the localization information as determined by the localization devices, it is possible to use a single device or more than one as infrastructure. The software generates a visualization on the screen as well as the protocol files. There is an overall protocol and a protocol in CSV format, providing the intermediate and final results of the localization processes. A room plan can be uploaded into the software. Here, the positions of the localization devices can be determined and the areas of interest can be entered.

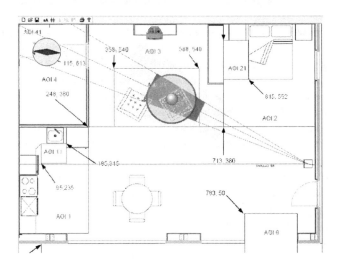

Fig. 8. Demo-software 'ArgusNetViewer'

4   Performance / Evaluation / Limits

The performance of the technology was tested in different environments. With an unobstructed line of view, a range of ca. 1500m was achieved in the city park of Ham-burg [5], in other, non-documented tests in the Alps, up to 5 km.

Indoor tests were run in airports, subway stations, in office buildings and underground parking garages. Here the ranges obtained very much depend on the structural conditions. In one office building a vertical range of ca. 7-8 floors was reached [6]. On the airport pier in Hamburg a reach of 550m horizontally, and three floors vertically was obtained [7]. In underground parking garages, a transponder was reliably located through 2-3 parking levels [8].

The accuracy of the distance measurement inside buildings typically amounts to 1-5m, depending on the wall materials and other conditions of the environment (for example, many people moving around). With an unobstructed view over distances of 100-500m, the maximum error typically lies around 10 to 20 meters. In the case of very long distances or strong signal attenuation respectively, a distance measurement is not always possible.

The accuracy of the integrated air-pressure sensors is around +/- 1m [9].

The technology has already been successfully tested in pilot projects with fire departments in Germany and the U.S.A., in searches for missing persons in buildings and in the Alps as well as in the Antarctica.

The accuracy of the measurement of angles of incidence was shown in the search for 'buried persons' (10*20*3cm-size bag). [10]. Further tests took place successfully under extreme conditions such as strong heat and water vapor in fire drills [11].

5   EvAAL Competition, Implementation and Findings

In the EvAAL competition, the handheld localization device, optimized for localization purposes in rescue applications, was used without any modifications. The handheld localization device was mounted on a tripod (Fig. 9), power supplied through a power adaptor, and its position in the room was measured. The handheld localization device then provided one direction and one distance approximately once per second for the transponder which was used in the process.

The transponder was attached to the actor's lower thigh (Fig. 10). The transponder can be worn anywhere on the body. Here, the foot was chosen, in order to achieve an optimum performance, when only one localization device is used. Generally, the localization device is suited to localize several transponders, in the given competition, however, the requirement was, that only one had to be localized.

Fig. 9. Handheld localization device   **Fig. 10.** Thigh mounted transponder

The information, as detected by the handheld localization device, was radio-transmitted to a laptop. Then, the demo-application 'Argus Netviewer' recorded said information on the laptop, entered it into a map (Fig. 8) and a protocol file, and transmitted it via telnet protocol to the EvAAL interface. The AOI was also determined in the application.

The accuracy of the individual localizations in this arrangement was excellent. Owing to the functional principle of the handheld localization device, this level of accuracy could only be achieved in slow motion or standstill. This arrangement could clearly demonstrate the enormous potential of AAL-field of application. With a few modifications in hardware and software, however, it is possible to fully realize this potential.

6   Future Pospects

The prototypes demonstrated here, are neither sufficiently robust, nor mature to go into productions. In order to develop the best possible product for a certain application, the prototypes can be adapted and further developed using features from a wide range of options.

For the AAL field, the transponder prototypes are already highly applicable in terms of size and power consumption. Furthermore, the compact transponder can readily be integrated into other products such as for example radio devices or mobile telephones, etc. In order to provide a better support for the tracking functionality, low-cost inertial sensors can be integrated into the transponder.

For this application, the localization devices can become substantially smaller (similar to the size of a WLAN router) and can be provided with a simpler layout. The localization quality can also be further improved by using an IMU and by adding several localization devices. Furthermore, algorithms specializing on the recognition of typically human movement can be used and optimized for the purpose.

The combination of distance measurement and inertial sensor technology makes it possible to achieve an excellent performance; major synergy effects between both technologies allow such achievements while offering extremely low costs.

References

1. Mewes, H.: Theoretische und experimentelle Untersuchungen von Peilverfahren für Mehrkanalempfänger im HF-Bereich, Verlag Shaker, Aachen (1994)
2. Introduction into Theory of Direction Finding, Radio Monitoring and Radio Location 2000/2001. Rhode & Schwarz GmbH & Co. KG (2000/2001)
3. Nickel, U.R.O.: Aspects of Implementing Super-Resolution Methods into Phased Array Radar. Int. J. Electron. Commun (AEÜ) 53(6), 315–323 (1999)
4. Wehner, M., Richter, R., Zeisberg, S., Michler, S.: High Resolution Approach for Phase Based TOF Ranging using Compressive Sampling. In: WPNC 2011 8th Workshop on Positioning, Navigation and Communication, Dresden (2011)
5. John, F.: Protokoll Feldtest Reichweite SW 1.76, Lambda:4-interne Feldtestprotokolle, Hamburg (Mai 23, 2012)

6. John, F.: Protokoll Feldtest L4 Bürogebäude über X-Stockwerke, Lambda:4-interne Feldtestprotokolle, Hamburg (May 10, 2012)
7. Ernst, M., John, F.: Protokoll Feldtest Flughafen Hamburg, Lambda:4-interne Feldtestprotokolle, Hamburg (April 19, 2012)
8. John, F.: Protokoll Feldtest Tiefgarage, Lambda:4-interne Feldtestprotokolle, Hamburg (März 2, 2012)
9. John, F.: Protokoll Feldtest Synchrontest Höhe, Lambda:4-interne Feldtestprotokolle, Hamburg (April 25, 2012)
10. Englisch, F.: Protokoll Feldtest Hangneigungstest Lawinen Genauigkeit, Lambda:4-interne Feldtestprotokolle, Davos (Dezember 03, 2008)
11. Ernst, M.: Protokoll Feldtest Brandhaus Berlin, Lambda:4-interne Feldtestprotokolle, Hamburg (2012)

The Smart-Condo™ Infrastructure and Experience

Iuliia Vlasenko, Meisam Vosoughpour Yazdchi, Veselin Ganev,
Ioanis Nikolaidis, and Eleni Stroulia

Department of Computing Science, 2-21 Athabasca Hall, University of Alberta,
Edmonton, Alberta, Canada, T6G 2E8
{vlasenko,vosoughp,vganev,nikolaidis,stroulia}@ualberta.ca

Abstract. The term "Smart Home" refers to a home equipped with sensors,
which observe the environment and the actions of its occupants, and actuators,
which automatically control the home ambience and devices. A Smart Home
can provide a variety of services to its occupants, based on information gleaned
from the data recorded by the sensors and using the automation afforded by the
actuators. Our work in the Smart-Condo™ project has been motivated by
healthcare concerns: we aim to support people with chronic conditions to live
independently longer. To that end, our first objective has been to develop an
accurate location- and activity-recognition method. In this paper, we describe
the Smart-Condo™ middleware architecture, focusing on its occupant-
localization feature. We report on simulation experiments with three sensor
placements, one of which was deployed at a recent indoor localization
competition. Finally, we draw a comparison between the simulated and real-
world results, showing the potential practical significance of our methodology.

Keywords: Smart Home, Ambient Assisted Living, Wireless Sensor Networks,
Indoor Localization, Virtual World, Simulation, Sensor Placement.

1 Introduction

The term "Smart Home" [5] refers to a home embedded with sensors, to observe the
environment and its occupants' activities, and actuators, to automatically control the
home ambience and devices in a way that improves the occupants' experience.
Sensor-based systems are being studied as a means of non-intrusively monitoring a
person's activity and providing this person, and his formal and informal caregivers,
with information, useful for making decisions regarding his care [6][8][9][14]. In our
work on the Smart-Condo™ project [3][4][15][16][17] we have been developing a
comprehensive platform for addressing exactly this research problem.

The first version of the Smart-Condo™ platform was deployed in 2009 in an office
reconceived (and sparsely refurnished) as the home of a three-person family. This
deployment included only motion sensors, pressure sensors and switches, and served
simply as a feasibility exercise.

In the summer of 2011, the platform was deployed in the Independent Living Suite
(ILS) of the Glenrose Rehabilitation Hospital, in Edmonton, Alberta, Canada [1] [17].

S. Chessa and S. Knauth (Eds.): EvAAL 2012, CCIS 362, pp. 63–82, 2013.
© Springer-Verlag Berlin Heidelberg 2013

The deployment was used to support discharge planning: patients, about to be discharged, stay in the ILS for several days, in order for the discharge team to determine whether they are ready to be discharged and live on their own, or whether they need to remain at the hospital longer. Typically, while patients stay in the ILS, nurses have to periodically check on them for the sake of their safety and wellbeing, which contradicts the purpose of the stay, namely for the patients to demonstrate their ability to live autonomously. The Glenrose clinicians have considered using video cameras to observe the patients' stay, however, some patients are unwilling to accept this technology out of privacy concerns. We deployed our platform and analyzed data recorded during the stay of two patients in the ILS. This deployment included a variety of sensors, through which we monitored movement, opening and closing of doors/drawers/kitchen cabinets, usage of electrical appliances, usage of furniture, bed occupancy, usage of the bathroom, and medication adherence. The collected data were used to generate reports and visualizations for the discharge team.

Between the two deployments, we have focused on two specific research problems, which have driven the evolution of our platform. First, we are concerned with extensibility of the platform, both in terms of the sensors that may be integrated in a home (including home-environment sensors, activity sensors and personal home-care devices), and in terms of the services that the platform may be required to support (including localization, activity recognition, alarm generation etc). In principle, standardization is required at (a) the sensor level, and at (b) the service-interface level. The former requirement is motivated by the need to seamlessly integrate new sensors, as they become available. When a new type of sensor reading and/or protocol is introduced to the system, the system must be able to use it and synthesize it with other pre-existing sensor data. The latter requirement captures the need for general-purpose platforms that can integrate a variety of services of differing computational complexity, as mentioned above. Second, we recognize that a major factor influencing the adoption of such technologies is the deployment and operational costs involved. To enable informed decision making on the part of potential adopters, we have developed a systematic process for simulating and evaluating the performance of the system under particular deployment conditions. Through this process, we can explore, in the pre-deployment phase, how we may reduce the number of sensors and yet be able to attain a certain performance level. To demonstrate the validity of our approach and compare the pre-deployment evaluation results with empirical results, we participated in the "Evaluating AAL Systems through Competitive Benchmarking" (EvAAL, http://evaal.aaloa.org/) competition in July 2012. The competition deployment became the third milestone for the Smart-Condo™ project; this paper highlights lessons learned while preparing for and during the competition.

In this paper, we discuss the high-level software architecture of the Smart-Condo™ platform (Section 2); we describe its support for simulation-based deployment configuration planning (Section 3); we explain its location-recognition algorithm (Section 4); we report on our experimental evaluation (Section 5); we review the most recent developments in the field of indoor localization (Section 6); and we conclude with a summary of our experience to date and some plans for future work (Section 7).

2   System Architecture

The high-level architecture of the Smart-Condo™ platform (shown in Figure 1) consists of three layers. The first layer corresponds to the sensor network, in the case of an actual deployment, or the sensor-network simulator, in the case of simulations for pre-deployment configuration planning. The sensor-network bridge component feeds the collected (or simulator-generated) data to the middle data-storage layer, using the MQTT[1] protocol. The top layer includes a variety of analyses and visualization tools for the purpose of extracting and communicating useful information to clinicians. These tools may rely on the archived data, accessed through a set of APIs supported by the data-storage layer, or on the run-time data accessed through a special-purpose client listening to the MQTT stream.

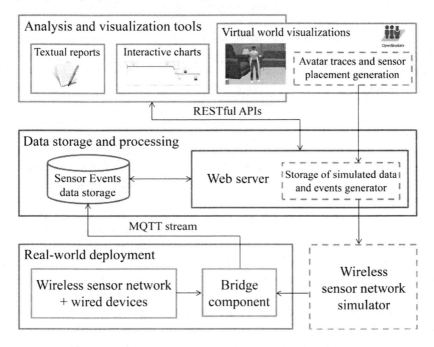

Fig. 1. The Smart-Condo™ Architecture

With the Smart-Condo™ architecture we provide two layers of abstraction to (i) flexibly integrate multiple (types of) sensors as necessary and (ii) to provide a range of services for health-care purposes. First, we have adopted a special-purpose bridge component, which already supports various adapters for collecting readings from different sensor protocols and produces as output an MQTT stream. Thus, the introduction of a new type of sensor involves the development of an intermediary software component that can read the sensor readings and communicate them in

---

[1] A lightweight publish/subscribe protocol, http://mqtt.org

MQTT. Second, we have developed a layer of REST APIs[2] through which the sensor data is accessed by our analyses and visualization tools. In addition to a typical web-based 2D visualization component, our toolkit includes a 3D virtual world, OpenSim[3], where an avatar driven by the activity information inferred by the sensor data can "replay" the occupant's activities in the real world. In the following subsections we discuss the crucial elements of the architecture in more detail.

2.1   The Sensor Network

The Smart-Condo™ platform currently uses (a) passive infrared motion sensors, (b) magnetic reed switches, (c) electrical-current sensors, (d) light, temperature and humidity sensors, (e) bed/chair occupancy pressure sensors, (f) medication-dispensing devices (introduced for the purposes of clinical study at the Glenrose), and is being augmented with (g) RFID readers. Its architecture is not limited to these sensors, but we have been able to produce reasonable results with just the sensors listed here.

The existing variety of sensors can be classified according to the principles of data transmission and available power sources into three categories: (a) wireless nodes with autonomous power supply (*e.g.*, motion sensors); (b) devices wirelessly transmitting their data, but powered from the power line (*e.g.*, electrical-current sensors); and (c) devices that require wiring for both power supply and data delivery (*e.g.*, medication adherence device). If a quick, low-labor deployment is necessary (as stipulated by the EvAAL competition rules) the sensors most favored are primarily motion sensors due to their independence of the apartment infrastructure. Other sensor types (reed switches, pressure sensors, RFID readers, etc.), although they may not need much cabling, tend to be more labor intensive because they require careful placement and embedding in the available furniture. Having chosen the motion sensors as the bare hardware minimum for a new deployment, we confine the discussion to a sensor network of wireless nodes only.

Each wireless node consists of a low-end microcontroller, a low-power radio transceiver, a battery and one or more sensors. In case of long-term deployment, the requirement to minimize energy consumption of the wireless nodes becomes crucial. For this purpose, wireless nodes buffer their readings until either a certain amount of time has passed since the last transmission or until the buffer is full (whichever occurs first). Buffering, as opposed to immediately transmitting sensed data, reduces the node's energy consumption, because every data transmission incurs the costs of (a) waking up the radio and preparing it for transmission, and (b) transmitting not only the actual sensed data and its timestamp but also a set of necessary packet headers. However, buffering complicates the processing of the readings since observations that were made at the same time by different nodes may be transmitted at different times, resulting in observations arriving out of order.

---

[2] The REST architectural style for web-based applications is described in Roy Fielding's 2000 thesis, http://www.ics.uci.edu/~fielding/pubs/dissertation/top.htm

[3] http://opensimulator.org

2.2   Bridge Component and Sensor-Readings Processor

The bridge is a hardware/software component with a variety of adaptors, through which data from different types of sensors and protocols can be collected. It enables us to integrate standard sensing devices, *e.g.*, electrical-current ZigBee-compliant sensors, along with custom-made and specifically programmed nodes running PicOS [2], for which we have developed our own PicOS-to-bridge adapter. A diverse landscape of other standard lower-layer protocols, *e.g.*, Bluetooth, ANT+, Z-Wave, as well as various proprietary protocols, can be equally easily integrated. The bridge's additional functionality is to provide a layer of data-storage redundancy, *i.e.*, an extra lightweight database in which all the raw sensor readings are stored prior to filtering and processing. This data storage constitutes an intermediate data format which can be used for tracing and debugging errors that may occur at different levels of the system architecture during execution.

To address the out-of order observations introduced earlier, the bridge uses a sliding-window buffer to (re)order raw sensor readings by their reported timestamps. Every t seconds (t is configurable), all readings in the buffer with a timestamp up to t seconds earlier than the current (wall clock) time are published to the MQTT broker.

The broker acts as a message queuing and filtering mechanism for clients that either (a) publish information updates under certain topics, or (b) subscribe to receive updates on topics of interest. Having decoupled producers and consumers of data, the MQTT-based middleware allows for greater modularity and heterogeneity to the extent that various devices with TCP/IP networking functionality[4] can be plugged into the system at the MQTT broker level, bypassing the bridge. In the current infrastructure, however, the bridge is an MQTT gateway for all the wireless devices. It publishes sensor readings under a pre-determined topic, and a special data-importing module, subscribed to that topic, gets notified and feeds the acquired data into a back-end implemented on top of WebSphere Sensor Events[5].

Readings imported into Sensor-Events are being processed by a set of database triggers and stored procedures, which are activated whenever a new entry is created in the raw sensor readings table. The triggers perform noise filtering and call stored procedures implementing activity-recognition logic. More specifically, in this paper we focus on "location and movement recognition", *i.e.*, determining the occupant's location, based on motion-sensor readings mainly. The Sensor-Events platform (with the underlying DB2 server) brings a benefit of implementing stored procedures in procedural SQL or Java, the latter being our language of choice for creating procedures of unconstrained flexibility and complexity.

The inferences generated as the application of location- and activity-recognition logic to the collected data through the triggers are stored in a separate database table, in a clear, client-independent format. These parsed readings are currently being used by a visualization client, implemented in the OpenSim virtual world, but they may be accessed by any type of a client via a call to an intermediary REST web service.

---

[4] Due to the fact that the MQTT is implemented on top of TCP/IP stack.

[5].WebSphere Sensor Events (http://www.ibm.com/software/integration/sensor-events) provides the core platform for developing, deploying, and managing end-to-end solutions that exploit the new real-world information available from networked sensors.

2.3   Virtual World Visualization

The virtual-world animation of the patient's activities has been developed as one of the visual-analysis tools of the Smart-Condo™ platform and addresses privacy issues associated with video surveillance. The generated animations provide sufficient level of detail comparable with video recording, yet have lower fidelity and are intrinsically non-personified. They are viewable both in real-time, *i.e.*, caregivers may monitor the avatar's actions and thus implicitly monitor the patient's actions as they occur, or off-line, *i.e.*, the caregivers can request a playback of a period in a patient's day based on the data stored in the Sensor-Events database. Figure 2 shows two alternative views of the 3D model of the apartment and the avatar (views are fully customizable).

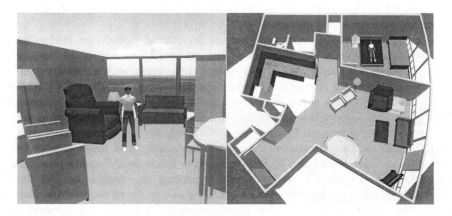

Fig. 2. Alternative views in the virtual world

The real-time virtual-world simulation of the patient's activities is generated as follows: when new sensor readings arrive to the Sensor-Events database, a special-purpose service is triggered to push specifically preformatted commands to the OpenSim server. The server parses the commands and updates the states and/or positions of the patient's avatar and the virtual objects corresponding to the furniture and appliances in the patient's real environment accordingly. The playback mode has to be initiated by the user who can select a desired time span and speed of replay; after the user request is issued, the rest of the procedure follows the same execution path as in the real-time mode.

3   The Smart-Condo™ Simulation Platform

Originally we conceived the virtual world as an environment for mirroring real-world activities. However, we have since expanded its functionality towards a simulation-based testing methodology, to support the planning of new potential deployments of the Smart-Condo™ platform. This became possible once we had developed virtual models of the real sensors. This functionality is especially important for accurate representation of motion sensors. The detection range of each motion sensor has a complex volumetric shape; as such, estimating the detection capability of a sensor at a given position and orientation using 2D placement tools is a challenge.

Overall, our simulation methodology involves the following sequence of steps.

1. We build a model of the deployment space in the virtual world based on CAD drawings and any additional information about furnishings, appliances, etc.
2. Next, we place virtual sensors in this model, following the same principles and practices that one would adopt to place the real sensors in the real world.
3. At (simulation) run time, these virtual sensors are triggered by the avatar. This interaction is tracked by in-world tools and converted into artificial sensor events.

In this procedure, the virtual world is used to generate realistic action traces and corresponding sensor data. Through the virtual-world client, the avatar can be controlled by a user to perform a sequence of activities. The avatar is equipped with an "action-tracking" device, which records movement, sitting/standing posture, and interaction with other virtual objects (opening/closing doors, switching on/off light switches, etc.) as a sequence of <time, action, location> tuples. The generated action log is used as the ground truth trace at the evaluation stage. At the same time, the virtual sensors generate their own events as they are programmed to mimic the real sensors behavior. For example, the virtual motion sensors sense collision events when a moving object penetrates the corresponding 3D shapes; the virtual RFID reader is able to identify different avatars located within the reader's range as if they were wearing RFID tags. All the virtual sensor readings are collected in a separate log as <time, sensorID, sensorReading> tuples. These sensor readings are further propagated through the sensor-network simulator, which helps to more accurately model the operating environment.

3.1   Wireless Sensor Network Simulator

Using PicOS substantially simplifies the software development for the low-end hardware used in wireless sensor networks through the use of its source-level simulator, Virtual Underlay Emulation Engine (VUE^2) [4]. VUE^2 implements the PicOS API and simulates many of the hardware components. It takes into account location and movement of nodes (if applicable), simulates wireless propagation characteristics and noise, and thereby makes it possible to determine data loss and delays rates anticipated in the real environment. The development of the PicOS-to-bridge adapter enabled us to integrate VUE^2 with the Smart-Condo™ system and, therefore, to easily experiment with new deployments in simulation mode.

Whenever any of the simulated sensors are triggered, a command specifying that event is sent to the VUE^2 simulator, which, in turn, invokes the event handler in the PicOS application for the particular sensor. From that point the simulated node registers the observation and eventually sends it to the bridge. As long as the wireless nodes used are running PicOS, this model follows closely the operation of the real sensor network, since the same code runs in the VUE^2 simulator and on the actual nodes. After the sensor reading has reached the bridge component, it is processed exactly the same way real readings are processed, including being published to the MQTT broker and eventually reaching the Sensor-Events database.

3.2   Closing the Loop via the Virtual World

The location estimates generated by the localization component (and activity inferences produced by activity-recognition components) are stored in a separate database table. Through an API, the virtual-world client can access them and convert them into a corresponding set of movements and actions for the avatar. That is, the virtual-world controller extracts and processes the readings, and then sends commands to relevant in-world objects to represent each action. Effectively, this procedure constitutes the playback visualization mode (subsection 2.3). Through this simulation path, we can directly compare the original avatar trace from the ground truth log to the trace replayed by the virtual world. Based on their differences, we can assess the accuracy of our monitoring infrastructure.

Given the negligible cost of placing virtual sensors in the virtual world, a variety of alternative placements can be experimented with; by comparing their relative location-recognition accuracy, the configuration with the most accurate anticipated location recognition may be selected for deployment.

This *closed-loop* development and refinement process enables us to perform experiments that systematically evaluate the accuracy of the inhabitant's activity record captured by the architecture and the capabilities of the assumed sensors, *before the actual deployment*. Experiments that involve trial runs with participation of human subjects are cumbersome to organize and difficult to assess. The virtualized alternative allows for arbitrary experiments prior to deployment (to reach a desired level of precision) and allows insights into alternative deployment strategies or alternative sensor technologies that best capture the needs of the client.

4   Location Recognition

Once the system hardware is deployed, the location of the condo occupant is inferred from the readings of motion sensors, light switches, reed switches on the doors/cabinets, and pressure sensors in the bed or chairs if the occupant is interacting with the respective elements of the furniture during movement. Location recognition can be improved with RFID readers, if the occupant wears an RFID tag. If the installation time is limited and it is preferable that furniture is kept intact (as was the case with the EvAAL competition), motion sensors become the minimal set of devices necessary for localization.

Motion sensors incorporated in our platform are commercially available passive infrared sensors chosen for their miniature size, fairly wide area of detection and low energy consumption [13]. Being passive, they do not emit infrared light but rather collect incident infrared radiation from within the coverage area. Thus when a moving object with temperature higher than that of the background enters this area, the sensor will detect an increase in the amount of radiation. The output of these sensors is therefore mapped to binary: 0 for no motion, and 1 for motion detected anywhere within the detection area; as a result, given a single sensor, the position of the moving object cannot be discerned with any higher precision than the "radius" of the sensor footprint.

If the localization accuracy is of crucial importance for the deployment, we opt for the sensors with the smallest available detection area. Besides minimizing this parameter, another way to improve localization granularity is to have the sensor footprints overlap. In this case, the floor space is segmented in a number of polygons each one annotated by a bit vector, a 0/1 in the n_{th} position of this vector signifies that the n_{th} motion sensor covers/does not cover the polygon. Hence, the bit vector is a "signature" of the motion-sensor readings that are expected to occur if a person steps in the corresponding polygon. Accordingly, the sensor placement that yields no overlap becomes a particular case of this assignment since each sensor covers a single polygon and thus at any given time of trace execution a signature of readings can contain at most a single 1 and the rest 0's unless the sensors are malfunctioning.

Apart from better localization granularity, the strategy of overlapping sensor footprints introduces synchronization issues. Ideally, to properly fuse the data from two sensors triggered by the same motion event, they must (a) arrive at the bridge at the same time and (b) be associated with identical timestamps. As discussed in section 2.1, buffering on the nodes causes the readings to arrive out of time order. This problem is alleviated by the sliding time window during which the readings are properly reordered and the expired readings are discarded. However, using buffering and a sliding window is acceptable only if the location estimates are not required immediately. When real-time performance of the system is important and energy conservation can be sacrificed (both are the case for the EvAAL competition which lasts only 3 hours for each competitor), the platform can be configured to deliver the sensor readings "instantaneously", *i.e.*, there is no buffering on the nodes and the only added time is for wireless transmission of the packets to the sink.

Having excluded buffering, we still have to work around the second requirement since there is no global synchronization across all nodes. Each node has its own internal clock, and the global timestamps at the bridge are inferred from the time of packet arrival and two timestamps reported: local time on the node when the packet was built and local time when the event was registered. If the first-time delivery of the packet was unsuccessful, the node will retransmit the same packet with an updated timestamp of its generation, accounting for the round-trip retransmission delays. However, there is no account for the usually unpredictable (due to medium access protocol behavior) one-way transmission time and extra processing times at the bridge: if two simultaneously issued packets travel in a crowded wireless environment or arrive at the bridge when it is under high load, they may end up with quite different global timestamps.

To better understand the trade-off of improved localization granularity *vs.* complications in data fusion and find the best suited for real-time deployment, we apply the closed-loop testing methodology to both overlapping and non-overlapping schemes of sensor placement.

5   Experiments

In preparation for the EVAAL competition, we systematically evaluated the localization accuracy of the Smart-Condo™ system through simulation. For each <time, action, location> tuple, as logged by the action-tracking device collecting the avatar traces, the error is defined as the distance, in meters, between the avatar's position, and the position of the corresponding action inferred by the localization component for the given timestamp (interpolated, if timestamps do not match). For the experiment as a whole, we consider the average error, as well as other descriptive statistics, such as standard deviation and error distribution. Assuming the sensors are all functioning properly, these metrics can give us an idea of the accuracy of the processed avatar locations, with respect to the original sensor readings. If a sensor is misbehaving, on the other hand, these readings can help us identify the malfunctioning sensor by returning a larger-than-expected error value for that sensor.

5.1   Simulation Results

During setup, the Smart-Condo™ localization component relies on knowledge of (a) the architectural diagram of the deployment space, (b) volumetric coverage models of the motion sensors, and (c) the coordinates and mounting angle of where the motion sensors have been placed to construct a special-purpose map of the space.

In preparation for the competition, we used the architectural diagram of the Living Lab[6] located in Madrid, Spain. From the four available types of passive infrared sensors varying in coverage area, we chose the one with the smallest detection range, that is, the spot type with footprint of 2x1.4m in cross-section at 2m away from the sensor. The more detailed inspection of the sensors datasheet revealed that the detection area of a sensor represents a grid of tiny detection zones and non-sensing strips. The spot type has the most regular and dense pattern of detection zones of all the sensors considered for deployment. Its coverage is well approximated by a rectangular-based pyramid; this pyramid is the geometric representation used by both the simulations in the virtual world and our localization component.

Due to installation time constraints in the competition, we narrowed down the variety of mounting techniques and opted for the mounting on the ceiling with sensors facing the floor in a way that the pyramid base is parallel to the floor plane. Therefore, the 2D sensor coverage map of the space becomes a grid of rectangles that may vary in orientation. Note that this type of mounting is not always possible or preferable. E.g., in previous deployments we have attached the sensors to the walls, hence, the projections of the pyramids on the floor are complex polygons (trapezoids in most generic cases) and the sensor map as a whole is highly irregular. This is when the virtual-world-based planning of deployment becomes an invaluable tool in terms of ease of operation, expressiveness and automation of otherwise manual tasks.

The next stage of simulation is the generation of alternative deployments. As we mentioned before, we focus on the two most important scenarios: overlapping and non-overlapping placements. In both cases, the objective is to minimize the number of sensors while still fully covering the space. Another alternative placement we would like to consider arises as we relax the latter requirement and cap the number of sensors at the fairly small but still reasonable number that covers at least 50% of the space. By this additional placement we would like to test (i) whether there exists a monotonic relation between the localization accuracy and the density of the deployed

---

[6] The floor-plan of the Living Lab
   http://evaal.aaloa.org/images/LL-coordinates.jpg

sensors, and (ii) whether the less crowded wireless environment will have noticeable effect on the accuracy. This third alternative deployment is also important if we consider the case when some number of the sensors prepared for the competition cannot properly function and there are no extra devices for a backup.

Therefore, we consider three placements (a) overlapping with 30 sensors, (b) dense non-overlapping with 22 sensors, and (c) non-overlapping with significant gaps in coverage with 13 sensors, shown in Figure 3.

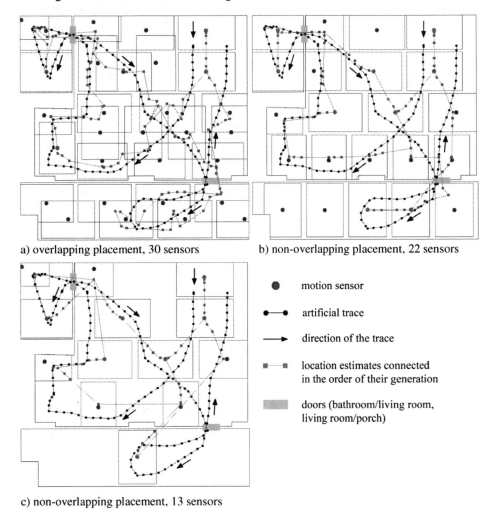

a) overlapping placement, 30 sensors   b) non-overlapping placement, 22 sensors

c) non-overlapping placement, 13 sensors

- ● motion sensor
- ●—● artificial trace
- → direction of the trace
- ▪—▪ location estimates connected in the order of their generation
- ▨ doors (bathroom/living room, living room/porch)

Fig. 3. Three alternative placements; an example of artificially generated trace execution

As our methodology suggests, we generated a number of artificial traces; each of them has been tested against all three placements under identical conditions; the results of our simulations are presented in Table 1. Figure 4 displays the error distribution for each of the tested placements.

Table 1. Descriptive statistics for three types of sensor placement

Description	# of sensors	Average error, m	Standard deviation, m
Overlapping, full coverage	30	0.5286	0.3155
Non-overlapping, full coverage	22	0.6127	0.3269
Non-overlapping, partial coverage	13	1.1619	0.9232

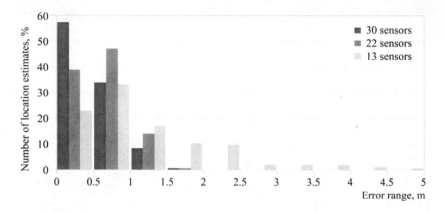

Fig. 4. Error distribution for three types of placements used in simulations

Overall we observe that the overlapping placement shows better results, as expected. However, it is worth noting that despite of our best effort to realistically model all non-software aspects of the system operation (*e.g.*, signal propagation in a wireless environment), certain issues intrinsic to overlapping sensor placement have not been properly addressed and only became evident during real-world tests.

More specifically, we noted two problems in the way that sensors get triggered: (i) the sensor will output 0 even if the person is within the coverage area but is completely still; (ii) the signal is rapidly oscillating between 1 and 0 (as fast as 10Hz) during continuous motion within a single sensor coverage area. These problems were not addressed in the simulations due to the basic assumption that as long as the avatar's location lies within the covered area, the sensor outputs 1 regardless whether the avatar is moving or not. The first type of idiosyncrasy is easily addressed by checking whether the avatar's location is not changing (the person is still), and the appropriate model of sensor behavior has been promptly applied. Unfortunately, signal oscillations have proved more intricate to model. Moreover, this behavior significantly undermined our data fusion mechanism, eventually forcing us to abandon the overlapping strategy of deployment.

Another important factor that influenced our sensor-placement decision was the number of sensors that needed to be transported to the remote location, reinforced by the limited time for their installation. In addition, the competition benchmarking tests included trials with two people when only one had to be localized. Considering that our system does not stipulate any wearable equipment (RFID readers have been left out during the initial phase of competition planning), non-overlapping placement becomes the most appealing strategy due to its ability to distinguish between adjacent sensor footprints and to fairly easily detect anomalies in sensor readings signatures.

On the software side, these simulations proved essential for debugging our localization algorithm. The algorithm's initial coarse estimate is the center of mass of the polygon corresponding to the overlap of the most recently triggered sensors. Subsequent estimates are generated along a physically plausible trajectory until reaching the center of mass of the next adjacent "triggered" area. Figure 3 depicts both the original trace and the results of our localization component calculations.

Closer inspection of Figure 3 suggests possible improvement both in terms of sensor placement and tweaking the algorithm. Note Figure 3a: besides rectangles of various sizes it has a number of polygons with slim protruding parts (as some at the very bottom of the map). The center of mass of such an oddly shaped polygon usually lies in its bigger section causing erroneous estimates when the sensor is triggered from the polygon's "slim" part. On the contrary, Figure 3b shows a generally smoother calculated trajectory (although with a bigger average error) which is, perhaps, due to regularity of the sensor coverage grid. This type of analysis prompts us to continue experimenting with both strategies of sensor placement.

As anticipated, the non-overlapping placement with 13 sensors is roughly twice as bad as the placement with 22 sensors. However, it can also be seen that the coverage grid is not regular and can be much improved even with the given number of sensors. One glaring issue in Figure 3c is that the localization algorithm is not taking into consideration the walls and doors (based on trace transitions from the living room to the porch or the bathroom). We are currently working to address this issue.

From the simulations, we learned that the most reliable placement should be the second type with 22 sensors and assured ourselves that even if a fairly big number of sensors are not working, our system will still be able to generate good results.

5.2 Experiment Results

The actual competition deployment was identical to the third placement considered in the previous section. According to the competition protocol, there were 8 tests overall, 4 with one person, 4 with two persons, and 2 more with one person which, however, assessed the ability of our system to detect the presence of the person in a number of predefined *areas of interest* (AoI). In this paper, we discuss the results of the tests with one person only since the other type of tests (with two people) was our first attempt to perform this sort of task and was neither thoroughly tested in the simulations nor was it our priority in this competition. Therefore, we considered 6 trials ("one person" and "AoI detection") for which we are reporting the average error and standard deviation in Table 2.

Note one clear outlier in this table, which is deemed to occur during a period of our system hardware malfunction. That is, trial "path2-1" has an average error of 3.4m whereas all other errors lie between 1.59 and 2.12m. This fact prompted us to exclude this trial from further consideration for reporting our results in this paper. For a total of 1321 location estimates from 5 valid traces, the overall average error is 1.9257m and standard deviation is 1.2423m. Figure 5 depicts the error distribution; 85% of all location estimates generated by our system lie within 3m-error range.

Table 2. Descriptive statistics for individual trials, one-person localization

Name of a trial	Average error, m	Standard deviation, m
path1-2	1.8470	1.1372
path1-3	1.5906	1.0486
path2-1	3.3999	1.6688
path2-3	2.1267	1.3809
pathRs-1	1.9004	1.1210
pathRs-2	1.9663	1.3406
Overall	**1.9257**	**1.2423**

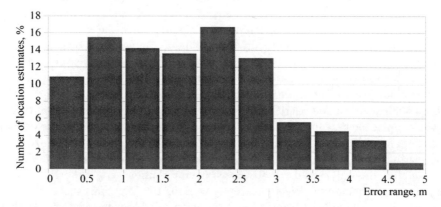

Fig. 5. Number of location estimates (%) *vs.* error range for the competition results

It is worth noting that the average error of experimental results exceeds the average error of simulations with identical placement by 66%. There are at least three factors that could have influenced the experimental results that we are aware of, and two of them had significant deteriorating effects: (i) imperfections in sensor installation and (ii) unanticipated delays in generation of location estimates by our system.

With regard to the sensor installation there was a problem with adhesive materials that we used for attaching sensors to the boxes with wireless nodes. These devices are assembled independently so that the sensors or the nodes are easily replaceable. The final custom device consists of a plastic box enclosing a node, and a sensor sitting outside of the box, attached to the node with a wire. When the deployment configuration is known, the sensor has to be firmly attached to the box with adhesive materials. During the competition, one sensor unglued from the box and freely hung on the ceiling causing a lot of misfiring. Figure 6 illustrates how in one of the trials this problem caused confusion of our localization component specifically at this sensor's location. This image was generated during trial "path2-3", and in comparison with images from other trials it clearly shows the effect of this mechanical failure on the operation of the localization component. To support this claim, trial "path2-3" has the largest average error and standard deviation of the five trials (without one outlier) considered for this paper.

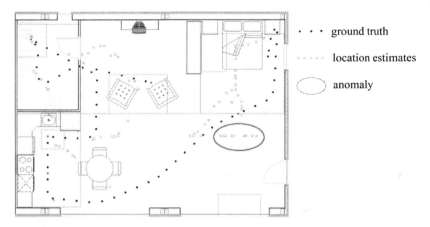

ground truth

location estimates

anomaly

Fig. 6. Anomaly in predicting location estimates due to the detached sensor (image generated and provided by the competition organizers)

Another problem that negatively impacted our results is both hardware-related and a matter of the error measure used. Due to the competition requirement for the competing systems to provide real-time updates of data, we chose not to use buffering on the nodes as explained in section 4. Therefore, this functionality was disabled during the simulations and real-world trials that we ran in preparation for the competition. The delays between the moment when a particular reading is registered on the node and when the location estimate is generated consists of the time needed for the packet delivery to the sink, and times for parsing the packet and calculating a new estimate, which all together sum up to 2s in the worst case (based on our real-world experiments). During the competition, however, we encountered certain hardware difficulties, which urged us to use the buffering period of 2s in order to reduce the number of packets being simultaneously transmitted. That is, the discrepancy between the timestamps of corresponding location estimates reported by our system and the timestamps when they were registered by the EvAAL server was about 4s. Unfortunately, the error computation stipulated by the competition implied that the reported location estimates should be associated with the EvAAL-registered timestamps, which also were used as the reference for comparing to the ground truth. The same error computation is used for the results shown above. In order to better understand our results, we also implemented an alternative error computation in which every timestamp reported by our system is matched against the ground truth data, if the exactly matching timestamp is not found, the estimate of the ground truth position is calculated as interpolation of two data points with the closest timestamps. Results of this alternative error computation are presented in Table 3.

Figure 7 compares the error distributions of the simulation experiment and the competition tests with identical sensor placements after applying the alternative error calculation scheme. These results bear more resemblance between each other, therefore, to certain extent proving the value of our methodology.

Table 3. Descriptive statistics based on matching reported timestamps

Name of a trial	Average error, m	Standard deviation, m
path1-2	1.0701	0.8726
path1-3	0.9147	0.5932
path2-3	1.2576	1.0323
pathRs-1	1.2079	0.9127
pathRs-2	1.4650	1.1727
overall	**1.2704**	**1.0193**

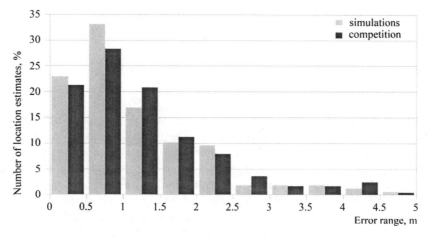

Fig. 7. Error distribution for identical placements in simulation and competition

There is one more factor that has affected these results but in a favorable way. One of the competition requirements was for each competitor to interface their system with the benchmarking system. This included optional integration with the contextual events created by sensors already installed in the Living Lab. The flexibility of our system architecture made this part fairly straightforward. We described the provided devices (light switches and a bicycle) in terms of our platform's sensor-specification language. Since other similar devices have already been successfully incorporated in our system (various switches, pressure sensors, etc.), there was no need to modify the localization component in order to use the information gleaned from the Living Lab devices. The integration went smoothly, was completely transparent to our system, and eventually paid off by improving our localization results. We cannot quantitatively estimate the effect of integration since, to our knowledge, every benchmark test contained a number of contextual events. Also, in our simulations we did not include devices unambiguously specifying action location (switches, etc.), since we focused primarily on the use of motion sensors. Therefore, it is not possible yet to draw any conclusive comparisons between simulations and experiments, but we tend to believe that our testing methodology, enhanced with additional models of hardware behavior and ability to detect various anomalies (even mechanical ones), will eventually eliminate costly real-world trials prior to final deployment.

6   Related Work

Having reviewed the crucial elements of the Smart-Condo™ platform and its location recognition feature, let us review parallel developments in the EvAAL community dedicated specifically to localization techniques.

The tendency to avoid optical tracking techniques is evident throughout recent work on localization, perhaps, due to similar privacy concerns that motivated our own system development. Thus, two major groups of techniques are (i) localization with wearable equipment, and (ii) ambient localization (*i.e.*, similar to our system). The majority of competitors, however, belong to the first group, and only one other competitor presented a device-free localization system [11].

Localization techniques that rely on wearable equipment most often consist of a network of transceivers (short-range radio signals, ultrasound, etc.) and a device installed on a moving target. A rather popular approach in such systems is received signal strength (RSS) fingerprinting, which was used by three competitors. Grupo TAIS from the University of Seville, Spain, develops a fingerprint-based system comprised of ZigBee devices. Similarly, the LOCOSmotion project from the University of Duisburg-Essen, Germany, relies on fingerprinting collected from Wi-Fi access points and uses a smartphone as a wearable device. Additional information is obtained from an accelerometer embedded in the smartphone. Although such systems are usually easy to deploy or can even exploit the existing infrastructure (most indoor environments already have multiple Wi-Fi access points), the fingerprinting phase can be rather tedious since a database of signal fingerprints for all possible mobile device locations has to be collected prior to localization tests. In addition, this approach is sensitive to any changes in the environment, thus, the created fingerprint database requires continuous maintenance. In order to overcome this limitation, the OwlPS system [7], has an auto-calibration mechanism, which eliminates manual fingerprint collection phase and continuously updates its fingerprint database during execution. The OwlPS deployment is one of the quickest in the competition, comprising of four Wi-Fi access points installed in the corners of the Living Lab. However, with respect to localization quality, the three fingerprint-based systems presented in the competition achieved the lowest accuracy scores among all teams.

The iLocPlus system [12] is an ultrasonic time-of-flight measurement system that comprises of reference nodes and an electronic badge/transmitter worn by the tracked person. Successful localization relies on the line-of-sight between the receiver nodes and the transmitter, therefore, the body of the badge wearer may cause deterioration of localization quality in certain positions. Overall, the accuracy score is better than of our system, however, installation is more time-consuming due to a large number of reference nodes required to overcome (i) the obstruction effects of the body and (ii) ultrasound interference caused by background noise.

The localization system developed by the Centre for Automation and Robotics (CAR), Spain [10], combines dead-reckoning with absolute-position estimation obtained from ambient infrastructure. That is, the wearable unit generates inertial data that translates into position estimates characterized by a distinctively smooth trajectory on one hand, and accumulated drift on the other. To minimize drift effects, the system is enhanced with RFID infrastructure that provides absolute position references. More specifically, a portable RFID reader is installed on the tracked person and active RFID tags are deployed in the space. This system requires minimum installation effort and has one of the best accuracy scores. However, as in the case with all the systems using wearable devices, it is arguable whether such a solution will become acceptable for everyday use in a typical AAL environment.

Particular to the Smart-Condo™ project is our motivation to keep the system minimally invasive, and therefore we avoid technologies that involve bulky wearable devices. For example, we are currently augmenting our system with the RFID technology; in our setup the readers are embedded in the ambient infrastructure, and the RFID tags are attached to the moving objects (as opposed to the CAR deployment with a portable reader). The tags are lightweight and cheap and can be easily incorporated into a variety of objects, *e.g.*, clothes, a wheelchair, a walker. The main purpose of integrating the RFID technology is to distinguish between the patient and all other people located in the condo. In a clinically-motivated scenario, the patient staying in the condo is visited by a nurse who has her own RFID tag (perhaps, sewn into the uniform). Therefore, we are able to distinguish between the object of localization interest (the patient) and the "disturber" (the nurse) while the patient remains unaware of the surrounding RFID infrastructure.

In this competition, only one other competitor was driven by a similar motivation. The RSS-based device-free localization system from the CPS Group of the University of Utah [11] consists of static nodes deployed along the inside perimeter of an apartment generating an interconnected graph of wireless links. When the person crosses the line-of-sight between any of the links, their baseline RSS values start fluctuating thus indicating a particular location upon fusion of the data from all the links. This system overcomes the typical for RSS-based approaches issues with dynamically changing environments thanks to continuous online self-recalibration. The localization accuracy of this system is among the best in the competition. There are a few shortcomings: a fairly big number of nodes required for high accuracy results (*e.g.*, 33 nodes in 58m^2), they are powered from the wall outlets which involves extra cabling, and they have to be installed along the walls on a fixed height not exceeding the tracked person height. The latter can be impossible due to existing furniture. On the contrary, our motion sensors can be installed on the ceiling, anywhere on the walls or even underneath a table/desk if we want to detect that specific location. They require no cabling. If a sensor needs to be moved, we only need to change the configuration file since our localization component by default takes into account every possible location and orientation of a sensor in 3D space.

We would like to note that even though our system did not prove to have the best localization accuracy, we managed to showcase the flexibility and interoperability of our architecture. Our system was the only deployment that was successfully integrated with the sensors pre-installed in the Living Lab. It is also worth noting that our system was conceived differently from the competing systems, in that localization is not its sole purpose but merely one of the features supported by the platform. Our work aims to develop a flexible architecture for supporting ambient-assisted living, on one hand, and experimentation with sensor development and sensor-network deployment, on the other. In this architecture, if we replace our existing motion sensor technology, the change will be transparent to the rest of the system.

7   Conclusions

The Smart-Condo™ project aims to support people with chronic conditions to live independently longer by developing a platform for unobtrusively observing the activities of a home's occupant (with a variety of sensors) and automatically controlling the home ambience and devices to improve the occupant's experience.

The Smart-Condo™ platform is architected in three layers. The sensor layer is responsible for collecting sensor readings, whether from a sensor-network actually deployed in a home or from a simulator. The middle layer analyzes the collected sensor data to infer the occupant's location and activities. The interactive-visualization layer communicates these inferences in a graphical manner and as avatar-based animations in a virtual-world model of the occupant's home. An important feature of the Smart-Condo™ platform is its support for simulating and evaluating a particular sensor deployment with respect to its inference accuracy. Through this feature, we are able to explore alternative deployments and their relative deployment-cost *vs.* inference accuracy trade-offs. To this end, the avenues for future work include (i) incorporating improved models for simulating the physical sensor behavior, (ii) overcoming the global synchronization issues for overlapping sensor footprints, and (iii) implementing detection of anomalies in sensor readings of various nature.

To date, the Smart-Condo™ platform has been deployed and evaluated three times in three different spaces. The results from the first two deployments were qualitative, because the experiment design did not allow knowledge of the ground truth of the occupant's activities. In the context of the EvAAL competition, we were able to precisely evaluate the utility and effectiveness of the simulation-based deployment-planning feature of our platform. Furthermore, the experiments demonstrated (a) the ease-of-deployment of our platform, (b) its flexibility and extensibility, as it was the single competitor able to integrate pre-existing sensors in the space, and (c) its high-quality (although not optimal) location-recognition accuracy.

Acknowledgments. We thank N. Boers, J. Huang, and P. Gburzynski for their work in developing the initial version of the Smart-Condo™ system. We thank L. Liu, S. King, and R. Lederer for their role in the broader Smart-Condo™ project. This research was supported by IBM, NSERC, iCORE and OlsoNet.

References

1. Abbey, B., Alipour, A., Gilmour, L., Camp, C., Hofer, C., Lederer, R., Rasmussen, G., Liu, L., Nikolaidis, I., Stroulia, E., Sadowski, C.: A remotely programmable smart pillbox for enhancing medication adherence. In: 2012 25th International Symposium on Computer-Based Medical Systems (CBMS), pp. 1–4. IEEE (2012)
2. Akhmetshina, E., Gburzynski, P., Vizeacoumar, F.: PicOS: A tiny operating system for extremely small embedded platforms. In: Proc. of ESA 2003, pp. 116–122 (2003)
3. Boers, N., Chodos, D., Huang, J., Gburzynski, P., Nikolaidis, I., Stroulia, E.: The Smart Condo: Visualizing Independent Living Environments in a Virtual World. In: Pervasive Computing Technologies for Healthcare, PervasiveHealth 2009, pp. 1–8. IEEE (2009)

4. Boers, N.M., Gburzynski, P., Nikolaidis, I., Olesinski, W.: Supporting Wireless Application Development via Virtual Execution. In: International Multiconference on Computer Science and Information Technology, IMCSIT 2008, pp. 853–860. IEEE (2008)

5. Chan, M., Campo, E., Estève, D., Fourniols, J.: Smart Homes — Current Features and Future Perspectives. Maturitas 64(2), 90–97 (2009)

6. Cook, D.J.: Health Monitoring and Assistance to Support Aging in Place. J. Univers. Comput. Sci. 12(1), 15–29 (2006)

7. Cypriani, M., Canalda, P., Spies, F.: OwLPS: A Self-calibrated Fingerprint-Based Wi-Fi Positioning System. In: Chessa, S., Knauth, S. (eds.) EvAAL 2011. CCIS, vol. 309, pp. 36–51. Springer, Heidelberg (2012)

8. Helal, S., Mann, W.C., El-Zabadani, H., King, J., Kaddoura, Y., Jansen, E.: The Gator Tech Smart House: A Programmable Pervasive Space. IEEE Computer 38(3), 50–60 (2005)

9. Hori, T., Nishida, Y., Murakami, S.: Pervasive Sensor System for Evidence-Based Nursing Care Ssupport. In: Proc. of the IEEE Int. Conf. on Robotics and Automation, ICRA 2006, pp. 1680–1685 (2006)

10. Jimenez Ruiz, A.R., Seco Granja, F., Prieto Honorato, J.C., Guevara Rosas, J.I.: Accurate Pedestrian Indoor Navigation by Tightly Coupling Foot-Mounted IMU and RFID Measurements. IEEE Transactions on Instrumentation and Measurement 61(1), 178–189 (2012)

11. Kaltiokallio, O., Bocca, M., Patwari, N.: Follow @grandma: Long-Term Device-Free Localization for Residential Monitoring. In: The 7th IEEE International Workshop on Practical Issues in Building Sensor Network Applications (2012)

12. Knauth, S., Kaufmann, L., Jost, C., Kistler, R., Klapproth, A.: The iLoc Ultrasound Indoor Localization System at the EvAAL 2011 Competition. In: Chessa, S., Knauth, S. (eds.) EvAAL 2011. CCIS, vol. 309, pp. 52–64. Springer, Heidelberg (2012)

13. Panasonic Electric Works, MP motion sensor "NaPIOn" (passive infrared), datasheet, http://pewa.panasonic.com/assets/pcsd/catalog/napion-catalog.pdf

14. Skubic, M., Alexander, G., Popescu, M., Rantz, M., Keller, J.: A Smart Home Application to Eldercare: Current Status and Lessons Learned. Technology and Health Care 17(3), 183–201 (2009)

15. Stroulia, E., Chodos, D., Boers, N., Huang, J., Gburzynski, P., Nikolaidis, I.: Software Engineering for Health Education and Care Delivery Systems: The Smart Condo Project. In: ICSE Workshop on Software Engineering in Healthcare, SEHC 2009, pp. 20–28. IEEE (2009)

16. Stroulia, E.: Smart Services Across the Real and Virtual Worlds. In: Chignell, M., Cordy, J., Ng, J., Yesha, Y. (eds.) The Smart Internet. LNCS, vol. 6400, pp. 178–196. Springer, Heidelberg (2010)

17. Woo, K., Ganev, V., Stroulia, E., Nikolaidis, I., Liu, L., Lederer, R.: Sensors as an Evaluative Tool for Independent Living. In: Duffy, V.G. (ed.) Advances in Human Aspects of Healthcare, pp. 612–621. CRC Press (2012)

The iLoc+ Ultrasound Indoor Localization System for AAL Applications at EvAAL 2012

Stefan Knauth[1], Aliaksei Andrushevich[2], Lukas Kaufmann[2], Rolf Kistler[2], and Alexander Klapproth[2]

[1] Stuttgart University of Applied Sciences - HFT Stuttgart
Schellingstr. 24, D-70174 Stuttgart, Germany
`stefan.knauth@hft-stuttgart.de`
[2] Lucerne University of Applied Sciences - iHomeLab
Technikumstr. 21, CH-6048 Horw, Switzerland
`firstname.lastname@iHomeLab.ch`

Abstract. iLoc+ is an ultrasound ranging based indoor localization system based on the iLoc system of the iHomeLab Living Lab. For example, the system can be used for visitor tracking: Visitors get an electronic name badge comprising an ultrasound transmitter. This badge can be localized with an average accuracy of less than 30 cm deviation in its spatial position, by means of reference nodes distributed in the lab rooms. iLoc among others received a 3rd prize at the 2011 EvAAL localization competition performed at the CIAMI Living Lab, Valencia. iLoc+ is a further development of the iLoc system. It specifically addresses AAL scenarios, where besides a high accuracy also low installation effort and affordable cost is important. Therefore iLoc+ reference nodes operate wireless. Node positions are self-determined with respect to a few given reference locations.

1 Introduction

Ultrasound time-of-flight (TOF) measurement is a proven technology for indoor ranging and has already been successfully applied to indoor localization systems in the past. Prominent ultrasound based localization projects are for example the CRICKET, CALAMARI and BAT systems ([10,12,11]) and the recently developed iLoc system [4,5]. They provide high and reliable accuracy, achieved with moderate effort. The iLoc+ ultrasound ranging based indoor localization system (Fig. 1) comprises mobile nodes (badges, name tags), detector nodes and a position server, as well as a time synchronization transmitter. The name tags (Fig. 3) are equipped with a microcontroller, a radio transceiver and an ultrasound transmitter. They emit ultrasound pulses at a configurable rate, for example 2 Hz, with a duration of 1 ms. These pulses are received by some of the detectors.

The detector nodes, also called reference nodes, are located at fixed positions. Their coordinates are self-determined by the system using an autolocation scheme (see chapter 4). The nodes comprise a microcontroller and an ultrasound

S. Chessa and S. Knauth (Eds.): EvAAL 2012, CCIS 362, pp. 83–94, 2013.

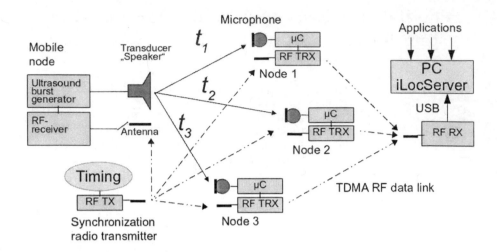

Fig. 1. Setup overview: A synchronization transmitter emits timing information via radio channel to the mobile node as well as to the receiver nodes (Node1 .. 3 shown in the image). The mobile node, for example a visitor badge, transmits a synchronized ultrasound burst. The receiver nodes detect the arrival time of this sound burst at their position and calculate the respective time of flights (TOF) t_1, t_2 and t_3. The TOF information is transmitted by radio to a receiver connected to the iLocServer. The server calculates the position and offers this information to interested applications.

receiver as well as a radio transceiver. The radio is used to receive time synchronization information and transmit data: The nodes record the reception times of ultrasound bursts transmitted by the badges, calculate the ultrasound time of flight (TOF) and transmit this information to the iLoc server. The server calculates position estimates from the received data by multilateration. The obtained position data may be used among others for visualization of visitor positions (see Fig. 2).

2   Hardware

2.1   Interactive Badges

The interactive badge (Fig. 3) comprises the following hardware blocks: a CC2430 Texas Instruments microcontroller including IEEE 802.15.4 radio transceiver, antenna and HF matching network, a Bosch SMB380 triaxial acceleration sensor, a charge pump chip to generate a higher voltage (20 V) to drive the 40 kHz piezoelectric ultrasound transducer, the transducer itself, the LCD unit, and a rechargeable 25 mAh lithium battery. The power consumption of the badge hardware is in the range of 1..10 μW in standby mode and raises to about 50 mW in operational mode, with transition times < 1 ms. The microcontroller comprises a 32 kHz crystal-based wake up timer. The badges are equipped with an inductive battery charging

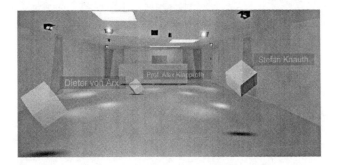

Fig. 2. 3D visualization of visitor positions in the iHome Living Lab. The positions are given as "hovering" cubes indicating the name of the badge bearer, embedded in a 3D visualization of the iHomeLab.

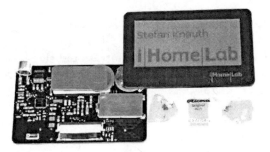

Fig. 3. Name badge with IEEE802.15.4 radio transceiver, ultrasound transmitter and LCD

circuity including a coil (part of the PCB layout), a rectifier and overvoltage protection. Charging of the badges takes place in their storage box equipped with two charging coils operating at a frequency of 125 kHz.

2.2 Reference Nodes

The reference nodes are Freescale HCS08GB60 Microcontroller based and equipped with a TI-CC2420 IEEE802.15.4 radio transceiver chip and an ultrasound preamplifier (see fig. 4). The ultrasound detection circuity generates two interrupts for two different sound levels. One level is just above the noise level, the second amplitude threshold is a bit higher. This allows to detect the reception time of the ultrasound pulse with a higher accuracy when compared to a single point detector: from the two thresholds the received amplitude of the signal can be estimated and used for correction of the time-of-flight. The transceiver is used to receive the timing information of the synchronization transmitter and to transmit the TOF information to the iLoc Server. As ultrasound reception is indicated by interrupts, the microcontroller can be at sleep mode while waiting for the ultrasound signal, waiting to perform time synchronization with the time transmitter, or waiting to transmit TOF data.

Fig. 4. Ultrasound receiver node assembly of battery, PCB and backplate for mounting. The PCB comprises microcontroller, ultrasound amplifier and 802.15.4 radio transceiver.

3   Operation, Timing and Synchronization

The maximum detection range of the iLoc ultrasound signal is about 15 meters. The pulse duration itself is about one msec, and this pulse propagates through air with the speed of sound (about 345 m/s at 22.5 °C). This corresponds to a maximum ultrasound pulse "livetime" of about 45 msec. This live time is given by the transmitter ultrasound amplitude, the sound path loss, and the receiver sensitivity, and is a consequence of the specific iLoc device parameters and the used sound frequency of 40 kHz. In order to avoid interference, a second ultrasound pulse should only be generated after this lifetime. For iLoc we chose 50 ms as the system time slot i. e. the pulse repetition rate.

There exist several design approaches for ultrasound localization systems with multiple mobile nodes. It is important to avoid ultrasound interference between the nodes (see for example [10]). One commonly used approach is to let the fixed infrastructure emit the pulses and send radio packets identifying the sending node. This has some advantages, for example privacy. The mobile node can detect its position without the system knowing that the mobile node exists. Also the number of mobile nodes is not limited in this case as they are passive. A disadvantage of this approach is that the mobile node has to listen for a certain time to radio and sound messages before being able to detect its position.

A main design goal of the original iLoc system was that the mobile nodes (currently the name badges) should consume as little energy as possible. Therefore we chose the opposite approach, using active mobile nodes and a passive detection infrastructure. The mobile nodes themselves emit the ultrasound pulse. For each node a 50 ms time slot is allocated, corresponding to the maximum lifetime of the propagating ultrasound pulse. The time needed for the position determination of n nodes is therefore $T = n \times 50$ms. A typical number of nodes in our lab is $n = 20$, so the position update rate for the nodes is 1 Hz. Other update rates are configurable, for example 10 Nodes with an update rate of 2 Hz each.

For correct TDMA operation and correct time-of-flight measurement, the whole system operates synchronized. A time synchronization accuracy of about

50 μs is achieved by the central synchronization radio transmitter. To establish this accuracy. the mobile nodes and the fixed nodes need to synchronize every 2-5 seconds. Actually the operation is as follows: The synchronization signal is sent with the slot rate, i.e. every 50 ms, containing also the number of the badge that shall send a pulse in the current slot. The mobile nodes therefore wake up just prior to the moment when they expect their next synchronization signal. They listen for the synchronization packet, readjust their clock, emit their ultrasound pulse and go to sleep again.

The whole sequence takes about 5 ms. Using a transmission rate of 1 Hz, this leads to a duty cycle of 1/200. The electric current in active mode is about 20 mA, leading to an average current of about 100 μA, at a voltage of 2.5 .. 3 V, enabling operation times of 10 days with a small lithium coin cell, and one update per second. Note that for the EvAAL competition, the update rate was 5 Hz, thus reducing lifetime by a factor of 5. The following table lists some operational times for the mobile node at 1 Hz update rate:

Battery type	Duty cycle	operational time
Lithium coin 25 mAh	1 sec	10 days
	10 sec	3 month
Lithium 500 mAh	1 sec	1/2 Year
	10 sec	> 2 Years
AA 2000 mAh	1 sec	2 Years

In the fixed nodes the ultrasound receiver is active at all times, and consumes a considerable current of about 1 mA, which restricts the lifetime to about 2 month, with AA cells. This is because the receiver nodes originally were designed for the older line-powered iLoc system. The remaining parts of the node, namely transceiver and microcontroller, are currently active four times per second, 5 ms each, leading to a duty cycle of 1/50. The four active times per second are used for TOF transmission to the iLoc server and for synchronization. During this active phases the node consumes about 20 mA. The nodes also wake up for a very short time after each time slot, i. e. 20 times per second, to check for- and evaluate TOF data of received ultrasound pulses.

A planned future version of the node hardware will comprise a much less "hungry" ultrasound circuity. Combined with an intelligent duty cycle algorithm, which adopts the update rate to the activity of the localized person, a battery lifetime of several years also for the receiver nodes seems possible.

4   Deployment Considerations and Real iLoc Installations

Basically, 3 range measurements from 3 different reference positions allow the determination of the tag position. Given the above mentioned 15 meter iLoc maximum ultrasound range, these conditions would be fulfilled for example by deploying the reference nodes in a lattice with a spacing of about 10 meters. Practically, depending on the desired accuracy, the density of reference nodes

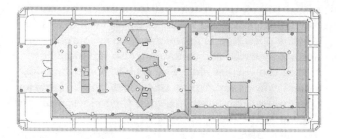

Fig. 5. Positions of the 70+ wired ultrasound receivers in the iHomeLab. The inner gray rectangle indicates the covered area (about 10m × 30m). The iHomeLab is located at Lucerne University of Applied Sciences at Campus Horw.

should be much higher. The typical node density used is one node per about 5 square meters. Then every point in the room is in the ultrasound range of more than 5 reference nodes, increasing the stability of the system against ultrasound interference for example by noise emitted from machinery or people. The ultrasound signal needs a line-of-sight for propagation, which can get lost by a shading caused by the body of the wearer of the tag or by other visitors in the same room. Also reflections have to be taken into account.

The iHome Living Lab setup is based on the older iLoc system, where the receiver nodes are wired by using the 2 wire ("IPoK") bus system [6] providing power supply and communication to the nodes. In the lab currently more than 70 nodes are arranged in 6 IPoK harnesses (fig. 5). Typically an emitted pulse is detected by about 5–15 receivers. Inconsistent range reports are rejected by the multilateration algorithm with a simple but computing intensive procedure: From the reported ranges for all permutations of 3 readings a position value is calculated. By stepwise removing of calculated positions lying outside of the mean value, the most probable readings are selected for the final trilateration [3].

In order to achieve a high accuracy of the system, the positions of the ultrasound receivers need to be accurately determined. Actually only a fraction of the positions have been manually measured. For the remaining positions only estimations have been entered to the database. Then the estimations have been adjusted by reference measurements: A mobile tag (name badge) was placed at a grid of known reference positions and time-of-flight results were recorded by the receivers. The position data of the reference receivers was then adjusted until the measured range values for a particular reference node matched best with the calculated distances. This fitting process was performed by minimizing the sum of the squared differences between measured range and calculated range.

For the EvAAL 2011 competition [2] the wired iLoc system was deployed at CIAMI Living Lab [1]. By using 3 pre-wired harnesses of about 10 nodes each, and placing the nodes more or less exactly on predefined positions, a 28 node system has been set up in about 1 hour, by 2 persons (fig. 6). In the competition, a localization accuracy of 80 cm (75th percentile) has been obtained by the system, during the tracking part of the competition.

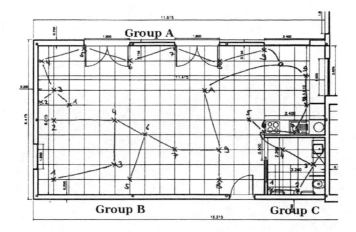

Fig. 6. Positions of the 28 iLoc receivers at CIAMI Living Lab (EvAAL 2011). The nodes were arranged in 3 wiring groups, as indicated in the image. The lab area covers 6 m × 11.2 m.

5   Autolocation of Reference Nodes

The manual position determination of the reference nodes can be a time consuming and error prone process. For AAL deployments, low installation costs are important to gain acceptance for a system. A possible automatic reference position determination solution is "leap-frogging" [9], especially feasible for temporary deployments: Here the position of some reference nodes for example at a corner of the deployment area is determined manually. Then a subsequent node is localized by the system using the already localized nodes, and so on. This mode requires the ability to use a given ultrasound transducer of a node not only as receiver, but also as transmitter. Unfortunately this simple approach accumulates positioning errors leading to quite inaccurate positions for distant nodes. More sophisticated algorithms use complex parallel evaluation of all measured node distances (see for example [8] for RF based ranging).

The iLoc+ system uses receivers mounted under the ceiling. The directional propagation characteristics of the used ultrasound transducers favors the indirect transmission path from transmitter to the floor and back to the receiver under the ceiling. Therefore direct observation of the inter-node distance by the nodes themselves is not feasible. The node autolocation procedure for iLoc+ is performed with the help of mobile nodes distributed temporary on the floor. Some of them are placed at known locations, others only help to link together the net of the distance measurements. For the Cricket ultrasound system [8] working autolocation with development of sophisticated algorithms and high obtained accuracy has been described by Mautz and Ochieng [7]. Our system currently uses the much simpler multilateration approach of selecting the most "believable" ranges by evaluating all possible permutations of three range readings, as described in this paper (Section 4) and more detailed in [3].

Fig. 7. Hardware used for the test run: Visible are 25 receiver nodes (table left side), 15 calibration nodes (table right side), 5 of them equipped with ultrasound booster amplifiers, and a notebook acting as iLoc server.

6   Setup and Test Run at Madrid University Living Lab

In a first step 19 positions were marked on the floor of the living lab by tape measure (see fig. 8 left). The coordinates of the positions were defined in advance. They were altered where necessary for example if a predefined coordinate was not usable due to furniture. A pre-engineered file containing these coordinates was manually adjusted to reflect the actual 19 calibration positions. Calibration transmitters were placed on the positions. Then 25 battery powered wireless ultrasound receiver nodes (fig 7) where blue-tacked under the ceiling or at the walls at a height of about 2 meters. This manual placement was performed using a sketch indicating desired positions, but the actual positions were not measured, as to save installation time. The actual installation time was about one man hour. The node positions have been documented by photos and have been determined by analysis after the competition.

Then the automatic position determination procedure was triggered. This worked by ultrasound determination of the distance matrix between the calibration nodes and the receiver nodes. Of course a particular node did receive signals only from a fraction of the calibration nodes. The determination procedure did consider the 9 nearest calibration nodes for calculation of the receiver position, or less if there were less reported distances.

In the right part of fig. 8 the receiver node positions are shown. Diamonds indicate "true" positions which have been roughly determined by evaluation of photos. Asterisks indicate positions obtained by the autolocation procedure. The following 11 node positions could be determined with an estimated error below

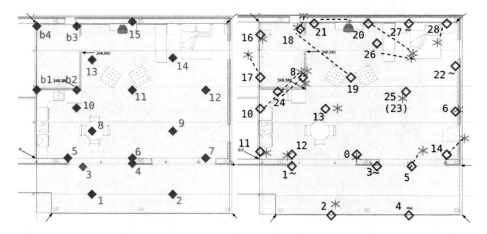

Fig. 8. Left: true positions of the calibration transmitters. They have been placed by tape measure. Right: Positions of ultrasound receiver nodes. Diamonds indicate true receiver node positions, asterisk indicate positions determined automatically by the autolocation procedure. Tilde signs indicate receiver opositions which were not determined by autolocation. For large displacements between true and calculated position the respective positions are connected with a dashed line.

1 meter: Nodes 0, 2, 5, 6, 8, 11, 12, 13, 16, 18, and 25. Medium accuracy (1m .. 2.5 m) has been obtained for the 6 nodes enumerated 14, 17, 21, 24, 26 and 28. The 3 Nodes numbered 10, 19 and 27 were beyond 2.5 m of error. The position of 5 nodes (1, 3, 4, 22 and 27) could not be determined by the autolocation procedure.

As it can be seen, only a minority of positions has been determined with displacements below one meter. Intentionally we expected more or less that all or at least the vast majority of the node positions would be determined with reasonable accuracy. During installation, auto-calibration and the test run a variety of sensor data has been logged. Among others this comprises the raw time-of-flight data, the node id's used for the lateration procedure and the measured distance matrix. From an analysis of this data, the following shortcomings could be identified:

- The outside area was equipped with four calibration transmitters. This turned out to be not enough: Only 2 out of 5 receivers placed outside have been located and therefore outside position determination was not possible during the test run.
- The bedroom area was also not well covered by calibration nodes, leading to failure in determination of the nodes 22 and 27.
- In the region of the two armchairs and the television, position determination was heavily distorted. Data analysis leads to the assumption that the signals of some more distant calibration nodes, namely Nodes 8, 9, 10, and 11 (with respect to the right side of fig 8) did not reach the nodes on the direct

way but "bounced" one time, e. g. they traveled from the calibration node on the floor to the ceiling, got reflected back to the floor and only then reflected to the detectors at the ceiling. This led to longer TOF values with the effect of "pushing" back the calculated positions from the calibration nodes. Especially sensor 19 with its central role has a large coverage, this influenced the test runs considerably.

– Also the kitchen area and the bathroom area suffered from displacements between true and detected positions. Here we assume that reflections at the walls in conjunction with long lasting ultrasound pulses (inter-slot interference) introduced the errors. This is under further investigation.

After auto-calibration, i.e. automatic determination of the 25 receiver node positions, the calibration transmitters had done their duty and were removed from the floor. The iLoc server was switched to normal position detection mode in order to track the position of the actor wearing the iLoc badge. As the time for the whole test run was limited, a manual determination of the node positions was not possible, and the tests had to be performed with the autocalibration generated position data. Obviously this limited the accuracy achievable during the test runs.

However, luckily, the effect of the deviation in node position determination is partly compensated as during the test run the error sources are the same. The transmitted signal of the node carried by the person to be tracked will undergo the same deviations as the signals from the calibration nodes. In that way, the system works like a fingerprinting system and accuracy is better than expected from the errors in node positions. Also, the multilateration algorithm comprises a "reasoning" mechanism which removes unlikely distance values which can arise for example from wrongly determined node positions.

Fig. 9 (left) displays a trace of the actor walking on path one from the entry to the bathroom. As it can be seen, the average accuracy is in the range of 1 meter. In fig. 9 (right) a trace of the third path is shown. Here it can clearly be seen that position determination at the outside area mostly failed. It worked a bit since the glass doors of the lab were opened and the ultrasound signal transmitted by the badge propagated also into the lab where it was detected by receivers 6, 13 and 25. In the entrance area the determination was also quite bad. The table and kitchen area performed reasonable. The two figures show that some areas were quite well covered, while others were not.

7   Results and Outlook

The iLoc+ indoor localization systems currently tracks for example 10 mobile nodes with a position update rate of two measurements per second per node, with an accuracy below about 30 cm, for single measurements with no temporal averaging applied. The system is designed for tracking of persons or assets in an AAL context. iLoc+ is a wireless system. Mobile nodes may operate several month without recharging of the battery. Fixed nodes battery lifetime is currently limited to about 2 months.

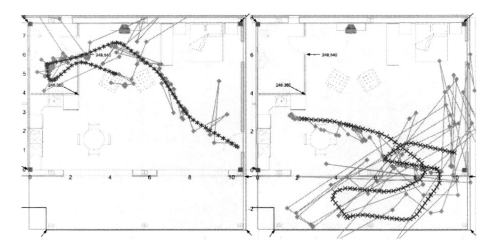

Fig. 9. Trace of the actor walking on path 3: Black squares indicate true positions, blue ones indicate iLoc+ determined positions.

The fixed infrastructure comprises at least 4 fixed nodes per room, for larger rooms a node should be placed for every 5 m^2 area. The iLoc+ system uses an autolocation procedure to determine the positions of the reference nodes after their placement. Therefore calibration nodes have to be placed at known positions for example on the floor.

The system is currently under development. The EvAAL 2012 competition run allowed us to test the system in a very different situation compared to our home lab. Even if the system was in a very early stage, we were able to install and run the system at the competition within the compact time frame. The observed performance of only 2 meters on average was well below our expectations with respect to the EvAAL 2011 result of 85 cm obtained with the older iLoc system. As a main reason we identified shortcomings of the autocalibration algorithm, and the yet time intensive procedure of calibration node placement as well as some software bugs attributed to the early development stage of the system. The test run has however shown that the principle idea to operate 25 or more wireless ultrasound receivers is quite possible and besides the autocalibration phase, the system is quite usable already.

The evaluation pointed out some shortcomings like the yet uncomfortable handling of the badge, suboptimal integrability and of course the yet to high duration of the installation phase. Nevertheless, in the accuracy score the iLoc+ system reached a third place.

The development includes the basic ranging electronic setup, firmware, system aspects, the timing- and multilateration algorithms, middleware and application software. Current applications of the system are visitor tracking and fall detection. Future planned developments include reducing the power consumption of the fixed nodes and test of further autolocation and multilateration algorithms. The ancestor of iLoc+, the iLoc ultrasound indoor localization system is deployed at the iHomeLab Living Lab at Lucerne University of Applied Science.

References

1. Ciami living-lab: Experimental research center in applications and services for ambient intelligence (2011), http://www.ciami.es/valencia/
2. Evaal: Evaluating aal systems through competitive benchmarking (2011), http://evaal.aaloa.org/
3. Knauth, S., Jost, C., Klapproth, A.: Range sensor data fusion and position estimation for the iloc indoor localisation system. In: Proc. 12th IEEE Intl. Conference on Emerging Technologies and Factory Automation (ETFA 2009), Palma de Mallorca, Spain (September 2009)
4. Knauth, S., Jost, C., Klapproth, A.: Iloc: a localisation system for visitor tracking and guidance. In: Proc. 7th IEEE Int. Conf. on Industrial Informatics, INDIN 2009, Cardiff, UK (June 2009)
5. Knauth, S., Kaufmann, L., Jost, C., Kistler, R., Klapproth, A.: The iLoc Ultrasound Indoor Localization System at the EvAAL 2011 Competition. In: Chessa, S., Knauth, S. (eds.) EvAAL 2011. CCIS, vol. 309, pp. 52–64. Springer, Heidelberg (2012), http://dx.doi.org/10.1007/978-3-642-33533-4_5
6. Knauth, S., Kistler, R., Jost, C., Klapproth, A.: Sarbau - an ip-fieldbus based building automation network. In: Proc. 11th IEEE Intl. Conference on Emerging Technologies and Factory Automation (ETFA 2008), Hamburg, Germany (October 2008)
7. Mautz, R., Ochieng, W.: Indoor positioning using wireless udistances between motes. In: Proceedings of TimeNav 2007 / ENC 2007, Geneva, Switzerland (May 2007)
8. Mautz, R., Ochieng, W., Brodin, G., Kemp, A.: 3d wireless network localization from inconsistent distance observations. Ad Hoc and Sensor Wireless Networks 3(2-3), 140–170 (2007)
9. Navarro-Serment, L., Grabowski, R., Paredis, C., Khosla, P.: Millibots. IEEE Robotics and Automation Magazine 9(4) (December 2002)
10. Smith, A., Balakrishnan, H., Goraczko, M., Priyantha, N.B.: Tracking Moving Devices with the Cricket Location System. In: 2nd International Conference on Mobile Systems, Applications and Services (Mobisys 2004), Boston, MA (June 2004)
11. Ward, A., Jones, A., Hopper, A.: A new location technique for the active office. IEEE Personal Communications 4(5), 42–47 (1997)
12. Whitehouse, K., Jiang, F., Karlof, C., Woo, A., Culler, D.: Sensor field localization: A deployment and empirical analysis. UC Berkeley Technical Report UCB//CSD-04-1349 (April 2004)

Open Source OwlPS 1.3: Towards a Reactive Wi-Fi Positioning System Sensitive to Dynamic Changes

Philippe Canalda, Matteo Cypriani, and François Spies

Institute FEMTO-ST UMR CNRS 6174, Département d'Informatique des Systèmes Complexes / Optimization Mobility NetworkIng Team, 1, Cours Louis Leprince-Ringuet 25200 Montbéliard - France
{Philippe.Canalda,Matteo.Cypriani,Francois.Spies}@femto-st.fr

Abstract. Since 2004, our team has been developing an academic positioning system (PS for short) for hostile environments. The techniques involved are mainly Wi-Fi based. While at the very beginning the system architecture was terminal centric, since 2008 it has become infrastructure centric, reducing the application part to being embedded in any Mobile Terminal (MT), focusing on intrusive localization and the illicit use of wireless network. Last year, we presented the OwlPS 1.2 version and the auto-calibration functionality which reduces the RSSI fingerprinting phase to the minimum. This year, the system proposed was enriched with, first of all dynamic changes exploitation, which means not only the last up-to-date RSSI- fingerprinting calibration, but also the instantaneous RSSI variation due mainly to human presence. Therein, the broken line of sight between Wi-Fi Access Points and MTs or the abnormal attenuation of Signal Strength between various references points are taken into account to configure the K-angle-weighted neighborhood proposed algorithm dynamically. Second, the RSSI cartography models the orientation of MT and the relative positioning of human presence. Third a tuning of OwlPS system development kit is performed in off-line phase. It makes use of a 3D dimensioning tool placing N-APs according to $GDOP_{RSSI}$ n-losses criteria and a Wi-Fi-adapted COST-231 propagation model. It also makes use of smartphone Android-based functionalities to calibrate, on demand, AOI reference points.

Keywords: Wi-Fi network, similarity function, fingerprinting method, RSSI cartography.

1 More Than a Wi-Fi Based Positioning System, an Evolutive Suite for Development and Experimentation

The OMNI[1] team has been engaged in a positioning program initiated by the Pays de Montbéliard Agglomération, since 2006.

The focus is on Wi-Fi based positioning techniques and algorithms applied to hostile environment. Two kinds of architectures have been studied, first, in a former

---

[1] OMNI stands for Optimization Mobility and NetworkIng. OMNI is a team from the DISC Department of Femto-st Institute.

S. Chessa and S. Knauth (Eds.): EvAAL 2012, CCIS 362, pp. 95–107, 2013.

phase, a Mobile Terminal (MT) centric one, and in a later phase, an infrastructure centric one. Several techniques and algorithms from the literature have been developed and integrated into an internal development suite, so that simulations, emulations and real experimentations are conducted following scenarios inside modern building and across indoor and canyon urban environments.

1.1 History and Internal Related Works

When, at the very beginning the system architecture was terminal centric, indoor positioning researches dealt with Wi-Fi positioning or GPS-based positioning. Since 2008, the architecture has become infrastructure-centric oriented, reducing the application part to being embedded in any MT, focusing on intrusive or non-intrusive localization, or on the illicit use of wireless network. Hence research activities have addressed combined positioning such as GPS and Wi-Fi in indoor environment, to improve the positioning service coverage significantly. Since 2010, we have investigated how to switch from one positioning system to another and how to dimension heterogeneous Wi-Fi infrastructure by adapting geometric and attenuation signal strength dilution of precision criteria.

Last year, we have competed with the 2nd evolution of our Wi-Fi based Positioning System named "OwlPS". Among the most innovative functionalities of this 1.2 version of OwlPS, the auto-calibration functionality reduces the off-line RSSI fingerprinting phase to the minimum.

1.2 New Problems Addressed

This year, the system proposed is first of all enriched with dynamic change exploitation, that means not only the last up-to-date RSSI- fingerprinting calibration, but also the instantaneous RSSI variation due mainly to human presence. Therein, the loss of the line of sight between Wi-Fi Access Points (AP for short) and MT or the abnormal attenuation of signal strength between various reference points dynamically configured the K-angle-weighted neighborhood algorithm proposed. Second, the RSSI cartography modeled the orientation of MT and the relative positioning of human. Third a tuning of OwlPS system development kit was performed in an off-line phase. It made use of a 3D dimensioning tool placing N-APs according to a GDOP_RSSI n-loss criteria and COST-231 propagation model. It also made use of a smartphone Android-based functionality to calibrate on-demand AOI reference points.

1.3 Summary of Our Proposal

In the sequel, we will briefly describe the core OwlPS system which competed at EvAAL'11. We will also summarize the techniques and algorithms which have been conceived, developed and experimented in real experiments in the last decade, such as the [16] navigator monitoring interface. Then we will explain the new contributions which may use the dynamic changes from radio-environment, the K-Weighted-Neighborhood algorithm, the smart Android Interface to pilot calibration processes and adaptive real-time positioning better, as well as the 3D dimensioning tooling.

Finally we will discuss internal laboratory experiments and list the perspectives of our proposal from a scientific view point and from the EvAAL'12 competition view point.

2   OwlPS 1.2 Version Which Competed at EvAAL'11

2.1   OwlPS Core Architecture

The OwlPS is an indoor positioning system based on the IEEE 802.11 radio network (Wi-Fi). It mainly exploits RSSI fingerprinting and indoor propagation models, helped by information such as the map of the building, the mobile path, etc. Fingerprinting location approaches provide a 4 meter mean error for a 3-D positioning, with only 5 Wi-Fi access points deployed in an area of 300m². The previous version of the system includes a self-calibration mechanism, which avoids the time-consuming manual fingerprinting phase.

The architecture of Owl Positioning System is infrastructure-centered. We first present its architecture and its deployment process, then the positioning algorithms implemented, and finally an explanation of the self-calibration mechanism. As summarized in Fig. 1, OwlPS is composed of several elements:

- Mobile terminals, such as laptops, PDAs, cell phones, hand-held game consoles, etc., which are equipped with Wi-Fi cards. These run the owlps-client software, which is a classical UDP/IP application.
- Access points (APs), which capture the frames of the Wi-Fi network by listening for any positioning request transmitted by the mobiles. These run the owlps-listener software, which uses the pcap library to capture the IEEE 802.11 frames. The SS values are extracted from the Radiotap [4] header of each frame; therefore the network interface driver must support Radiotap [5]. It is possible to have as many APs as desired: as long as they are only listening to the radio network, they do not cause any interference.
- The aggregation server, to which the APs forward the captured positioning requests; its task is to gather and format these requests. It runs the owlps-aggregator software.
- The positioning server (or computation server), which computes the position of each mobile from the information forwarded by the aggregation server, thanks to the owlps-positioner software.

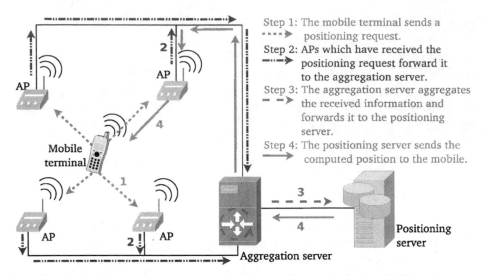

Step 1: The mobile terminal sends a positioning request.

Step 2: APs which have received the positioning request forward it to the aggregation server.

Step 3: The aggregation server aggregates the received information and forwards it to the positioning server.

Step 4: The positioning server sends the computed position to the mobile.

Fig. 1. OwlPS infrastructure-centric architecture and Signal Strength acquisition process

2.2   The OwlPS Processes

The Signal Strength Acquisition process (SSA-process for short) is used during the (auto-) calibration phase and the positioning/tracking phase. It helps to build the Signal Strength Cartography (SSC for short) from the signal transmitted either by an AP to other Aps or an MT to all APs. The auto-calibration phase eliminates the costly off-line calibration of fingerprinting based positioning algorithm. In this previous version of OwlPS, the auto-calibration is executed recurrently, according to a time period. A token ring-based algorithm assigns to each AP the right to deliver an explicit calibration packet to the aggregator. The positioning functionality runs under two modes, an explicit one and an implicit one. The former requires the MT to send a packet in a specific format [13], whereas the latter accepts any UDP-like packets which are intercepted and analyzed by APs, then transmitted to the aggregator. Hence the aggregator temporally collapses the SS received and transmits it to the calculator which computes the SS tuple respectful of an off-line configuration. The tuple represents the t means of n UDP packets transmitted by either an AP or the MT, with t the number of Aps (each visible by (t-1) others). m tuples are registered in an SSC, with m the size of the grid depending on the distance between each RP in a 2D-plan. As an illustration, if we consider[2] a rectangular room of l by L m^2, where l = 5.8 m., and L = 10.6 m., then the number of RPs nbRP= $(l+1)*(L+1)$, considering a grid meshing of 1 m.

---

[2] This room is located in our Multimedia Development Center NUMERICA, at the -1 level, our laboratory used this space to experiment automatic indoor AR-Drone navigation, and also to evaluate the optimal sizing and positioning of APs, and also to design and compare the techniques and algorithm of positioning.

Around the SSA-Process, numerous other processes are articulated, from the deployment of infrastructure and its configuration to the automated off-line calibration, the periodic on-line auto-calibration, the positioning and tracking of authorized or intrusive MTs.

2.3   OwlPS Descriptions and Functionalities

These processes are achieved making use of a bulk of functionalities and descriptions among which: wired and wireless 802.11.x communications, the description of the hardware characteristics (antenna gain, transmitted power, coordinates of the fixed elements), the description of the size and topology of the deployment area if available, and manual on-line calibration (fingerprinting) only if auto-calibration is not selected,

When running the system, one positioning algorithm has to be selected among several[3] implemented in the positioning server:

- Nearest neighbor in Signal Strength (NSS), based on RADAR [3], a simple cartography-based algorithm.
- Trilateration using the propagation formula proposed by Interlink Networks [1].
- Trilateration using the FBCM [2, 7] (Friis-Based Calibrated Model), which adapts the propagation formula to match the deployment area's characteristics better.
- Basic FRBHM [8, 7, 9] (FBCM and Reference-Based Hybrid Model), a combination of the NSS and the FBCM which allows to adapt the propagation formula dynamically to the characteristics of the room where the MT is supposed to be.

2.4   OwlPS Techniques and Tool Set Box

When designing and developing a new positioning algorithm, some other techniques are usable to serve as a basis or to compare performance such as support for the Viterbi-enabled algorithms:

- NSS with Viterbi-like [10],
- Discrete and Continuous FRBHM [7, 9].

At the previous competition EvAAL'11, we presented a Wi-Fi based navigation monitoring and, in addition, an AR-Drone navigator using an itinerary scenario description [13].

---

[3] These algorithms were described and compared in [6].

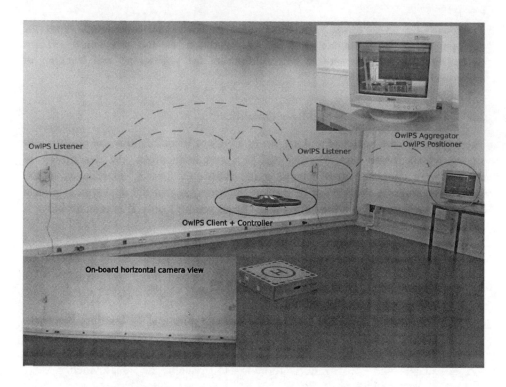

3   New Contributions

3.1   OwlPS Latest Version Exploits the Dynamic Changes of the Radio Environment Better

Exploitation of the Dynamic Radio Changes. OwlPS implements an auto-calibration mechanism that allows the system to be operational within a few seconds after its deployment. Since the self-calibration is a continuous process, it also guarantees that the system is aware of the modifications occurring in the radio environment. In the previous competition, we proved that the self-calibration process annihilates the costly previous off-line calibration phase, without altering the accuracy of the positioning (for a mean accuracy of 4m, for 4 APs deployed in the competition area). The positioning server builds a matrix of the SSs received by each APRx from each APTx (with Rx and Tx $\in$ [1,N] and N the number of deployed APs). Several matrixes are computed:

- MAPs represent the SSC of APs. We recommend to register an initial one, iMAP, performed when no human is present in the experimentation area, and another incrementally modified one of MAPs (CurrentTime) for which the refreshing period can be parameterized to 4 per second.

  Then, the Radio-Environment Sensible Positioning Algorithm (RESP-algorithm for short) being invoked at CurrentTime consecutively to an explicit positioning demand from an MT, the RESP-algorithm first identifies which APRx-APTx is attenuated when differentiating iMAPs with MAPs(CurrentTime), and second the relative positioning of the MT with the human presence. Then the K-angle weighted neighborhood (KAWN) algorithm [13] is more appropriately applied.

- MAPs+RPs represent the SSC of APs and RPs. The SSC of RPs is obtained by applying the KAWN algorithm considering a position of a virtual MT M which matches the RPs position defined from the topology of the experimentation area and the meshing of the SSC's grid.

Extended K Angle Weighted Neighborhood Algorithm. As already introduced, the KAWN algorithm is extended when identifying a rupture of the line of sight between two APs, and considering where the human could be positioned when using the MT being tracked.

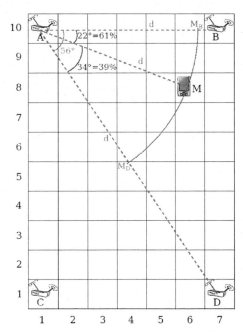

Fig. 2. Selection and weighting of the referenced APs to compute the SS received by AP_A from the virtual MT *M*

3.2   Smart Android Interface Suited to Wi-Fi Indoor Positioning Data Repository

Fig. 3 describes the functionalities of OwlPs-SAI. From now on, experimenting the current OwlPS version, the deployment is guided when configuring the refreshing frequency of any SSCs, calibration is performed on demand, either automatically or manually. The manual calibration allows to insert a specific RP or modify one, and itmay be previously set during the initial auto-calibration phase. The MT interface proposes two modes of interaction, a declarative one, and a smart-sensor one. The Wi-Fi indoor positioning data repository is extended (see Fig.4) with the orientation and positioning of both the APs, and the MTs. The relative positioning of the human is registered depending on either the explicit declaration or the sensor equipment available

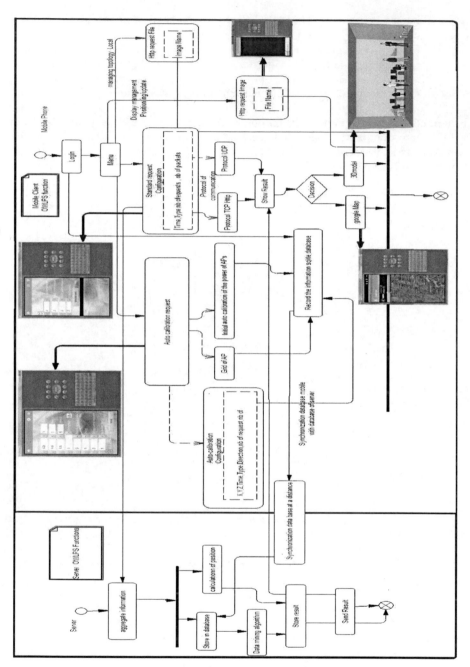

Fig. 3. Schema and screen shots of the OwlPS Smart Android interface suited to Wi-Fi indoor positioning data repository

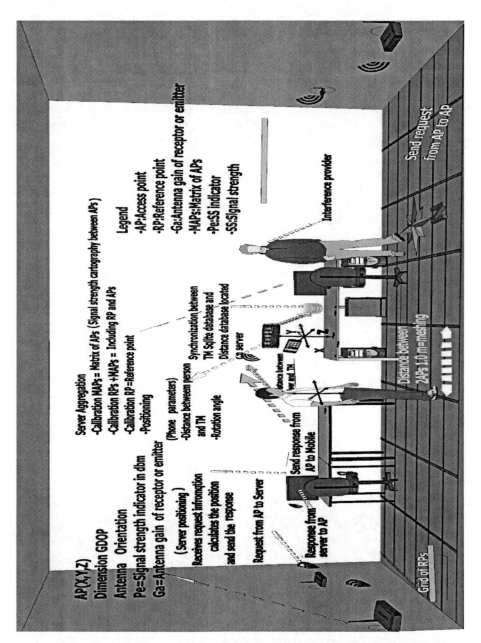

Fig. 4. 3D OwlPS deployment within FEMTO-ST internal experimentation area, with OwlPS data repository definition

on the MT. Last but not least, data repository synchronization is performed between the SQLite local data repository on the MT, and the distant SQL-based server-side data repository. This is more robust in the face of any Wi-Fi communication disturbances, and respectful of the privacy and confidentiality of the user's data.

3.3   3D Dimensioning Wi-Fi Infrastructures

As mentioned before, the OwlPS is completed by other tools. The last decade positioning program has provided our team with a geometric and SS attenuation dilution of precision criteria for the Wi-Fi positioning system combined or not with a GPS positioning system. With this in mind, we have modeled and implemented a 2D AP placement optimizer. It optimizes the geometric positioning of APs and its impact on the indoor positioning accuracy. A study has been performed in a real room inside our laboratory, sustained by a simulation platform which involves:

- Radio propagation models such as Friis and COST231-Hata.
- The planning of the Wi-Fi network inside an indoor 2D topology, with or without walls. We will exploit this tool to determine how many APs can be used and where to position them in order to optimize both the maximal and mean Wi-Fi GDOP values.

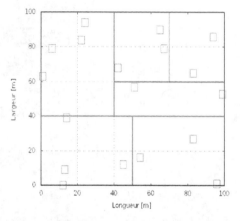

Fig. 5. mean GDOP$_{WiFi}$=7.73341-maximal GDOP$_{Wi-Fi}$=14.0826

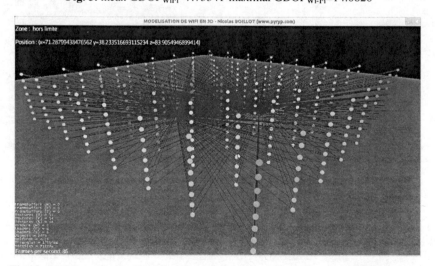

Fig. 6. GDOP$_{WiFi}$distribution for an indoor-outdoor environment with human presence

4   3rd Place at EvAAL'12 Benchmarking Competition

With OwlPS 1.3 Version, this RSSI based fingerprinting Positioning System becomes an open source and academic Positioning System. Among operational functionalities, numerous algorithms from the literature have been implemented (Interlink Networks, Radar, Fingerprinting, and Propagation Model). This year, new functionalities were experimented: the auto-calibration phase facilitates the installation process. However, the accuracy was not improved due to:

Table 1. OwlPS' result at EvAAL'2012 Competition

Positioning System evaluated	Accuracy	Availability	Installation complexity	User's acceptance	Integrability in AAL	Final Score and rank
OwlPS 1.3 Version	0,8	10	9,7	6,4	6,9	6,29 3rd/7

- An insufficient number of disseminated APs : only 5 Fonera APs were configured, where more APs were used, the better the positioning accuracy was;
- The AP placing, based on the Geometric Dilution of Precision Wi-Fi, to improve the covering and the positioning accuracy was not operational;
- Last but not least, the similarity function was not operational. This similarity function was based on a K-Weighted Neighborhood algorithm used during the static phase to build the RSSI fingerprinting.

However, during the competition, the system was easy to install and provided an excellent availability. The user's acceptance was quite satisfying, but the signal-receiving Fonera placed at hip caused many human shadow disturbances.

The 2nd best positioning system of the EvAAL'12 competition has shown that the radio free line of sight Positioning System S requires a significant quantity of APs (around 10).

5   Conclusion and Perspectives

Our current proposal composed of the OwlPS' latest 1.3 version, and augmented by 3D dimensioning APs tools, tends to improve OwlPS v1.2 which competed last year. This Year the Open source OwlPS 1.3 version obtained the third place at EvAAL'12, one place better than the fourth place obtained with the OwlPS 1.2 version at EvAAL'2011.

This year, the auto-calibration functionality reduced the static installation phase. During the dynamic phase, the auto-calibration was performed to build an RSSI fingerprinting reference. Hence, tuning the frequency of fingerprinting regeneration allowed reacting when human presence, temperature, new furniture, door or windows status changed. During the competition, the new similarity function was not operational to match dynamically actualized fingerprinting reference points better.

We expect that the weighted angle-based positioning system will be operational for the next EvAAL'13 competition. We also expect that, by better placing a growing number of APs (from 5 up to ten), using our indoor/outdoor GDOP-based tool, to dimension the Wi-Fi infrastructure, we will increase the positioning system accuracy by 20%. Laboratory tests were conducted [14] in a reproducible environment. A set of 26 benchmarking scenarios allow to evaluate the 3D positioning, the variation of temperature, the human shadow of one or 2 men, and any occurring Wi-Fi disturbances.

Apart from the OwlPS evolution and tuning, a Real-Time image analysis based positioning system has been developed to make use of a natural marker [15]. In an indoor environment, lit by a 60-watt ampoule per room of 8 m. by 8 m., the positioning accuracy is under 10 cm.

Acknowledgement. The authors want to thank Soumaya Zirari, Hakim Mabed, Honoré Bizagwira, Nicolas Boillot, Mouhannad Kazmouz, Florian Bataillard which contribute to produce the multi-positioning prototype, and the optimizing and placing libraries. This work has been, for part, supported by the Pays de Montbéliard Agglomeration and the European project G-Navis FP7 Collaborative Project, grant agreement No. 287203.

References

1. Interlink Networks, Inc.: A practical approach to identifying and tracking unauthorized 802.11 cards and access points. TR (2002)
2. Lassabe, F., Baala, O., Canalda, P., Chatonnay, P., Spies, F.: A Friis-based calibrated model for WiFi terminals positioning. In: Proceedings of IEEE Int. Symp. on a World of Wireless, Mobile and Multimedia Networks, Taormina, Italy, pp. 382–387 (June 2005)
3. Bahl, P., Padmanabhan, V.N.: RADAR: An in-building RF-based user location and tracking system. In: INFOCOM, vol. 2, pp. 775–784 (2000)
4. Radiotap website, http://www.radiotap.org/
5. Radiotap on Linux Wireless website, http://linuxwireless.org/en/developers/Documentation/radiotap
6. Cypriani, M., Lassabe, F., Canalda, P., Spies, F.: Open Wireless Positioning System: a Wi-Fi-based indoor positioning system. In: VTC-fall 2009, 70th IEEE Vehicular Technology Conference, Anchorage, Alaska. IEEE Vehicular Technology Society (September 2009)
7. Lassabe, F., Canalda, P., Chatonnay, P., Spies, F.: Indoor Wi-Fi positioning: Techniques and systems. Annals of Telecommunications 64(9/10), 651–664 (2009)
8. Lassabe, F., Charlet, D., Canalda, P., Chatonnay, P., Spies, F.: Refining WiFi indoor positioning renders pertinent deploying location-based multimedia guide. In: Proceedings of IEEE 20th Int. Conf. on Advanced Information Networking and Applications, Vienna, Austria, vol. 2, pp. 126–130 (April 2006)

9. Cypriani, M., Canalda, P., Lassabe, F., Spies, F.: Wi-Fi-based indoor positioning: Basic techniques, hybrid algorithms and open software platform. In: Mautz, R., Kunz, M., Ingensand, H. (eds.) IPIN 2010, IEEE Int. Conf. on Indoor Positioning and Indoor Navigation, Switzerland, pp. 116–125 (September 2010)
10. Bahl, P., Balachandran, A., Padmanabhan, V.: Enhancements to the RADAR user location and tracking system. Technical report, Microsoft Research (February 2000)
11. MadWifi website, http://www.madwifi-project.org/
12. Cypriani, M., Canalda, P., Zirari, S., Lassabe, F., Spies, F.: Open Wireless Positioning System, version 0.8. Technical Report RT2008-02, LIFC – Laboratoire d'Informatique de l'Université de Franche Comté (December 2008)
13. Cypriani, M., Canalda, P., Spies, F.: OwLPS: A Self-calibrated Fingerprint-Based Wi-Fi Positioning System. In: Chessa, S., Knauth, S. (eds.) EvAAL 2011. CCIS, vol. 309, pp. 36–51. Springer, Heidelberg (2012)
14. Cypriani, M., Canalda, P., Spies, F., Ancuta, D.: Benchmark Measurements for Wi-Fi Signal Strength based Positioning System. In: Rizos, C., Mautz, R. (eds.) IPIN 2012, Int. Conf. on Indoor Positioning and Indoor Navigation, Sydney, Australia, 8 p. IEEE (2012)
15. Canalda, P., Salem, A., Spies, F., Tabbane, S.: An IMA-based Centimeter Precise Positioning for Smart Mobile Devices in Hostile Environments. In: Rizos, C., Mautz, R. (eds.) IPIN 2012, Int. Conf. on Indoor Positioning and Indoor Navigation, Sydney, Australia, 5 p. IEEE (2012)
16. Parrot Ar-Drone specification,
    http://ardrone.parrot.com/parrot-ar-drone/en/technologies

Radio Tomographic Imaging for Ambient Assisted Living

Maurizio Bocca[1], Ossi Kaltiokallio[2], and Neal Patwari[1]

[1] SPAN Lab, ECE Department, The University of Utah
50 S. Central Campus Drive, Salt Lake City, UT 84102, USA
maurizio.bocca@utah.edu, npatwari@ece.utah.edu
[2] Automation and Systems Technology Department,
Aalto University Otaniementie 17, 02150 Espoo, Finland
ossi.kaltiokallio@aalto.fi

Abstract. Accurate localization of people in indoor and domestic environments is one of the key requirements for ambient assisted living (AAL) systems. This chapter describes how the received signal strength (RSS) measurements collected by a network of static radio transceivers can be used to localize people without requiring them to wear or carry any radio device. We describe a technique named radio tomographic imaging (RTI), which produces real-time images of the change in the radio propagation field of the monitored area caused by the presence of people. People's locations are inferred from the estimated RTI images. We show results from a long-term deployment in a typical single floor, one bedroom apartment. In order to deal with the dynamic nature of the domestic environment, we introduce methods to make the RTI system self-calibrating. Experimental results show that the average localization error of the system is 0.23 m. Moreover, the system is capable of adapting to the changes in the indoor environment, achieving high localization accuracy over an extended period of time.

Keywords: Wireless Networks, Indoor Localization, Received Signal Strength, Radio Tomographic Imaging.

1 Introduction

For ambient-assisted living (AAL) and elderly care applications, accurate localization of people in indoor and domestic environments is one of the most important requirements. The location information can be used for multiple purposes, *e.g.*, to monitor the daily activities and observe the tendencies of people, to alert caretakers and doctors in case of abnormal behavior of events, to automate lights, appliances and air conditioning systems in order to reduce the electricity consumption, etc. Indoor localization has received considerable attention in recent years from the research community, and different systems and sensing technologies have been applied in the context of AAL. In this chapter, we present our research on received signal strength (RSS) based device-free localization (DFL) and we show how it can be successfully applied in real-world scenarios for AAL and elderly-care applications.

S. Chessa and S. Knauth (Eds.): EvAAL 2012, CCIS 362, pp. 108–130, 2013.
© Springer-Verlag Berlin Heidelberg 2013

In an RSS-based DFL system, multiple low-power, wireless transceivers are deployed in the area to be monitored as to form a mesh network. Each device broadcasts packets and stores the RSS of the packets received from all the other devices forming the network. When people are located or move in the environment, they modify the way the radio signals transmitted by the nodes propagate [1, 2], by shadowing [3], reflecting [4], diffracting [5], or scattering [6] a subset of their multipath components [1–9]. The effect of people on the wireless links is reflected in the RSS measurements collected by the nodes [10]. By knowing the position of the nodes, an RSS-based DFL system is capable of estimating the position of the people found in the monitored area by processing the changes over time of the RSS measurements of all the links of the network [11–17]. Since in this type of system the only source of information is the RSS provided by the radio module of the wireless transceivers, we refer to the transceivers as *sensors*, and to the network as a radio frequency (RF) sensor network [18].

In the context of AAL and elderly-care applications, DFL systems provide considerable advantages over other technologies. Unlike other systems, they accurately localize and track the people in the environment without having them to carry or wear any radio device or sensor. This feature makes these systems more suitable to monitor the activities of elder people without causing them physical discomfort or requiring them to remember each day to activate or wear these devices [19] (something particularly challenging for elder people affected by dementia or other neuro-degenerative diseases). Compared to video-camera systems [20], DFL systems do not raise the same privacy concerns, as they can not identify the person or recognize in detail what she is doing. DFL systems are also minimally invasive, since the small wireless sensors composing the network can be embedded in the walls of the house or into furniture, appliances, and other every day objects found in common domestic environments. Moreover, they can localize people also through-wall and in furnished environments which would be hard to cover with infrared motion detectors. Besides their limited invasiveness and flexibility, DFL systems are also considerably cheaper than *e.g.* ultra-wideband (UWB) radar devices.

Accurate indoor localization is even more challenging in the domestic environment. As people perform various activities during their every-day life, objects of various size, shape, and material are constantly moved, changing the propagation patterns of the radio signals. Thus, RSS-based systems have to monitor and dynamically adapt to these changes, providing high localization accuracy in the long-term. For systems using fingerprinting methods or statistical models of the relationship between distance and RSS [21–24], these sudden changes of the radio environment make sub-meter accuracy difficult to achieve and ultimately lead to the need of time-consuming recalibrations of the models. In addition, from a system perspective, the communication protocol run by the sensors composing the network has to be robust to sensors' failures, interference from overlapping wireless networks, and faulty links. Overall, the system must reliably provide its service over the long-term, without requiring manual re-configurations, re-calibrations or even re-starts.

In this chapter, we describe how the temporal changes in the radio propagation field of a wireless mesh network caused by the presence of people, measured by means of RSS, can be used to estimate their positions. Our discussion starts from the observation of how a person crossing a wireless link between two communicating RF sensors affects the RSS measured by the two devices. We show that the change in RSS depends on the frequency channel, and we provide a theoretical framework to combine the information collected on different frequency channels into a unique measurement for the link. The RSS measurements of all the links of the network are then processed in real-time to generate images of the changes in the propagation field of the monitored area - a process named radio tomographic imaging (RTI).

We present the experimental results obtained during a long-term deployment of a DFL system in an apartment. In this testbed, we apply methods to perform an on-line recalibration of the reference RSS of the links of the network. This allows separating the changes in the RSS introduced by the movements of people from the ones due to changes in the domestic environment. Besides achieving high localization accuracy over the entire length of the deployment, we show how the position estimates provided by the system can be processed in order to derive higher-level information about the daily activities and tendencies of the monitored people.

1.1   Outline of the Chapter

In Section 2, we first show how the RSS measured by two communicating sensors is affected by the presence of a person in the proximity of the link line, *i.e.*, the straight imaginary line connecting the two devices. We then describe how, for the same transmitter and receiver pair, the change in RSS varies depending on the frequency channel. The remainder of the section presents the RTI process, in which the RSS measurements collected on all the links of the network on multiple frequency channels are combined to form images of the change in the propagation field due to the presence of people in the monitored area. We also introduce the methods that make our DFL system self-calibrating in order to achieve accurate localization over the long-term in highly dynamic indoor environments. The long-term deployment carried out in an apartment is described in Section 4.1, and the results are presented in Section 4.2. Section 5 concludes the chapter.

2   Radio Tomographic Imaging

2.1   Link Line Crossing and Fade Level

An RTI system uses the RSS measurements collected on the links of a wireless mesh network to localize and track people found in monitored area. In AAL applications, RTI has to be carried out in indoor environments where multiple objects and obstructions are normally found. Thus, in this type of environments, multipath propagation of the radio signals is predominant. The RSS measured at the receiving end of a link is the result of a phasor sum of the waves impinging on its antenna. The result depends on the position of the receiver and the center frequency of the radio signal. When the waves have the same phase, the phasor sum is constructive; when the waves have opposite phase, the phasor sum is destructive. For link l, the RSS measured on channel c at time instant k, $r_{l,c}(k)$, can be modeled as:

$$r_{l,c}(k) = P_c - L_{l,c} - S_{l,c}(k) + F_{l,c}(k) - \eta_{l,c}(k), \quad c \in \mathcal{F} \tag{1}$$

where P_c is the transmit power of the nodes, $L_{l,c}$ the large scale path loss, $S_{l,c}$ the shadowing loss, $F_{l,c}$ the fading gain (or *fade level* [25]), $\eta_{l,c}$ the measurement noise, and $\mathcal{F} = \{1, \ldots, C\}$ is the set of measured radio frequencies.

The RSS, which usually does not show consistent variations when the environment is stationary [26], is otherwise affected by the presence and movement of people in the proximity of the link line [10], *i.e.*, the straight imaginary line connecting two communicating devices. The link line here defined differs from the definition of line-of-sight (LoS), which refers to an obstruction free direct path between the transmitter and receiver of the link. Figure 1 shows the RSS measurements collected on three different radio frequencies for the same link when this is crossed two times by a person. The dynamics of the RSS varies significantly depending on the considered frequency channel. Channel A (blue solid line) shows two consistent (8 dBm) drops of the RSS when the person crosses the link line and no significant variation when the person is located far away from it. Channel B (red dashed-dotted line) shows a more consistent variation even when the person is located slightly away from the link line. However, the average RSS remains approximately the same even when the link line is crossed. Channel C (black dashed line) shows a very large variation of the RSS even when the person is very far from the link line. Moreover, when the person crosses the link line, the RSS tends to increase.

The relation between human-induced RSS changes and steady-state narrowband fading has been modeled in [25] by using the concept of *fade level*. The fade level of a link varies in between two extremes, namely an *anti-fade* state and a *deep fade* state. The RSS of a link in anti-fade is the result of constructive multipath interference. For such a link, $F_{l,c}$ in (1) is positive. When the link line is obstructed by a person, the RSS on average decreases. On the contrary, the RSS of a link in deep fade is the result of destructive multipath interference. For such a link, $F_{l,c}$ in (1) is negative. When the link line is obstructed by a person, the RSS on average increases. Since both the large scale path loss $L_{l,c}$ and the shadowing loss $S_{l,c}$ change very slowly with the center frequency and the frequency channels available with the ZigBee, 802.15.4-compliant nodes used in this work span over 80 MHz in the 2.4 GHz band, we assume that both do not depend on the measured frequency channel c. Thus, $F_{l,c}$ can be calculated as:

$$F_{l,c}(k) = r_{l,c}(k) - P_c + \eta_{l,c}(k). \tag{2}$$

Due to the measurement noise, $\eta_{l,c}(k)$, we can not directly measure the fade level of a link. To estimate it, we use the average RSS, $\bar{r}_{l,c}$, measured in an

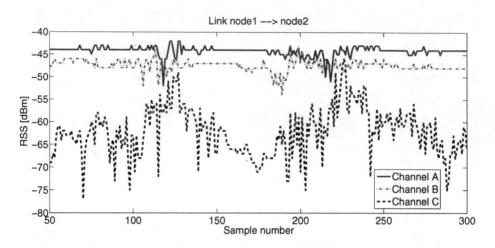

Fig. 1. The RSS measurements collected on three different radio frequencies for the same link when it is crossed two times by a person. The nodes are elevated 1 m from the floor and are 1.5 m apart. Channel A is ZigBee channel 15 (2425 MHz). Channel B is ZigBee channel 22 (2460 MHz). Channel C is ZigBee channel 26 (2480 MHz).

initial calibration of the system performed in stationary conditions, *i.e.* when the monitored area is empty. For each link l, the lowest $\bar{r}$ measured on the channels in $\mathcal{F}$ is used as a reference to derive the fade level during calibration $\bar{F}$ of channel c:

$$\bar{F}_{l,c} = \bar{r}_{l,c} - \min_c \bar{r}_{l,c}. \tag{3}$$

A link is in a *deeper* fade on channel c_1 than on channel c_2 if $\bar{r}_{l,c_1} < \bar{r}_{l,c_2}$. Thus, in figure 1, channel A is the most anti-fade of the three, while channel C is the most deep fade. By definition, $\bar{F}_{l,c} \geq 0$ and $\bar{F}_{l,c} = 0$ for one channel c on each link.

For the purpose of localization, the difference between anti-fade and deep fade channels is substantial. As shown in Figure 1, for anti-fade channels, a person crossing the link line causes attenuation of the RSS, *i.e.*, a sudden drop of several dBm, which can be easily detected. Moreover, the area in which this change is measured is limited around the link line. Thus, anti-fade channels are the most informative to achieve an accurate localization. For deep fade links, the variation of the RSS is consistent even when the person is located at some position far away from the link line [16]. Thus, deep fade links are less suitable for accurate and timely detections of link line crossings, but can successfully be used to detect motion in the monitored environment, especially in sparse deployments, *i.e.* large areas covered by a small number of sensors. The difference between anti-fade and deep fade channels is illustrated also in Figure 3.

The dynamics of the RSS measured on anti-fade and deep fade channels is affected also by the distance of the two communicating devices, as shown in Figure 2. As the distance becomes larger (5 m), the RSS drop measured on the anti-fade channel A (blue solid line) when the person crosses the link line

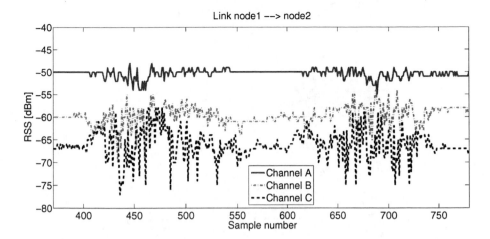

Fig. 2. The RSS measurements collected on three different radio frequencies for the same link when it is crossed two times by a person. The nodes are elevated 1 m from the floor and are 5 m apart. Channel A is ZigBee channel 15 (2425 MHz). Channel B is ZigBee channel 22 (2460 MHz). Channel C is ZigBee channel 26 (2480 MHz).

is smaller (4 dBm) and less predictable. Moreover, even the anti-fade channel measures a small variation of the RSS when the person is slightly far from the link line. Again, the channels having a deeper fade level pick up the presence of the person even when she is very far from the link line.

2.2   Image Estimation

An RTI system composed of S static RF sensors deployed at known positions $\{\mathbf{z}_s\}_{s=1,\ldots,S}$ uses the RSS measurements $r_{l,c}(k)$, collected at time instant k on all the L links of the network on channel $c \in \mathcal{F}$, to estimate a discretized image of the change in the propagation field of the monitored environment, $\mathbf{x}$. The estimation problem can be modeled as:

$$\mathbf{y} = \mathbf{Wx} + \mathbf{n}, \qquad (4)$$

in which $\mathbf{y}$ and $\mathbf{n}$ are $L \times 1$ vectors representing the RSS measurements and noise of the L links of the network, $\mathbf{x}$ is the $N \times 1$ discretized image to be estimated, where N is the number of voxels of the image, and $\mathbf{W}$ is the $L \times N$ weight matrix, which tells how each voxel's attenuation impacts each link. Each element x_n of $\mathbf{x}$ represents the change in the propagation field caused by the presence of a person in voxel n. The linear model for the change in the propagation field is based on the correlated shadowing models introduced in [11, 27] and the work in [12].

The change in RSS caused by the presence of people can be quantified using different methods. In *attenuation-based* RTI [12], the change in RSS is estimated as the difference between the RSS measured at time k, $r_{l,c}(k)$, and the average RSS measured during the initial calibration of the system, $\bar{r}_{l,c}$:

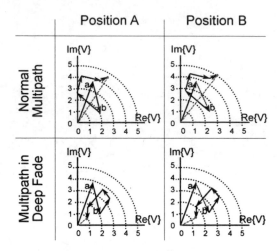

Fig. 3. Multipath contribute complex voltages to a phasor sum, the squared magnitude of which is the received power. Here, a person in Position A causes a frequency channel to have complex voltages as given in the left column. When the person moves to Position B (right column), they change path b by 10 degrees. For the normal multipath channel (top row) the multipath amplitude increases from 4.6 to 5.0, *i.e.*, an increase of 0.7 dB. For the channel in a deep fade, the same change in path b causes the amplitude to change from 1.0 to 1.5, *i.e.*, an increase of 3.5 dB. Thus the same change is more noticeable when the channel's multipath are situated in a deep fade.

$$\Delta r_{l,c}(k) = r_{l,c}(k) - \bar{r}_{l,c}. \tag{5}$$

This method allows localizing both stationary and moving people, but requires an initial calibration of the system for the estimation of $\bar{r}_{l,c}$. In *variance-based* RTI [9], the change in RSS is quantified as the short-term unbiased sample variance of the RSS measurements:

$$\hat{s}_{l,c} = \frac{1}{N_s - 1} \sum_{p=0}^{N_s-1} \left(r_{l,c}(k - p) - \mu_{l,c}(k) \right)^2, \tag{6}$$

where:

$$\mu_{l,c}(k) = \frac{1}{N_s} \sum_{p=0}^{N_s-1} r_{l,c}(k - p). \tag{7}$$

is the mean of the last N_s RSS measurements of link l on channel c. This method does not require an initial calibration of the system and can localize moving people, but is not capable of localizing stationary people. In *histogram distance-based* RTI [28], the change in RSS is quantified as the kernel distance [29] between the histogram of the most recently collected RSS measurements (the *short-term* histogram) and the histogram of RSS measurements collected during the calibration phase (the *long-term* histogram). Similarly to attenuation-based RTI, histogram distance-based RTI can localize both moving and stationary people, but also requires an initial calibration of the system.

Both attenuation-based RTI and histogram distance-based RTI are more suitable to AAL applications than variance-based RTI, since people living in a house can spend considerable amounts of time without moving, e.g., sleeping during the night or sitting on the couch. In this chapter, we consider only attenuation-based RTI and we introduce methods to make the system self-calibrating in order to achieve long-term accurate localization also in highly dynamic domestic environments.

For each link l, the RSS measurements collected on different frequency channels are combined into a unique RSS measurement y_l. As discussed in Section 2.1, anti-fade channels are more informative for localizing the people in the environment. In [16], the channels in $\mathcal{F}$ are ranked based on their fade level, from the most anti-fade to the most deep fade. If $\mathcal{A}_i$ is the set of size m containing the indices of the m top channels in the fade-level ranking, the link RSS measurement y_l at time k is calculated as:

$$y_l(k) = \frac{1}{m} \sum_{c \in \mathcal{A}_i} \Delta r_{l,c}(k). \tag{8}$$

The results in [16] show that the optimal value of m, i.e. the number of channels considered in the computation of y_l, is different for each deployment of the RTI system. In the deployment described in this chapter, we include in the computation of y_l the measurements collected on all the channels in $\mathcal{F}$, and we use the fade level $\bar{F}_{l,c}$ calculated as in (3) to weight them:

$$y_l(k) = \frac{1}{\sum_{c \in \mathcal{F}} \bar{F}_{l,c}} \sum_{c \in \mathcal{F}} \bar{F}_{l,c} \cdot |\Delta r_{l,c}(k)|. \tag{9}$$

The vector $\mathbf{y}$ is formed as follows:

$$\mathbf{y} = [y_1, ..., y_L]^T. \tag{10}$$

In RTI, the change in RSS measured on a link is assumed to be a spatial integral of the radio propagation field in the monitored area [11, 27]. Due to this, some voxels of the discretized image affect the RSS of a specific link, while some others do not. Each link's change in RSS is assumed to be a linear combination of the change in voxels' attenuation:

$$y_l = \sum_{n=1}^{N} w_{l,n} x_n + \eta_l, \tag{11}$$

where x_n is the change in attenuation of voxel n, $w_{l,n}$ the weight of voxel n for link l, and η_l the measurement noise of link l.

The weighting matrix $\mathbf{W}$ in (4) represents a spatial impact model between the L links of the network and the N voxels of the image. Each element $w_{l,n}$ of the matrix indicates how the change in RSS of voxel n affects the RSS measurements

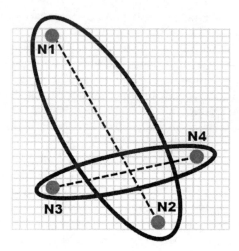

Fig. 4. The spatial impact model used in RTI is an ellipse having the foci located at the transmitter and receiver. The voxels located outside of the ellipse have their weight set to zero, while the voxels that are located within the ellipse have their weight set to a constant inversely proportional to the area of the ellipse. Thus, the shorter links (N3-N4), which are more informative for localization, are weighted more than the longer ones (N1-N2).

of link l. The spatial model used in RTI [9, 11, 12, 16, 30, 31] is an ellipse having the foci located at the transmitter and receiver. According to this model, the voxels that are located outside of the ellipse have their weight set to zero, while the voxels that are located within the ellipse have their weight set to a constant which is inversely proportional to the area Γ_l of the ellipse:

$$w_{ln} = \begin{cases} \frac{1}{\Gamma_l} & \text{if } d_{l,n}^{tx} + d_{l,n}^{rx} < d_l + \lambda \\ 0 & \text{otherwise} \end{cases}, \tag{12}$$

where d is the distance between the transmitter and receiver, d_{ln}^{tx} and d_{ln}^{rx} are the distances from the center of voxel n to the transmitter and receiver of link l, respectively, and λ is the excess path length of the ellipse, i.e., the parameter defining the width of the ellipse. In Section 2.1, we discussed how the shorter links are more informative for localization. In (12), by using a constant inversely proportional to the area of the ellipse, the shorter links are weighted more than the longer ones. The spatial impact model used in RTI is shown in Figure 4.

Since the number of links is considerably smaller than the number of voxels, estimating the image vector $\mathbf{x}$ is an ill-posed inverse problem, which requires regularization [32]. In this work, we use a regularized least-squares approach [11, 16, 30, 31]. The estimated image of the change in the propagation field is calculated as:

$$\hat{\mathbf{x}} = \mathbf{\Pi}\mathbf{y}, \tag{13}$$

where the inversion matrix is:

$$\mathbf{\Pi} = (\mathbf{W}^T\mathbf{W} + \mathbf{C}_x^{-1}\sigma_N^2)^{-1}\mathbf{W}^T, \tag{14}$$

in which σ_N^2 is the regularization parameter. The *a priori* covariance matrix $\mathbf{C}_x$ is calculated by using an exponential spatial decay:

$$[\mathbf{C}_x]_{j,i} = \sigma_x^2 e^{-d_{j,i}/\delta_c}, \tag{15}$$

where σ_x^2 is the variance of voxel measurements, $d_{j,i}$ is the distance from the center of voxel j to the center of voxel i, and δ_c is the voxels' correlation distance. The linear transformation $\mathbf{\Pi}$ is computed only once before real-time operation. The calculation of $\hat{\mathbf{x}}$ in (13) requires $L \times N$ operations and can be performed in real-time.

When only one person is in the monitored environment, her position $\hat{p}$ is estimated as:

$$\hat{p} = \arg\max_{n \in N} \hat{\mathbf{x}}, \tag{16}$$

i.e., the person's position estimate is at the voxel n of the discretized image $\hat{\mathbf{x}}$ having the highest value. In [9, 15, 31], the estimated trajectory followed by the person is smoothed by recursively applying a Kalman filter [33] on the position estimates. In this chapter, we present results related only to the localization of one person. For multiple people localization and tracking with RTI, the reader is invited to refer to the works in [17, 25, 34, 35].

2.3   On-line Calibration for AAL Applications

One of the main challenges in using an RTI system in real-world indoor and do-mestic environments is represented by the fact that they are highly dynamic, *i.e.*, people working or living in these environments constantly change the position of objects of various size, shape and material while carrying out their activities. This changes dramatically over time the *reference* RSS of the links on the mea-sured frequency channels, *i.e.* the RSS measured in stationary conditions. Figure 5 provides an example of the effect of environmental changes on the reference RSS: a person moves towards the link line carrying a metallic chair with her, then places the chair in the middle point of the link and moves away from the link line. The new position of the chair in the environment changes dramatically the RSS measured on the three different channels: for channel A (blue solid line), the reference RSS drops by 6 dBm; for channel B (red dashed-dotted line), the reference RSS drops by 5 dBm; for channel C (black dashed line), the reference RSS drops by 10 dBm.

By affecting the reference RSS, environmental changes modify also the fade level of the frequency channels. Before the chair is placed in the middle point of the link, channel C is the one in the deepest fade; after, channel B is the one in the deepest fade. Consequently, the fade level-based ranking of the channels derived during the initial calibration of the system which is used in [16] can be drastically modified even by environmental changes. In this work, the fade level

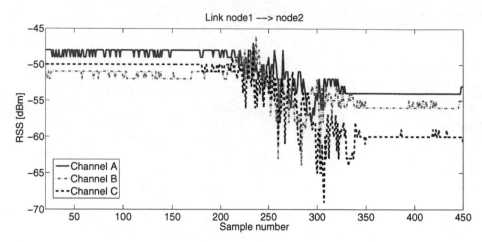

Fig. 5. The effect of environmental changes on the RSS measured on different radio frequencies for the same link. The nodes are elevated 1 m from the floor and are 4 m apart. At sample 200, a person carrying a chair starts moving towards the link line and places the chair in the middle point of the link. At sample 300, the person moves away from the link line leaving the chair behind. The presence of the chair on the link line changes considerably the RSS measured on the three channels.

is used in (9) to weight the RSS measurements of all the channels in $\mathcal{F}$. Thus, environmental changes modify also the weight assigned to the RSS measurements of the different channels.

These observations require methods to make the RTI system able to adapt to the changes in the propagation patterns of the radio signals and recalibrate on-line both the reference RSS and fade level of the frequency channels. Without recalibration, the RTI system would not be able to achieve accurate localization over an extended period of time and would need to be stopped, recalibrated and restarted frequently. In [9, 30, 36, 37], different methods to adapt to the dynamic environment are presented. In [30], the reference RSS $\bar{r}_{l,c}(k)$ of link l on channel c at time k is calculated using a moving average:

$$\bar{r}_{l,c}(k) = (1 - \alpha)\bar{r}_{l,c}(k - 1) + \alpha r_{l,c}(k), \tag{17}$$

where $\alpha \in [0, 1]$ is a parameter defining the rate of adaptation of the reference RSS, i.e., slow for low values, e.g., $\alpha = 0.01$, fast for higher values, e.g., $\alpha = 0.2$. In this work, we extend the on-line recalibration of the system to the fade level of the channels. The fade level $\bar{F}_{l,c}(k)$ of link l on channel c at time k is calculated using the reference RSS calculated in (17):

$$\bar{F}_{l,c}(k) = \bar{r}_{l,c}(k) - \min_c \bar{r}_{l,c}(k). \tag{18}$$

Consequently, at time k, the link measurement y_l becomes:

$$y_l(k) = \frac{1}{\sum_{c \in \mathcal{F}} \bar{F}_{l,c}(k)} \sum_{c \in \mathcal{F}} \bar{F}_{l,c}(k) \cdot |\Delta r_{l,c}(k)|, \tag{19}$$

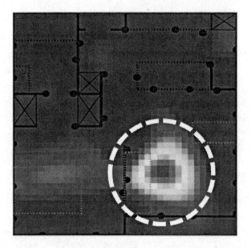

Fig. 6. A typical RTI image produced by the RTI system. The red blob indicates the area occupied by the person. The white dashed circle, centered at the current position estimate, represents the gating area outside of which the links are recalibrated on-line.

where:

$$\Delta r_{l,c}(k) = r_{l,c}(k) - \bar{r}_{l,c}(k). \tag{20}$$

Figure 6 shows a typical RTI image produced by the system. The red *blob* in it indicates the area in which the person is located. When the person is stationary, the RSS measurements of the links intersecting the area occupied by the person are approximately constant. Due to the on-line recalibration of the reference RSS, if the person will not move for an extended period of time, *e.g.*, while sleeping or sitting on the sofa, the RSS attenuation on those links, $\Delta r_{l,c}(k)$, will be very small, since the on-line reference RSS, $\bar{r}_{l,c}(k)$, will have a value very close to the current RSS measurements. Thus, the link measurement y_l will also have a very small value and the red blob indicating the position of the person will vanish in the background, making the position estimate $\hat{p}$ calculated in (16) noisy and unreliable.

To avoid the disappearing of the blob when the person is stationary for an extended period of time, we center a circular *gating area* of radius ω at the current position estimate $\hat{p}(k)$. The gating area is used as a spatial filter for the on-line recalibration of the reference RSS and fade level of the channels, as follows:

$$\bar{r}_{l,c}(k) = \begin{cases} (1-\alpha)\bar{r}_{l,c}(k-1) + \alpha r_{l,c}(k) & \text{if } l \notin \mathcal{P}_l \\ \bar{r}_{l,c}(k-1) & \text{otherwise} \end{cases}, \tag{21}$$

and similarly for the fade level of the channels:

$$\bar{F}_{l,c}(k) = \begin{cases} \bar{r}_{l,c}(k) - \min_c \bar{r}_{l,c}(k) & \text{if } l \notin \mathcal{P}_l \\ \bar{F}_{l,c}(k-1) & \text{otherwise} \end{cases}, \tag{22}$$

Table 1. Image reconstruction parameters

Description	Parameter	Value
Pixel width [m]	p	0.20
Ellipse excess path length[m]	λ	0.02
Voxels standard deviation [dB]	σ_x	0.2236
Noise standard deviation [dB]	σ_N	1
Correlation coefficient	δ_c	3
Moving average coefficient	α	0.05
Gating area radius [m]	ω	1

where $\mathcal{P}_l$ is the set of links of the network intersecting the circle of radius ω centered at the current position estimate $\hat{p}(k)$. Thus, the links of the network not intersecting the gating area are recalibrated on-line, while the ones intersecting the gating area are not recalibrated. Thanks to this spatial filter, the red blob does not disappear from the image and the position estimate $\hat{p}$ remains on the spot occupied by the person even when she is stationary for an extended period of time. The values of the parameters used in methods described in this Section are listed in Table 1.

3   Hardware and Communication Protocol

In this section, we describe the RF sensors composing the RTI system and the communication protocol used to collect the RSS measurements of all the links of the nework on multiple frequency channels.

3.1   Hardware

The experiments described in this chapter are carried out with Texas Instruments CC2531 USB dongle nodes [38], shown in Figure 7. The nodes are equipped with a low-power, 802.15.4 [39] compliant radio operating in the 2.4 GHz ISM band. In the experiments, we set the transmit power of the nodes to the maximum nominal value, *i.e.*, 4.5 dBm.

The 802.15.4 standard defines 16 frequency channels, 5 MHz apart and having 2 MHz of bandwidth. The carrier frequency (in MHz) of channel c is:

$$f_c = 2405 + 5(c - 11), c \in [11, 26]. \tag{23}$$

Due in part to the differences in antenna impedance matching across an 80 MHz frequency band [40], the CC2531 nodes measure lower RSS values on the lower frequency channels than on the higher ones. Thus, to avoid bias in estimating the fade level of the channels, normalization is required. We experimentally derived the linear relationship $P_c = 0.145c + 1.733$, which closely matches the measured transmit power.

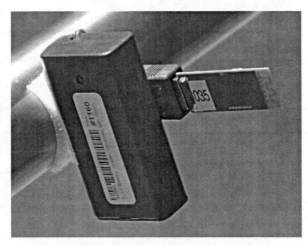

Fig. 7. Two figures of the CC2531 USB dongle node used in the experiments. On the left, a node plugged into an electricity socket through an USB power adapter. On the right, a node powered by two AA batteries.

In [30], we had noticed that the propagation pattern of the antenna of the nodes was heavily affected by the proximity to metallic surfaces and walls. This made the RSS measurements more noisy and decreased the localization accuracy. The new battery pack, visible in Figure 7, is now designed such that the antenna is pointing away from the surface or wall to which it is attached through velcro. This compact and lightweight design allows us reducing the time required to deploy the nodes and increase the quality of the RSS measurements.

3.2   Communication Protocol: *multi*-Spin

The RF sensors composing the RTI system run *multi*-Spin, a multi-channel TDMA protocol which defines the order of transmission of the nodes and synchronizes their switching on different frequency channels. In *multi*-Spin, time is divided into *slots*, *cycles* and *rounds*: a round includes $|\mathcal{F}|$ TDMA cycles; a TDMA cycle includes S slots. In each slot, only one of the nodes transmits a packet, while all the other nodes are in receiving mode. The order of transmission of the nodes in a TDMA cycle is based on their built-in ID number. The set of measured frequency channels $\mathcal{F}$ is pre-defined by the user before deployment and stored as a list in the memory of the nodes.

In each cycle, the nodes communicate on one of the frequency channels of the list. At the end of the cycle, they switch synchronously on the next channel of the list. The first channel in the list acts as a backbone channel: if a node does not receive any packet for S consecutive slots, it will assume to have lost synchronization with the network and will immediately switch back to the backbone channel, waiting for packets. In this way, when the other nodes will switch

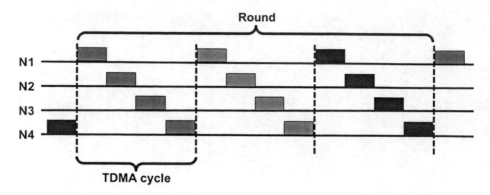

Fig. 8. In *multi*-Spin, time is divided into *slots*, *cycles* and *rounds*: a round includes $|\mathcal{F}|$ TDMA cycles; a TDMA cycle includes S slots. In each slot, only one of the nodes of the network is transmitting (solid block), while the others are in receiving mode. The order of transmission is based on the built-in ID number of the nodes. At the end of a TDMA cycle, the nodes switch synchronously on the next frequency channel in the list pre-defined by the user.

again to the first channel of the list, the node previously fallen out-of-sync will be able to rejoin the network. This mechanism ensures that even when one or more nodes stop receiving packets from the others, *e.g.*, because they have run out of power or have accidentally been unplugged from the electric socket, they will be able to rejoin the network without requiring a manual restart by the user.

multi-Spin starts when at least two nodes are turned on (if battery-powered) or plugged into electric sockets. Each node repeatedly calculates a random back-off time and transmits a packet on the backbone frequency channel until it receives a packet from another node. The reception of the first packet allows the nodes to synchronize themselves and communicate on the frequency channels of the list.

The payload of each packet includes the ID number of the transmitting node and the most recent RSS measurements of the packets received from the other nodes. A node connected to a laptop switches channels synchronously with the network of RF sensors and overhears all the traffic, collecting and processing in real-time the RSS measurements of all the links. By knowing the total number of sensors S composing the network and the ID number of the transmitting node ID_{TX}, at the reception of a packet each node is able to calculate the number of slots until the next switching of frequency channel, Δ_c, and the number of slots until the next transmission, Δ_{TX}, as follows:

$$\Delta_c = S - ID_{TX}, \tag{24}$$

$$\Delta_{TX} = \begin{cases} ID_{RX} - ID_{TX} - 1 & \text{if } ID_{TX} < ID_{RX} \\ S - ID_{TX} + ID_{RX} & \text{otherwise} \end{cases}, \tag{25}$$

where ID_{RX} is the ID number of the receiving node. This mechanism makes the network tolerant to packet drops, due *e.g.* to the interference of other coexisting wireless networks [41, 42], as the nodes can keep on communicating and on being synchronized even when dropping packets.

The features described above make *multi*-Spin an autonomously starting, synchronizing and healing communication protocol tolerant to interference from coexisting wireless networks. With the CC2531 nodes, the average time length of a slot is approximately 3 ms. For a network composed of 33 RF sensors communicating on five frequency channels, such as the one described in Section 4.1, the total length of a TDMA cycle is approximately 100 ms, making the total length of a round approximately equal to 500 ms. Thus, an RTI system composed of 33 nodes collects two RSS measurements per link per second.

4   Experimental Results

4.1   Deployment

To evaluate the performance of the methods described in Section 2, we use the data collected during a three months deployment of an RTI system composed of 33 nodes in a typical 58 m² single floor, one bedroom apartment inhabited by a single person. The nodes are set to communicate on five frequency channels, *i.e.*, $\mathcal{F} = \{11, 15, 18, 21, 26\}$. The blueprint and an image of the apartment are shown in Figure 9.

4.2   Localization Accuracy

In the beginning of the deployment, we evaluate the accuracy of the RTI system in localizing the person in different areas of the apartment. We define 14 spots of evaluation, in which the person stands without moving for a pre-determined amount of time before walking to the next position. Figure 10 shows the average position estimates provided by the RTI system in each of the 14 points of evaluation. The average localization error is 0.23 m. It has to be noted that the localization error remains below 0.40 m in 13 of the 14 points of evaluation. The largest error, 0.92 m, is measured when the person stands in the kitchen, where a large marble counter (visible also in Figure 9) has a remarkable impact on the propagation of the radio signals.

The effect of the on-line recalibration of the reference RSS and fade level of the measured frequency channels is shown in Figure 11. The RTI images (a) and (b) are formed using the on-line recalibration methods described in Section 2.3, while the images (c) and (d) are formed using the reference RSS and fade levels estimated during the initial calibration of the system. Images (a) and (c) are formed six hours after the system is started ($\Delta T = 6$ h), while images (b) and (d) are formed 18 hours after the system is started ($\Delta T = 18$ h). Without on-line recalibration, the images formed by the RTI system rapidly become more noisy: while in image (a) the image shows only one clear blob in the position occupied

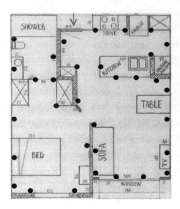

Fig. 9. On the left, the blueprint of the single floor, one bedroom apartment in which the RTI system has been deployed for over three months. The black dots represent the position of the 33 RF sensors. On the right, an image of the apartment.

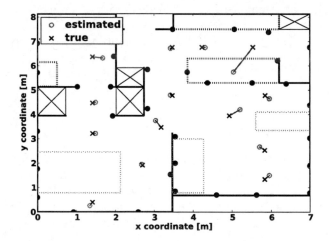

Fig. 10. The true and estimated position of the person in 14 different points of the apartment. The average localization error is 0.23 m.

by the person, image (c) shows other three small blobs due to changes in the environment. After 18 hours, the effect of the on-line recalibration is even more evident: in image (b), the system can still correctly localize the person, forming an image that shows only one clear blob in the correct position. Without on-line recalibration (image (d)), the system forms a very noisy image with multiple blobs and provides a position estimate very far from the true location of the person. We invite the reader to view a video showing the movements of the person living in the apartment over a ten minutes time interval at [43].

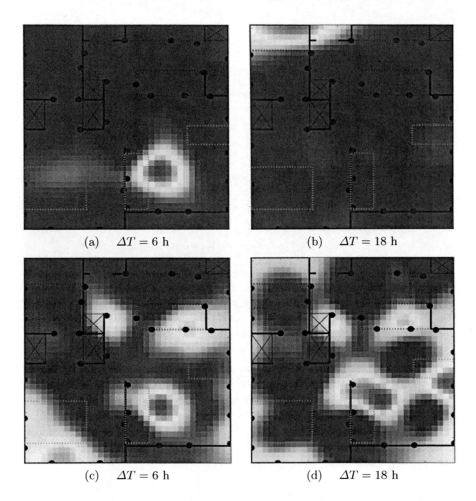

(a) $\Delta T = 6$ h   (b) $\Delta T = 18$ h

(c) $\Delta T = 6$ h   (d) $\Delta T = 18$ h

Fig. 11. The effect of the on-line recalibration of the reference RSS and fade level of the measured frequency channels on the long-term localization accuracy. Without on-line recalibration (images (c) and (d)), the RTI images formed by the system rapidly become more noisy and ultimately lead to position estimates far from the true location of the person. On the other hand, a system using the on-line recalibration methods described in Section 2.3 can maintain high localization accuracy over an extended period of time despite the several environmental changes due to the daily activities carried out by the monitored person.

The location information can be used in AAL applications to infer about the daily routine and the health of the monitored person. The apartment can be divided into areas-of-interest (AoI), *e.g.*, the kitchen, bathroom, bedroom, living room, etc. The highly accurate localization provided by an RTI system allows further dividing each AoI into smaller *sub*-areas which can be associated to specific activities, *e.g.*, cooking on the stove, washing laundry, taking a shower,

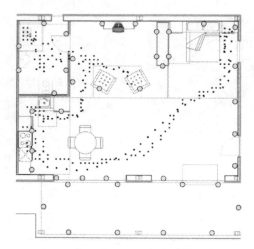

Fig. 12. The blueprint of the home in which the tests of the second *EvAAL* competition were carried out. The yellow circles represent the RF sensors. The black dots represent the true position of the person during the test at 1 s intervals. The red dots represent the true position of the person at spots in which she was stationary for five seconds. The blue dots represent the position estimates returned by the RTI system.

riding a stationary bike, etc. For example, an RTI system can be used by doctors and caretakers as a non-invasive way to monitor the eating habits and the level of mobility of an obese person while at home. The movements of a person in different AoIs can be reliably detected by using a finite-state machine [30], in which each state is associated to a different AoI. The temporal sequence of state transitions the and time spent in each AOI measured by the RTI system can be used to extract spatiotemporal activity patterns [44].

4.3   EvAAL Competition Deployment

The RTI system described in this chapter participated to the second *EvAAL* (Evaluating AAL Systems through Competitive Benchmarking) competition [45] in the track on indoor localization and tracking. Figure 12 shows the blueprint of the home in which the experimental evaluation was carried out. In it, the yellow circles represent the RF sensors, the black dots the true position of the person during the test at 1 s intervals, the red dots the true position of the person at spots in which she was stationary for five seconds, and the blue dots the position estimates returned by the RTI system. The 42 RF sensors were installed by one person in approximately 43 minutes. The position of the nodes was decided before their deployment in order to be able to pre-calculate the inversion matrix Π in (14). However, in order to speed up the deployment, the installer positioned the nodes by using the furniture found in the home as reference, *i.e.*, without precisely measuring the distances among the nodes. This inevitably introduced an error for some nodes between their real coordinates and the ones used in the computation of Π. Despite this small errors, the RTI system was able to accurately track the person moving around the home, as shown in Figure 12.

5 Conclusion

This chapter explores the use of radio tomographic imaging (RTI) in the context of ambient assisted living (AAL) applications. In RTI, the received signal strength (RSS) measured on the links of a mesh network composed of static wireless transceivers are used to accurately localize and track people without requiring them to wear or carry any sensor or radio device. The presence of a person on the link line, *i.e.*, the straight imaginary line connecting the transmitter and receiver, changes the measured RSS. We show that this change in RSS depends on the *fade level* of the measured frequency channel and the distance between the two communicating devices. Based on these findings, the spatial impact area of a link is modeled as an ellipse having the foci at the transmitter and receiver. This ellipse is more narrow for shorter links, and wider for longer links. The concept of fade level is used to weight the RSS measurements collected on different frequency channels: the *anti-fade* channels are weighted more than the *deep fade* ones, since their RSS measurements are more informative for localization. By applying a regularized least-square approach, we are able to estimate in real-time a discretized image of the change in the propagation field of the monitored area due to the presence a person. The voxel of the RTI image having the highest intensity represents the estimated position of the person.

RSS-based indoor localization becomes even more challenging in highly dynamic domestic environments, since the propagation patterns of the radio signals can be drastically changed even by small environmental modifications. In this chapter, we introduce methods to make the RTI system able to recalibrate on-line and adapt to the environmental changes introduced by the monitored person during her daily activities. We deploy a system for over three months in a typical single floor, single bedroom apartment inhabited by a single person. Experimental results demonstrate that the average localization error is 0.23 m. In addition, the system provides a high localization accuracy over an extended period of time despite several environmental changes introduced by the person during her daily activities, as shown in the video in [43]. The ability of the RTI system to accurately localize the person without requiring her to participate in the localization effort makes this technology a very attractive solution for AAL and elder-care applications.

Acknowledgments. This work is supported by the US National Science Foundation Grants #0748206 and #1035565.

References

1. Bultitude, R.J.: Measurement, characterization, and modeling of indoor 800/900 MHz radio channels for digital communications. IEEE Communications 25(6), 512 (1987)
2. Hashemi, H.: A Study of Temporal and Spatial Variations of the Indoor Radio Propagation Channel. IEEE International Symposium on Personal, Indoor and Mobile Radio Communications, 127–134 (1994)
3. Rappaport, T.: Wireless Communications: Principles and Practice, 2nd edn. Prentice Hall PTR, Upper Saddle River (2001)
4. Liberti, J.C., Rappaport, T.S.: A Geometrically Based Model for Line-of-Sight Multipath Radio Channels. In: 46th IEEE Vehicular Technology Conference, vol. 5, pp. 844–848 (1996)
5. Molisch, A.: Wireless Communications, 2nd edn. John Wiley & Sons Ltd. (2011)
6. Nørklit, O., Andersen, J.B.: Diffuse Channel Model and Experimental Results for Array Antennas in Mobile Environments. IEEE Transactions on Antennas and Propagation 46(6), 834–840 (1998)
7. Hashemi, H.: The indoor radio propagation channel. Proceedings of the IEEE 81(7), 943–968 (1993)
8. Ghaddar, M., Talbi, L., Denidni, T.: Human Body Modelling for Prediction of Effect of People on Indoor Propagation Channel. Electronics Letters 40, 25 (2004)
9. Wilson, J., Patwari, N.: See-Through Walls: Motion Tracking Using Variance-Based Radio Tomography Networks. IEEE Transactions on Mobile Computing 10(5), 612–621 (2011)
10. Woyach, K., Puccinelli, D., Haenggi, M.: Sensorless Sensing in Wireless Networks: Implementation and Measurements. In: 4th International Symposium on Modeling and Optimization in Mobile, Ad Hoc and Wireless Networks (2006)
11. Patwari, N., Agrawal, P.: Effects of Correlated Shadowing: Connectivity, Localization, and RF Tomography. In: IEEE/ACM International Conference on Information Processing in Sensor Networks, pp. 82–93 (2008)
12. Wilson, J., Patwari, N.: Radio Tomographic Imaging With Wireless Networks. IEEE Transactions on Mobile Computing 9(5), 621–632 (2010)
13. Kanso, M.A., Rabbat, M.G.: Compressed RF Tomography for Wireless Sensor Networks: Centralized and Decentralized Approaches. In: Krishnamachari, B., Suri, S., Heinzelman, W., Mitra, U. (eds.) DCOSS 2009. LNCS, vol. 5516, pp. 173–186. Springer, Heidelberg (2009)
14. Chen, X., Edelstein, A., Li, Y., Coates, M., Rabbat, M., Aidong, M.: Sequential Monte Carlo for Simultaneous Passive Device-free Tracking and Sensor Localization Using Received Signal Strength Measurements. In: ACM/IEEE Information Processing in Sensor Networks (2011)
15. Kaltiokallio, O., Bocca, M.: Real-Time Intrusion Detection and Tracking in Indoor Environment Through Distributed RSSI Processing. In: 17th IEEE International Conference on Embedded and Real-Time Computing Systems and Applications, pp. 61–70 (2011)
16. Kaltiokallio, O., Bocca, M., Patwari, N.: Enhancing the Accuracy of Radio Tomographic Imaging Using Channel Diversity. In: 9th IEEE International Conference on Mobile Ad Hoc and Sensor Systems (2012)
17. Zhang, D., Liu, Y., Ni, L.: Rass: A Real-Time, Accurate and Scalable System for Tracking Transceiver-Free Objects. In: IEEE International Conference on Pervasive Computing and Communications, pp, pp. 197–204 (2011)

18. Patwari, N., Wilson, J.: RF Sensor Networks for Device-Free Localization and Tracking. Proceedings of the IEEE 98(11), 1961–1973 (2010)
19. Li, Q., Stankovic, J.A., Hanson, M.A., Barth, A.T., Lach, J., Zhou, G.: Accurate, Fast Fall Detection Using Gyroscopes and Accelerometer Derived Posture Information. In: 6th International Workshop on Wearable and Implantable Body Sensor Networks, pp. 138–143 (2009)
20. Anderson, D., Keller, J., Skubic, M., Chen, X., He, Z.: Recognizing falls from silhouettes. In: 28th International Conference of the IEEE Engineering in Medicine and Biology Society, pp. 6388–6391 (2006)
21. Bahl, P., Padmanabhan, V.: RADAR: an In-building RF-based User Location and Tracking System. In: 19th Conference of the IEEE Computer and Communication Societies, vol. 2, pp. 775–784 (2000)
22. Youssef, M., Mah, M., Agrawala, A.: Challenges: Device-Free Passive Localization for Wireless Environments. In: ACM International Conference on Mobile Computing and Networking, pp. 222–229 (2007)
23. Barsocchi, P., Lenzi, S., Chessa, S., Giunta, G.: A Novel Approach to Indoor RSSI Localization by Automatic Calibration of the Wireless Propagation Model. In: 69th IEEE Vehicular Technology Conference, pp. 1–5 (2009)
24. Viani, F., Rocca, P., Benedetti, M., Oliveri, G., Massa, A.: Electromagnetic Passive Localization and Tracking of Moving Targets in a WSN-Infrastructured Environment. Inverse Problems 26(7) (2010)
25. Wilson, J., Patwari, N.: A Fade-Level Skew-Laplace Signal Strength Model for Device-Free Localization with Wireless Networks. IEEE Transactions on Mobile Computing 11(6), 947–958 (2012)
26. Baccour, N., Koubâa, A., Mottola, L., Zúñiga, M.A., Youssef, H., Boano, C.A., Alves, M.: Radio link quality estimation in wireless sensor networks: A survey. ACM Transactions on Sensor Networks 8(4), 1–34 (2012)
27. Agrawal, P., Patwari, N.: Correlated Link Shadow Fading in Multi-hop Wireless Networks. IEEE Transsactions on Wireless Communications 8(8), 4024–4036 (2009)
28. Zhao, Y., Patwari, N.: Demo Abstract: Histogram Distance-Based Radio Tomographic Localization. In: IEEE/ACM International Conference on Information Processing in Sensor Networks, pp. 129–130 (2012)
29. Phillips, J.M., Venkatasubramanian, S.: A Gentle Introduction to the Kernel Distance. Technical Report arXiv:1103.1625, Arxiv.org (2011)
30. Kaltiokallio, O., Bocca, M., Patwari, N.: Follow @Grandma: Long-Term Device-Free Localization for Residential Monitoring. In: 7th IEEE International Workshop on Practical Issues in Building Sensor Network Applications (2012)
31. Zhao, Y., Patwari, N.: Noise Reduction for Variance-Based Device-Free Localization and Tracking. In: 8th IEEE Conference on Sensor, Mesh and Ad Hoc Communications and Networks, pp. 179–187 (2011)
32. Wilson, J., Patwari, N., Vasquez, F.G.: Regularization Methods for Radio Tomographic Imaging. In: Virginia Tech. Wireless Symposium (2009)
33. Kalman, R.E.: A New Approach to Linear Filtering and Prediction Problems. Transactions of the ASME Journal of Basic Engineering (Series D) (82), 35–45 (1960)
34. Thouin, F., Nannuru, S., Coates, M.J.: Multi-target Tracking for Measurement Models with Additive Contributions. In: International Conference on Information Fusion (2011)

35. Nannuru, S., Li, Y., Zeng, Y., Coates, M., Yang, B.: Radio Frequency Tomography for Passive Indoor Multi-Target Tracking. IEEE Transactions on Mobile Computing (2012), http://doi.ieeecomputersociety.org/10.1109/TMC.2012.190
36. Zheng, Y., Men, A.: Through-Wall Tracking with Radio Tomography Networks Using Foreground Detection. In: IEEE Wireless Communications and Networking Conference (2012)
37. Edelstein, A., Rabbat, M.: Background Subtraction for Online Calibration of RF Sensing Networks. IEEE Transactions on Mobile Computing (accepted September 2012)
38. Texas Instruments.: A USB-Enabled System-on-Chip Solution for 2.4GHz IEEE 802.15.4 and ZigBee Applications, http://www.ti.com/lit/ds/symlink/cc2531.pdf
39. IEEE 802.15.4 Standard Technical Specifications, http://www.ieee802.org/15/pub/TG4Expert.html
40. Texas Instruments.: Small Size 2.4 GHz PCB antenna. www.ti.com/lit/an/swra117d/swra117d.pdf
41. Srinivasan, K., Dutta, P., Tavakoli, A., Levis, P.: Understanding the Causes of Packet Delivery Success and Failure in Dense Wireless Sensor Networks. In: 4th ACM Conference on Embedded Networked Sensor Systems, pp. 419–420 (2006)
42. Xing, G., Sha, M., Huang, J., Zhou, G., Wang, X., Liu, S.: Multichannel Interference Measurement and Modeling in Low-Power Wireless Networks. In: IEEE Real-Time Systems Symposium, pp. 248–257 (2009)
43. Kaltiokallio, O.: Follow @Grandma: Long-term Device-Free Localization for Residential Monitoring (YouTube Video), http://www.youtube.com/watch?v=XuMBRm6S_6g
44. Lymberopoulos, D., Bamis, A., Savvides, A.: Extracting Spatiotemporal Human Activity Patterns in Assisted Living Using a Home Sensor Network. Universal Access in the Information Society 10(2), 125–138 (2011)
45. Second EvAAL (Evaluating AAL Systems through Competitive Benchmarking) Competition, http://evaal.aaloa.org/2012/2012-competition

Evaluating Human Activity Recognition Systems for AAL Environments

Juan Antonio Álvarez-García*

Computer Languages and Systems Department, University of Seville, Spain
`jaalvarez@us.es`

Abstract. EvAAL Activity Recognition track's main goal is to evaluate one of the pillars of Ambient Assisted Living (AAL): human activity recognition (AR). In this edition 4 teams from United States, Ireland, Spain and Japan participated in the competition. Results show that accelerometer based solutions are promising due to their small size and their integration in complex devices such as mobile phones or elastics wearable straps.

Keywords: AAL, activity recognition, tracking.

1 Introduction

Activity Recognition (AR) is a research area where the objective is to recognize human activities. The automatic and unobtrusive identification of users activities is one of the challenging goals of context-aware computing [1] and is expected to be a practical solution to monitor aged people: According to UNFPA[2] although currently only Japan has an older population of more than 30 per cent, by 2050, 64 countries are expected to join Japan.

Our objective is to measure AR hardware and software performance through a competition. Since competitions in computer science have a long-established tradition, the design of EvAAL has been inspired by other successful competitions. Some past and current competitions have been analyzed in order to identify successful practices, specifically: HARL [3],OPPORTUNITY [4], HASC [5] and BSN Contest [6]. The main difference with the preceding ones is that this track addresses both software and hardware so that whole state of the art of activity recognition can be examined.

The main objective of this competition is to implement an activity recognition system (ARS) that recognizes the following activities: lie, sit, stand, walk, bend, fall and cycle (using a stationary bike).

The competition took place from 9 to 13 July, 2012 at the CIAmI Living Lab [7] in Valencia (Spain). In this track there is no limitation to the number of devices that can be used and competing solutions can be based on a variety of

---

* This work was supported in part by the European Commission in the framework of the FP7 project universAAL under Contract 247950.

S. Chessa and S. Knauth (Eds.): EvAAL 2012, CCIS 362, pp. 131–136, 2013.

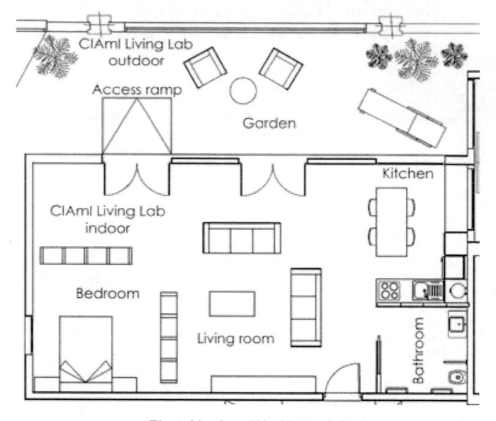

Fig. 1. Map from CIAmI Living Lab

sensors and technologies, including: accelerometers, gyroscopes, magnetometers, pressure sensors, microphones, sensor networks, mobile phones, cameras, etc.. Other technologies or combinations of them are also considered acceptable provided they are compatible with the constraints of the hosting Living Lab. Figure 1 shows the CIAmI map.

2   Benchmarks

Competitors are invited to install and run their ARS during a time slot, in this case for two hours and a half, divided in three subslots: Installation, Benchmark and Removal phases.

During the second phase, the ARS are evaluated. An actor (an evaluation committee member) performs a predefined physical activity trip across the smart home. Audio signals synchronize the actor movements in each performance (twice per team) in order to get the same ground truth for all the participants. The path followed by the actor and the activities are the same for each performance, and they were not disclosed to competitors before the application of the benchmarks.

Similarly, the position of the stationary bike and the place of the fall are not revealed either.

Once the two performances are executed, the one with better overall mark is used to compare each team.

A critical issue (that was communicated in advance to the competitors) is the age of the actor, that is required in order to train and prepare their algorithms properly. The actor was also trained to repeat the activities in the benchmarks always in the same way (following the mp3 file explained in Section 3). The fall is also critical, because many different kind of falls are possible [8]. For this reason we published in advance a video of the fall that had been executed by the actor during the experiment. A recorded performance can be seen in this video[1].

3   Reference Localization System

The reference ARS is used to obtain the ground truth data. In order to get approximately the same ground truth for all the contestants, audio signals were used to synchronize the actor movements. An mp3 file indicates the next activity that the actor must perform and a countdown ("three, two, one, now") to perform it. When the actor hears the word "now", he begins the transition to the next activity. In some cases, such as BSN Contest, researchers identify transitions to recognize the next activity. In our case with 7 activities, the number of possible transitions (some of them not very probable) is 42. Since the number of transitions is high and it is not trivial to evaluate them, we decided not to evaluate the transitions but only the activities.

To retrieve competitor and ground truth data, a local server accepts sockets with the activity code and the time when it is identified. A competitor system only need to send this information to the server. A local NTP server is also available to synchronize the time. To obtain ground truth data, an evaluator uses an Android application to mark the activities (activity code) or transitions (-1 code) through his mobile phone and to send this information to the socket server.

To this purpose, the evaluator follows the actor to see exactly when he starts the activities or transitions. For instance, if the actor is standing still and hears "Cycling 3, 2, 1, now!" he begins to hold the handlebars and move his leg to go up the bike. When the word "now" is spelled, the evaluator pushes the button in the application to identify the end of previous activity and the beginning of a transition. The evaluator later on pushes again the button to mark the end of the activity.

4   Evaluation Criteria

The following criteria and weights were used to evaluate the system of every team:

Accuracy (0.25) It evaluates the recognized activity instances (500 ms) using F-measure $\frac{2*precision*recall}{precision+recall}$ to compute it.

---

[1] http://vimeo.com/52843550

Recognition delay (0.2) It refers to the elapsed time between the instant in which the user begins an activity and the time in which the system recognizes it.

Installation complexity (0,15) It is a measure of the effort required to install the ARS in a flat, measured by the evaluation committee as a function of the person-minutes of work needed to complete the installation.

User Acceptance (0.25) It captures how much invasive the ARS is in the users daily life and thereby the impact perceived by the user; this parameter is evaluated by the Evaluation Committee using a questionnaire.

Interoperability with AAL systems (0,15) It is evaluated using a questionnaire that measure the use of open source solutions, use of standards, availability of libraries for development and integration with standard protocols.

5   Contestants and Results

After peer review, five teams were accepted but one of them withdrew due to financial cutbacks of its institution. Hence only four competitors participated in the challenge, CUJ (from Chiba University, Japan), CMU (from Carnegie Mellon and Utah Universities, USA), DCU (from Dublin City University, Ireland) and USS (from University of Seville, Spain). The technology used by every team is described here:

5.1   DCU Team

Title of paper Visual Experience for Recognising Human Activities

List of Authors and affiliations Na Li, Martin Crane, Heather Ruskin from Centre for Scientific Computing and Complex Systems Modelling, School of Computing, Dublin City University.

Brief description DCU Team uses a SenseCam[2] hanging from the actor's neck to evaluate off-line the activities. The DCU system worked offline and therefore no accuracy and delay score was assigned.

5.2   CUJ Team-Bronze

Title of paper Human Behavior Recognition by a Mobile Robot Following Human Subjects.

List of Authors and affiliations Myagmarbayar Nergui[1], Nevrez Imamoglu[1], Yuki Yoshida[1], Jose Gonzalez[2], Masashi Sekine[2], Kazuya Kawamura[1] and Wenwei Yu[1].

1. Medical System Engineering Department, Graduate School of Engineering, Chiba University.
2. Research Center for Frontier Medical Engineering, Chiba University.

Brief description CUJ Team uses a robot (initially a Pioneer 3-AT[3] but due to difficulties in transport from Japan, a Roomba[4] was used instead) with

---

[2] http://research.microsoft.com/en-us/um/cambridge/projects/sensecam/
[3] http://www.mobilerobots.com/researchrobots/p3at.aspx
[4] http://store.irobot.com/family/index.jsp

two kinects[5]. The first Kinect is used to avoid obstacles when following the actor and the other to recognize their activities. After the Evaal experience CUJ decided to use only one Kinect.

5.3 CMU Team-Silver

Title of paper An Activity Recognition System for Ambient Assisted Living Environments

List of Authors and affiliations Jin-Hyuk Hong, Julian Ramos, Choonsung Shin, Anind Dey from Human-Computer Interaction Institute Carnegie Mellon University.

Brief description CMU Team proposes a solution composed by three subsystems: A chest wearable elastic strap[6] capable of measuring several physiological signals, an Android mobile phone and a system for indoor localization based on Radio tomographic imaging[7].

5.4 USS Team-Gold

Title of paper Activity recognition system using AMEVA method

List of Authors and affiliations Luis Miguel Soria[1], Luis Gonzalez-Abril[2], Miguel Ángel Álvarez de la Concepción[1],, Juan Antonio Ortega Ramírez[1]

1. Computer Languages and Systems Department, University of Seville.
2. Applied Economics I Department, University of Seville.

Brief description USS Team uses an android mobile phone placed on the right hip. The user activities are recognized by means of the accelerometer embedded in the mobile phone.

5.5 Results

Table 1 shows the results for each team and criteria for the best of both performances. The winner (USS team) obtained acceptable results in performance, but its simplicity (although it uses multiple mathematical methods it only rely on accelerometers) and interoperability give good marks in all the evaluated criteria. Gold and Silver teams used accelerometer-based solutions.

Table 1. Best performance result

Team	Accuracy	Delay	Installation	User Acceptance	Interoperability	Final Score
USS	4,33	9	10	7,47	7,63	7,3945
CMU	7,17	9	0	7,93	6,15	6,4975
CUJ	2,59	2	0	5,6	5,09	3,5235
DCU	0	0	10	5,2	1,25	2,9875

---

[5] http://en.wikipedia.org/wiki/Kinect

[6] http://www.zephyr-technology.com/bioharness-bt

[7] http://span.ece.utah.edu/radio-tomographic-imaging

6   Conclusions

Next edition some improvements may regard the kind of activities (some more complex activities can be taken into account) and the possibility to simulate an aged actor using specifics kits to avoid rapid movements. Results suggest that there is still space for other editions of this competition in the future, and encourage us to continue in this track for the next year.

References

1. Brush, A.B., Krumm, J., Scott, J., Saponas, S.: Recognizing activities from mobile sensor data: Challenges and opportunities. In: Ubicomp 2011 (2011)
2. United Nations Population Fund and HelpAge International, ed.: Ageing in the Twenty-First Century: A Celebration and A Challenge. United Nations Population Fund (December 2012)
3. Wolf, C., Mille, J., Lombardi, L., Celiktutan, O., Jiu, M., Baccouche, M., Dellandrea, E., Bichot, C.E., Garcia, C., Sankur, B.: The liris human activities dataset and the icpr 2012 human activities recognition and localization competition. Technical Report RR-LIRIS-2012-004, LIRIS Laboratory (March 2012)
4. Sagha, H., Digumarti, S.T., del R. Millán, J., Chavarriaga, R., Calatroni, A., Roggen, D., Tröster, G.: Benchmarking classification techniques using the opportunity human activity dataset. In: 2011 IEEE International Conference on, Systems, Man, and Cybernetics (SMC), pp. 36–40 (2011)
5. Kawaguchi, N., Ogawa, N., Iwasaki, Y., Kaji, K., Terada, T., Murao, K., Inoue, S., Kawahara, Y., Sumi, Y., Nishio, N.: Hasc challenge: Gathering large scale human activity corpus for the real-world activity understandings. In: ACM AH 2011 (2011)
6. Vitali, L., Roozbeh, J.: Power aware wireless data collection for bsn data repositories. In: International Conference on Body Sensor Networks (2011)
7. Martínez, A., Llorente, M.A., Lázaro, J.P.: Ciami living lab: an economically sustainable technological tool for open innovation. In: I ENoLL Living Lab Summer School (2010)
8. Noury, N., Fleury, A., Rumeau, P., Bourke, A.K., ÓLaighin, G., Rialle, V., Lundy, J.: Fall detection - principles and methods. In: Proceedings of the 29th Annual International Conference of the IEEE Engineering in Medicine and Biology Society (EMBS 2007), pp. 1663–1666 (2007)

Activity Recognition System Using AMEVA Method

Luis M. Soria Morillo[1], Luis González-Abril[2],
Miguel A. Álvarez de la Concepción[1], and Juan A. Ortega Ramírez[1]

[1] Computer Languages and Systems Dept., University of Seville, 41012 Seville, Spain
{lsoria,malvarez,jortega}@us.es
[2] Applied Economics I Dept., University of Seville, 41018 Seville, Spain
luisgon@us.es

Abstract. This article aims to develop a minimally intrusive system of care and monitoring. Furthermore, the goal is to get a cheap, comfortable and, especially, efficient system which controls the physical activity carried out by the user. For this purpose an innovative approach to physical activity recognition is presented, based on the use of discrete variables which employ data from accelerometer sensors. To this end, an innovative discretization and classification technique to make the recognition process in an efficient way and at low energy cost, is presented in this work based on the χ^2 distribution. Entire process is executed on the smartphone, by means of taking the system energy consumption into account, thereby increasing the battery lifetime and minimizing the device recharging frequency.

1 Introduction

Just 30 minutes of moderate activity five days a week, can improve your health according to the Centers for Disease Control and Prevention. By enabling activity monitoring on an individual scale, over an extended period of time in a ubiquitous way, physical and psychological health and fitness can be improved. Studies performed by certain health institutes initiative [7,3,10,6] have shown significant associations between physical activity and reduced risk of incident coronary heart disease and coronary events. Their results can be seen in Figure 1, where the inverse correlation between the risk of cardiovascular incidents and physical activity level is shown through the comparison of four separate studies.

In recent years, thanks largely to the increased interest in monitoring certain sectors of the population such those of as elderly people with dementia and of people in rehabilitation, activity recognition systems have increased in both number and quality. Furthermore, communication between relatives, friends and professionals can be improved by means of graphs of weekly activity (high relevant for sportsmen and for the relatives of elderly people) whereby the doctor can be automatically alerted if any strange activity is detected. By using data acquired from accelerometer, *NFC*, or even microphone sensors and applying

S. Chessa and S. Knauth (Eds.): EvAAL 2012, CCIS 362, pp. 137–147, 2013.

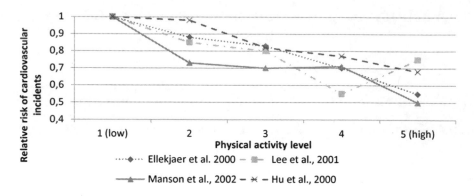

Fig. 1. Associations between physical activity and reduced risk of incident coronary heart disease and coronary events

some classification algorithm, it is possible to recognize human activities. Artificial neural networks (ANN) method will be analyzed and compared with our work. Results show the main differences between different studies, and certain drawbacks are determined which rules them out for development on users' smartphones To reduce the cost related to process accelerometer signals, this paper opts for an innovative technique, through which the work is performed in the field of discrete variables. Thanks to a discretization process, the classification cost is much lower than that obtained when working with continuous variables. Any dependence between variables during the recognition process is therefore eliminated and, on the other hand, energy consumption from the process itself is minimized.

2 Activity Recognition

2.1 Data Collection

Certain related studies attain results on activity recognition off-line. A comprehensive training set from the accelerometer output is first needed before data can be classified into any of the recognized activities. However, this paper has sought to minimize the waiting time for recognition, thereby providing valid information of the activity very frequently. To this end, both training and recognition sets are obtained using time windows [8] of fixed duration. After having conducted a performance and system accuracy analysis, it is determined that the optimum length for these windows is 5 seconds. Five seconds windows was chosen due to for our system it's extremely important to ensure that in each time window there is, at least, one activity cycle. Where activity cycle is define as an complete execution of some activity pattern. For instance, two steps are an activity cycle for walking and one pedal stroke is the activity cycle for cycling. If at least one activity cycle can not be ensure in each time window, it's not possible to determine, basing on accelerometer patterns, the activity performed. This statement could be seen in the next example. Suppose a two second cycle is having and the actor is jumping continuously, that is, we have a cadence of one jump for each two seconds. The system is configured with one second time window and thus, for each activity cycle will have two windows. In the first one, while the user is rising, vertical acceleration is negative. In the other one, because the user is falling, vertical acceleration will positive. If user increase the cadence by two, mean between acceleration set is close to , due to vertical positive and negative accelerations will be counteracted. For this reason, it's very important to ensure that one cycle of all activities, regardless of the speed performed, is contained in a time window. Segmentation process and activity cycle is shown in Figure 2.

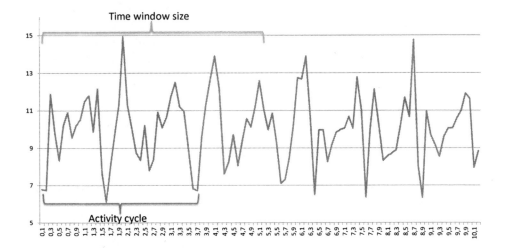

Fig. 2. Time windows split method over accelerometer signal

Based on these time windows, which contain data for each accelerometer axis, the signal module has been chosen in order to reduce the computational cost of the new solution. In addition to rendering the system more efficient, this choice of module eliminates the problem caused by device rotation [5,4]. Furthermore, user comfort with the system is decreased by removing the restriction that forces its orientation to be maintained during the process of learning and recognition. Using the accelerometer module, a data from each of the different readings taken within a time window $a_i = (a_{x,i}, a_{y,i}, a_{z,i})$ for the x, y, and z axes is defined as follows

$$|a_i| = \sqrt{(a_{x,i})^2, (a_{y,i})^2, (a_{z,i})^2} \tag{1}$$

For each temporal window is obtained Arithmetic Mean, Minimum, Maximum, Median, Std deviation, Geometric mean and other measures. In addition to the above variables, hereafter called temporal variables, a new set of statistics from the frequency domain of the problem is generated. This second set of variables will be called frecuencial variables. In order to obtain the frequency characteristics, the Fast Fourier Transform (FFT) for each time window is applied. In this way, and based on the frequency components obtained.

2.2 Set of Activities

Far from being a static system, the number and type of activities recognized by the system depends on the user [9]. However, to carry out a comparative analysis of the accuracy and performance of the discrete recognition method proposed below, 8 activities were taken into account. These activities are immobile, walking, running, jumping, cycling, drive, walking-upstairs and walking-downstairs. The learning system allows the user to decide what activities he/she wants the system to recognize. This is highly useful when the determination of certain very specific activities on monitored users is required. Examples of this situation include patients in rehabilitation who are monitored during their period of learning the various physical tasks prescribed by their doctors.

3 Qualitative Method

3.1 Ameva Algorithm

Let $X = \{x_1, x_2, \ldots, x_N\}$ be a data set of a continuous attribute $\mathcal{X}$ of mixed-mode data such that each example x_i belongs to only one of ℓ classes of the variable denoted by

$$C = \{C_1, C_2, \ldots, C_\ell\}, \quad \ell \geq 2$$

A continuous attribute discretization is a function $\mathcal{D} : \mathcal{X} \to C$ which assigns a class $C_i \in C$ to each value $x \in \mathcal{X}$ in the domain of the property that is being discretized.

Let us consider a discretization $\mathcal{D}$ which discretizes the continuous domain of $\mathcal{X}$ into k discrete intervals:

$$\mathcal{L}(k; \mathcal{X}; C) = \{[d_0, d_1], (d_1, d_2], \cdots, (d_{k-1}, d_k]\}$$

In this discretization, d_0 is the minimum value and d_k is the maximum value of the attribute $\mathcal{X}$, and the d_i values are in ascendent order.

If L_1 is the interval $[d_0, d_1]$ and L_j is the interval $(d_{j-1}, d_j]$, $j = 2, 3, \ldots, k$, then

$$\mathcal{L}(k; \mathcal{X}; C) = \{L_1, L_2, \cdots, L_k\}$$

Therefore, the aim of the Ameva method [1] is to maximize the dependency relationship between the class labels C and the continuous-values attribute $\mathcal{L}(k)$, and at the same time to minimize the number of discrete intervals k.

As a result from applying the above algorithm to each statistical value of the system, a series of intervals associated with a particular C tag is obtained. Thus, after processing all system statistics, a three-dimensional matrix is obtained. In the first two dimensions, the label of the activity C associated with the interval

$L_i = (L_i^l, L_i^s]$, as well as with the lower limit L_i^l and the upper limit L_i^s of that range is stored. In a third dimension, the matrix contains the above data for each statistic $\mathcal{S} = \{S_1, S_2, ..., S_\mathbb{S}\}, \mathbb{S} \geq 2$. This three-dimensional matrix containing the set of interval limits for each statistic is called the *Discretization Matrix* and is denoted by $Dm\{\mathcal{C}, L^{l,s}, \mathcal{S}\}$. The *Discretization Matrix* therefore determines the interval to which each item of data belongs with respect to each statistical value, by means of carrying out a simple and fast discretization process.

Class Integration. The next step of the algorithm determines the probability associated with the statistical data for each of the activities based on previously generated intervals. To this end, each element of the training set $x = \{\mathcal{X}; \mathcal{C}\}$ is processed, to which, in addition to the value of each statistic whose calculation is based on the time window, is also associated the label of the specific activity in the training set. In order to carry out this process, *Class-Matrix* is denoted by $Cm\{x, L_i, \mathcal{S}\}$ and is defined as a three-dimensional matrix that contains the number of data x from the training set associated with each L_i interval for each statistical $\mathcal{S}$ of the system. This matrix is defined as follows,

$$Cm_{x,i,s} = |x \in \mathcal{X}|x \geq L_i^l \wedge x < L_i^s \wedge x\{\mathcal{C}\} = C_s \qquad (2)$$

Therefore, by this definition, each position in the *Class-Matrix* is uniquely associated with a position in the *Discretization-Matrix*, as determined by its range.

At this point not only is it possible to determine the discretization interval likelihood, but the *Class-Matrix* also helps to obtain the probability associated with the discretization process performed with the *Ameva* algorithm.

Activity-Interval Matrix. The next step in the learning process is to obtain the matrix of relative probabilities. This three-dimensional matrix, called the *Activity-Interval Matrix* and denoted by $AIm\{x, L_i, \mathcal{S}\}$, determines the likelihood that a given value x associated to an $\mathcal{S}$ statistic corresponds to a specific C_i activity. This ratio is based on the quality of the discretization performed by *Ameva*, and in order to determine the most probable activity from the generated data and the intervals of the training set. First the contents of the array AIm is defined as follows,

$$AIm_{c,i,s} = \frac{Cm_{c,i,s}}{total_{c,s}} \cdot \frac{1}{\ell - 1} \sum_{j=1, j \neq c}^{\ell} (1 - \frac{Cm_{j,i,s}}{total_{j,s}}) \qquad (3)$$

where $total_{c,s}$ is the total number of time windows of the training process labeled with the c activity for the $\int$ statistic.

Figure 3 shows the overall process described on this section for carry on data analysis and interval determination.

3.2   Classification Process

Having obtained the discretization intervals and the probabilities of belonging to each interval, the process by which the classification is performed can be

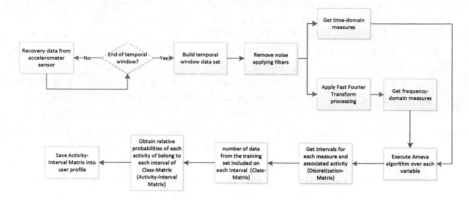

Fig. 3. Overall process of data analysis and interval determination

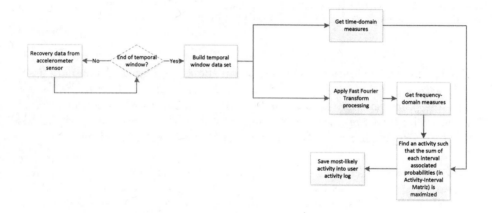

Fig. 4. Overall recognition process from data sensors

described. This classification is based on data from the analysis of time windows. The process is divided into two main steps: the way in which to perform the recognition of physical activity is first described; and the process to determine the frequency at which some particular activity is then presented.

Classifying Data. For the classification process, the most probable activity is decided by a majority voting system. This process starts from the *Activity-Interval Matrix* and uses a set of data $x \in \mathcal{X}$ for each of the statistics belonging to the $\mathcal{S}$ set. The process consists of finding an activity $mpa \in \mathcal{C}$ such that the likelihood is maximized. The above criterion is included in the following expression,

$$mpa(\mathcal{X}) = \max \sum_{s=1}^{s} AIm_{c,i,s}|x_s \in (L_i^l, L_i^s] \qquad (4)$$

The expression shows that the weight contributed by each statistic to the calculation of the probability is identical. This can be carried out under the assumption that all statistics provide the same information to the system, and that there is no correlation between them. Thus, the most probable activity, or *mpa*, represents those activities whose data, obtained through the processing time window, is more suited to the *AIm* set values. In this way, the proposed algorithm not only determine the *mpa*, but also its associated probability. From this likelihood, certain activities that do not adapt well to sets of generic classification can be identified. This could be an indication that the user is carrying out new activities for which the system has not been previously trained.

Figure 4 shows the overall process described on this section for recognition process from Activity-Interval Matrix calculated in the previous stage.

4   Method Analysis

Now that the basis of the activity recognition algorithm has been laid out, an analysis of the new proposal can be performed. To this end, the new development is compared with a widely used recognition system based on neural networks [2]. In this case, both learning and recognition is performed by continuous methods. The test process is conducted on *Google Nexus S, Samsung Galaxy S2, and Google Nexus One* devices for a group of 40 users. Notably, the activity habits of these users are radically different, since 10 of them are under 25 years old, 20 users are between 25 and 40 years old, and the rest are over 40. An approximate distribution of the data for each subject regarding the eight activities in the study are: immobile (2800 min, 70 min per user), walking (2600 min, 65 min per user), running (2400 min, 60 min per user), jumping (2400 min, 60 min per user), cycling (2200 min, 55 min per user), driving (2200 min, 55 min per user), walking-upstairs (2400 min, 60 min per user), and walking-downstairs (2000 min, 50 min per user). Annotations are performed using a mobile application installed on the device itself with speech recognition software through which users dictate the name of the new activity when the physical activity being performance changes. Those unrecognizable activities conducted during the test process are dismissed to analyze the system accuracy. Data collection is obtained during four weeks.

Moreover, it is crucial to consider energy consumption and the processing cost of the system when it is working on a mobile device. In this case, after comparing the above methods, the conclusion reached is that the method based on *Ameva* reduces the computational cost of the system by about 50%, as can be seen in Figure 5. The time needed to process a time window by using the *Ameva*-based method is 0.6 seconds, while, for methods based on neural networks this figure is 1.2 seconds.

As can be seen in 6, Ameva battery consumption is lower than neural networks. For the first one, the battery lifetime is close to 25 hours while for the last one, it's only 16 hours. In the comparison can be observed the battery lifetime for decision tree but the main problem of this method, based on statistics chosen, is the low accuracy, not higher than 60%.

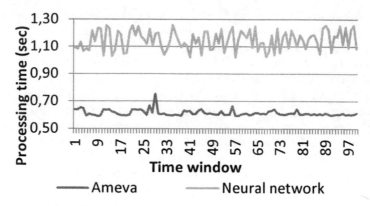

Fig. 5. Processing time of the Ameva and neural network methods on the device

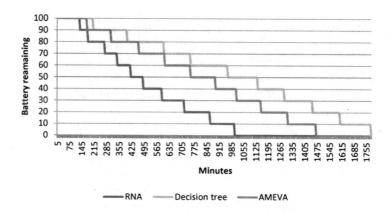

Fig. 6. Battery life for Ameva compared to neural network and decision tree methods

Based on Accuracy, Recall, Specificity, Precision, and F measure, Table 1 is presented. In this table, differences between the two methods, *RNA* and *Ameva* can be observed. Most values presented for each measure and activity show that the *Ameva* method performs better than *RNA*, especially as regards precision. That is to say, the number of false positive in the *Ameva* method is lower than that using the *RNA* method. *Immobile* and *Drive* are controversial activities due to their similar characteristics. Even under observation, it is difficult to differentiate between these two activities. For this reason and due to temporal nature of the *Immobile* activity, results from these two activities present a high level of disturbance in contrast to other activities.

Table 1. Performance comparison by using measures of evaluation

Activity	Accuracy		Recall		Specificity		Precision		F-measure (F_1)	
	Ameva	RNA	Ameva	RNA	Ameva	RNA	Ameva	RNA	Ameva	RNA
Walk	98.77%	97.93%	97.92%	93.95%	98.91%	98.57%	93.50%	91.36%	95.66%	92.64%
Jump	99.35%	98.87%	97.03%	96.44%	99.70%	99.25%	98.00%	95.12%	97.51%	95.77%
Immobile	98.69%	99.50%	94.57%	97.37%	99.42%	99.88%	96.60%	99.29%	95.58%	98.32%
Run	99.27%	98.35%	97.61%	92.62%	99.49%	99.14%	96.36%	93.64%	96.98%	93.13%
Up	98.93%	98.17%	95.40%	90.79%	99.43%	99.22%	96.00%	94.35%	95.70%	92.54%
Down	98.64%	98.25%	95.20%	92.68%	99.04%	98.89%	91.95%	90.62%	93.55%	91.64%
Cycle	99.32%	99.03%	96.13%	95.67%	99.73%	99.47%	97.91%	95.89%	97.01%	95.78%
Drive	98.14%	98.74%	90.02%	95.01%	99.20%	99.23%	93.63%	94.16%	91.79%	94.58%

5   Conclusions and Future Work

In this work, a highly successful recognition system based on discrete variables is presented, which uses the *Ameva* discretization algorithm and a new *Ameva*-based classification system. It has therefore been possible to achieve an average accuracy of 98% for the recognition of 8 types of activities. Furthermore, working with discrete variables has significantly reduced the computational cost associated to data processing during the recognition process. By using this process to increase recognition frequency, it has been possible to obtain a physical activity reading every 5 seconds and to enter these readings into the user activity log. However, the main problem of this system based on statistical learning is the limit to the number of activities that can be recognized. Working only with accelerometer sensors implies a limit to the number of system variables and therefore may lead to a strong correlation between these variables.

6   AMEVA Running in EvAAL Competition

During the competition, two test sessions were executed. In the first one, the training was performed prior to competition by an external actor not related to evaluation process. The training actor was 31 years old and the entire training process was performed with the smartphone in the hip, attached to the user's belt. In the competition, the actor was in a similar age range and thus, the way in that physical activity was executed was very similar. In other case, the system should be retrained for a better accuracy. Once finished the first evaluation session, intermediate data was analyzed. From this analysis, it was concluded that some activities was not well-recognized such as bending or cycling. This was a substantial impact in the accuracy due to cycling session was long. The accuracy for the other activities was promising but we detect that something was wrong for cycling detection. By using discrete techniques to perform the activity recognition, cycling is a easy activity to be detected because of the acceleration patterns presents an evident component in the advancing direction. Unfortunately, cycling activity was carried out on a stationary bike and thus, accelerations presented in movement direction was not detected. For the other controversial activity, bending, the system was not training to detect it because it was a important conflict with sitting activity. Both activities have a very similar acceleration profile and it can not be determine which is the right activity with a proper accurate. In the second test process, the system was retrained in order to achieve a most accurate recognition. Unfortunately, the Internet connection was not good enough to connect with training server placed at the University of Seville. For this reason, dataset from time windows was not properly sent to the server and therefore, the training parameters were wrong. After checking this problem, we decided to go on with the evaluation process to determine the impact of this problem in the accuracy. As it was thought, the second evaluation had a very low accuracy due to that problems. Furthermore, by studying intermediate data after the evaluation, temporal windows was misconfigured and it was set to 3 seconds and thus, some "fast activities" such as walking or cycling wasn't well recognized. Finally, EvAAL competition was a great chance to make a real stress test of AMEVA system since It's not usual in humans to make a long activities set in so quickly and so fast. In this regard, statistical-discrete classification for activity recognition based on AMEVA algorithm was designed to medium-long time activities. Transitions in discrete classification systems are really difficult to detect and, in AMEVA case, was not implemented any change activity detector. In conclusion, EvAAL offered a junction to test many systems and generate new ideas for competitors' systems. On the other hand, is very good to know other techniques in activity recognition and new perspectives about this field.

Acknowledgments. This research is partially supported by the projects of the Spanish Ministry of Economy and Competitiveness ARTEMISA (TIN2009-14378-C02-01) and Simon (TIC-8052) of the Andalusian Regional Ministry of Economy.

References

1. González Abril, L., Cuberos, F.J., Velasco, F., Ortega, J.A.: Ameva: An autonomous discretization algorithm. Expert Syst. Appl. 36(3), 5327–5332 (2009)
2. Altun, K., Barshan, B., Tunçel, O.: Comparative study on classifying human activities with miniature inertial and magnetic sensors. Pattern Recogn. 43(10), 3605–3620 (2010)
3. Ellekjaer, Holmen, Vatten: Physical activity and stroke mortality in women. Stroke 31(1), 14–18 (2000)
4. He, Z., Jin, L.: Activity recognition from acceleration data based on discrete consine transform and SVM. In: 2009 IEEE International Conference on Systems, Man and Cybernetics, pp. 5041–5044. IEEE (October 2009)
5. Khan, A.M., Lee, Y.-K., Lee, S., Kim, T.-S.: Accelerometer's position independent physical activity recognition system for long-term activity monitoring in the elderly. Medical & Biological Engineering & Computing 48(12), 1271–1279 (2010)
6. Lee, I.-M., Rexrode, K.M., Cook, N.R.: Physical activity and coronary heart disease in women. JAMA 285(11), 1447–1454 (2001)

7. Manson, J.E., Greenland, P., LaCroix, A.Z., Stefanick, M.L., Mouton, C.P., Ober-
man, A., Perri, M.G., Sheps, D.S., Pettinger, M.B., Siscovick, D.S.: Walking compared with vigorous exercise for the prevention of cardiovascular events in women.
The New England Journal of Medicine 347(10), 716–725 (2002)
8. Paiyarom, S., Tungamchit, P., Keinprasit, R., Kayasith, P.: Activity monitoring
system using Dynamic Time Warping for the elderly and disabled people, pp. 1–4.
IEEE (2009)
9. Ravi, N., Nikhil, D., Mysore, P., Littman, M.L.: Activity recognition from accelerometer data. In: Proceedings of the Seventeenth Conference on Innovative
Applications of Artificial Intelligence(IAAI), pp. 1541–1546 (2005)
10. Sattelmair, J.R., Kurth, T., Buring, J.E., Lee, I.-M.: Physical Activity and Risk of
Stroke in Women. Stroke 41(6), 1243–1250 (2010)

An Activity Recognition System
for Ambient Assisted Living Environments

Jin-Hyuk Hong, Julian Ramos, Choonsung Shin, and Anind K. Dey

Human-Computer Interaction Institute
Carnegie Mellon University
5000 Forbes Ave., Pittsburgh, PA 15213
{hjinh7,choonsung2}@gmail, {julian,anind}@cs.cmu.edu

Abstract. Ambient assisted living facilities provide assistance and care for the elderly, where it is useful to infer their daily activity for ensuring their safety and successful aging. In this work, we present an activity recognition system that classifies a set of common daily activities, where it is designed to be comfortable and non-intrusive, and is comprised of commercial, robust and well known devices. A hybrid model of Bayesian networks and support vector machines for activity recognition with calibration is proposed to provide a high recognition accuracy and fast adaptation for new users. On the data collected from 15 participants, we have compared our approach to other two ways of building activity recognition systems, and shown its superiority.

Keywords: activity recognition, ambient assisted living facility.

1   Introduction

Activity recognition for ambient assisted living facilities is necessary for supporting the well-being of occupants at short and long term, since there are many situations that could endanger or halt successful aging of the elderly, like falls. While this could become dangerous by itself, depending on the impact and the health state of the elder, it is worst when the person cannot stand up again by herself. Therefore, supervision or monitoring of an elderly person at risk for such problems is required to be able to recognize and provide assistance in such situations. Other less common daily activities could easily aggravate the health of the elder; for example, if an Alzheimer's patient simply forgets to take a pill [1], his condition could be exacerbated in the long term. These kinds of activities are much more subtle and harder to recognize by means of commonly used sensors like accelerometers. Another kind of situation that arises outside of the scope of commonly used sensor systems for activity recognition is exercising. While for most people, exercising seems standard and harmless, it is known in the medical sports community that increasing one's maximal heart rate by more than 75% increases the chance of a cardiovascular or pulmonary attack [2], and that this likelihood increases with age, particularly when other cardiovascular problems like high blood pressure are present.

S. Chessa and S. Knauth (Eds.): EvAAL 2012, CCIS 362, pp. 148–158, 2013.
© Springer-Verlag Berlin Heidelberg 2013

In this paper we present a system for real-time recognition of daily activities by using a wearable sensing platform including accelerometers worn by users. The activities that will be recognized in our system are comprised of: Walking, standing up, sitting down, lying down, bending, falling and bicycling (using a stationary bike). A hybrid model is used for precise activity recognition, and a calibration-based model construction approach is proposed for the easy setup of the system.

2 Activity Classification Problem

Activity classification is well known and it has been studied thoroughly in the area of ubiquitous and mobile computing. Many systems have been created by using accelerometers located at different parts of the body [3–5]. However, few of them use a combination of physiological signal sensors, accelerometers and localization devices (GPS, radio tomography). The setup with the three kinds of sensors can improve the classification of activities that have a higher physical demand, since physiological signals such as heart rate, temperature and respiration change according to the physical activity [6], still physiological sensors alone tell only part of the story. For example, an increase of heart rate does not necessarily imply engagement of the subject in physical activity. Instead, it could be pure emotion triggered by watching a movie [7]. In the other hand the user may be engaged in a demanding Yoga session where accelerometer's readings will not easily tell apart that there is a physical activity going on. To tackle this problem, a localization system using radio tomographic imaging (RTI) [8–10] has been included, this system can tell with an accuracy of +/- 20 cms the location of one person or more in its area of coverage. With this localization system, and a map of the living environment of the user, it will help the classifiers to discern the context of the sensor data captured by the Bioharness.

Furthermore, conventional recognition systems sometimes use an excessive number of features, but some of them are unnecessary or redundant [11] in the sense that they do not necessarily help in the classification task but instead lead to increased computation time, implying a slower system response, increased memory usage and a shorter battery life for a mobile device performing real-time analysis and sensing. In this work, we propose a system centered on overcoming all of these problems by evaluating features and selecting those relevant to the problem and to every activity. A hybrid model composed of Bayesian networks and support vector machines is exploited to model the relationship between sensory signals and activity. In modeling activity, we consider the issues of accuracy, responsiveness and comfort or wearability of the system by keeping at a minimum the quantity and complexity of data being processed.

3 Hardware/Sensing Platform

Our system is comprised of one popular physiological signals recording device, a novel system for indoor/outdoor localization and a laptop/smartphone for data logging and processing. The signals used are: electro cardiograph, breathing (chest expansion and compression), skin conductivity, skin temperature and relative localization coordinates(x,y). From these, different features are extracted (Table 1). In previous studies [6-7], these features have proven to help in the classification problem we are trying to solve.

Table 1. Features used in our activity recognition system

Signals	Features extracted	Sampling rate
Electrocardiogram	Heart rate, ECG amplitude, ECG noise, statistics (Std, mean, max, min)	250 Hz
Respiration	Breathing rate, breathing wave amplitude, statistics	18Hz
Temperature	Skin temperature, statistics	
Acceleration	XYZ acceleration minimums and peaks, posture, vector magnitude, peak acceleration, statistics	1Hz 100Hz
Coordinates	X, Y position in the living area	10Hz
Noise	Measurement of the reliability of the system generated coordinates	10Hz
Acceleration	XYZ acceleration statistics	20Hz

As shown in Fig. 1, our system consists of a Bioharness BT, a RTI system and a laptop/smartphone. The laptop/smartphone is used only to process the data from the sensing systems, extract features and perform activity classification. The Bioharness BT is a chest wearable elastic strap capable of measuring several physiological signals as well as physical quantities: heart rate, breathing rate, acceleration and skin temperature. Furthermore, it is also capable of wireless transmission of the logged data through Bluetooth. This device has been used before by our team to recognize stressful [12] situations and physical activities. It has outstanding electronic properties like long lasting battery life of up to 18 hours. The sensing frequency varies among the different physiological signals but provides at least a sample per second and at most 250 samples per second for the ECG.

Radio tomographic imaging [8–10], is a novel technique that measures the variation of the signal strength of a network of radio devices for localization purposes. RTI works by placing a network of small and inexpensive radios around an area of interest. Each radio communicates with the others in the network creating a dense net of links passing through the area. Objects moving within the area will either reflect or absorb the wireless signal creating a measurable disruption that is used to measure the location of the interfering object. A laptop/smartphone will be used as the main data processing device. On it, an application will be running at all times, logging the data sent by the Bioharness and the Radio tomographic imaging system. Data logging, visualization and classification will be performed on this main application. The laptop and the smartphone will be running on Windows and Android OS, respectively.

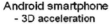

Bioharness BT
 - physiological responses: HR. BR. Temperature. etc.
 - 3D acceleration: 20 samples in every 400ms

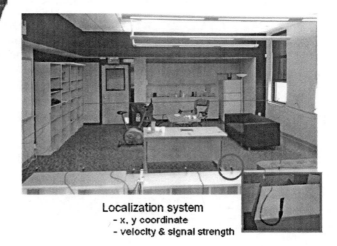

Android smartphone
 - 3D acceleration

Localization system
 - x, y coordinate
 - velocity & signal strength

Fig. 1. Sensing platform

4   Activity Recognition System

As shown in Fig. 2, the system is composed of three phases including modeling, calibration, and online recognition. For practical use of the system, we propose a new approach to personalize the system instead of training an activity model for new users. In the modeling phase, we build a pool of activity models from a group of people. 3D acceleration data from the bioharness are collected through the android smartphone where videos are captured for the manual labeling of the data. An activity model composed of Bayesian networks and support vector machines is constructed through the process of preprocessing and model training. The preprocessing module filters out noise, segments the data every half second, and extracts statistical features (minimum, maximum, average, median, standard deviation) from the 3D acceleration.

Instead of conventional approaches that construct a population model or train an individual model for a new user, we apply a most matching activity model in the pool of activity models already constructed from the other people. The new user is only required to perform each activity shortly for the calibration process by using a simple labeling interface on the Android smartphone. In the calibration phase, it calculates the recognition performance of activity models on this new data, and selects one with the highest accuracy. Finally, the system recognizes the user activity in 2 stages by integrating two additional modules of the localization system and the accelerometer of the Android. The hybrid model of Bayesian networks and support vector machines with the 3D acceleration of bioharness, which is selected from the calibration process, first carries out the activity recognition. This recognition result is refined by several rules that are designed with the localization system and the additional 3D acceleration of the Android across the population.

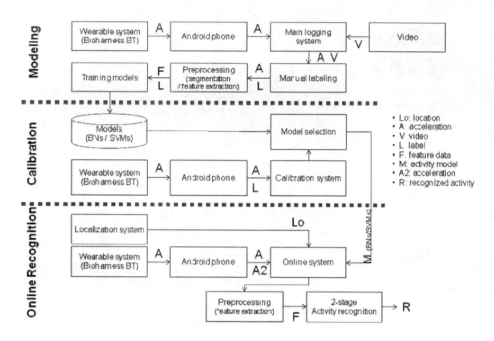

Fig. 2. Overview of the general system

4.1   Hybrid Model for Activity Recognition

As shown in Fig. 3, our hybrid model to provide a preliminary recognition result has a number of expert models, each of which is optimized to recognize the corresponding activity, and a control model that regulates those multiple expert models to output a final decision. For the given segments of extracted features, the control model estimates the probability of all activities and orders the expert models according to the probabilities. As its subsumption architecture [13], the expert models perform the classification of activities in order until an activity is recognized. This modular architecture leads to accurate modeling of each activity with an expert model, as well as effective management of those multiple expert models by the control model. Also, the proposed method has been verified its usefulness to address the ambiguity of integration of multiple models through several previous works on multiclass problems [14,15].

In constructing this hybrid model, we use Bayesian networks as the control model and support vector machines (polynomial kernel with degree = 3) for expert models to find the complex relationship between the features and activities, accompanied with a feature selection process since not all features are useful for recognizing each activity.

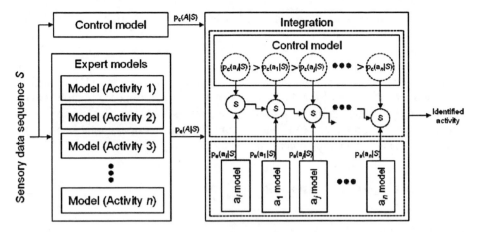

Fig. 3. Classification scheme

4.2   Additional Refining Process

After getting the preliminary recognition result from the hybrid model, we apply several rules based on the information from the Android smartphone and localization system. The rules are designed based on the general characteristics of activities and the additional sensory information as shown in Fig 4.

Localization information-based
   IF UserLocation isn't around BIKE, it is impossible to bicycle
   IF UserLocation is around CHAIR or COUCH, it is more probable to sit down
   IF UserLocation is around BED or COUCH, it is more probable to lie down
   IF UserVelocity < $\theta1$, it is less probable to walk

Android smartphone acceleration-based
   IF avg(ZX) > $\theta2$, it is less probable to stand up or walk
   IF avg(ZX) < $\theta2$, it is less probable to sit down or lie down
   IF std(XYZ) > $\theta3$, it is more probable to walk or bicycle

For two different types of bending activities
   IF Type 1 bend: avg(ZX) < $\theta2$ &
      IF 1st stage result∈{bend, lie_down},
      THEN it could be bending
   IF Type 2 bend: avg(ZX) > $\theta2$ &
      IF 1st stage result∈{stand, sit_down},
      THEN it could be bending

Fig. 4. Refining rules

The localization system provides the user's indoor location and its related contextual information on the indoor environment. Some specific activities are limited for the user to perform, e.g., bicycling is only available around the stationary bike and lying down has more chances when the user is on the bed or couch. The walking activity surely has certain speed due to the user's movement. The additional acceleration information of the Android in the user's pocket may help an ambiguity between some activities such as standing up and sitting down, which are often hard to differentiate based on the chest movement only. The recognition can be improved by considering the lower and upper body movement together.

5   Experiment and Analysis

5.1   Data Collection

For the validation of our system, we have collected the data in a furniture room by using our sensing platform, especially with the Bioharness. Data collection has been carried out in a large room with various furniture including a desk, different types of chairs, a couch, bookshelves, a bed, a table, a stationary bike, a sink and a refrigerator, where there are also various objects such as books, golf and tennis balls to provide a more realistic data collection environment. A camera was installed in the room to capture the video of participants' performing activities to get the ground truth through post labeling.

During data collection, participants were asked to wear the Bioharness and perform a set of tasks for about an hour. For more realistic movements, any explicit instruction or restriction was not given to the participants so that they could freely complete the tasks. 30 different tasks given to the participants include common daily activities such as walking around the room, sitting on the chairs and reading a book, lying down on the couch and taking a rest, rearranging books in the bookshelves, picking up golf or tennis balls, bicycling on the stationary bike, falling down onto the bed, having a small meal in the couch and washing hands. Especially for a falling task, a short demonstration was given by the experimenter and the participants were asked to fall down onto the bed for safety. These tasks were specially intended as a way to make the participants execute them in a naturalistic way in which they were not restricted by time or form constraints, neither they were aware of the tasks we intended to gather. After collecting the sensory data, we analyzed the video captured during the data collection and obtained the ground truth data in terms of 7 activities including standing up, sitting down, lying down, walking, bending, bicycling, and falling.

Fifteen people were recruited for the data collection, where total 112,592 samples were collected. As shown in Fig. 5, three common activities including standing, walking and sitting account for more than 20 percent, but some activities like bending and falling account for very little since they are very short activities.

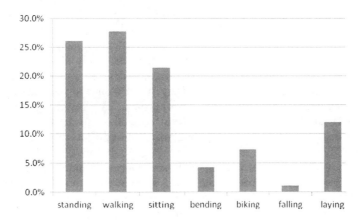

Fig. 5. Activity class distribution

5.2   Experimental Result

In 2-fold cross validation, we have compared our system with two other approaches of building activity models: population and individual. On each run for a participant, the population model was trained with the data from other people (14 participants in this study) and one fold data for training from the participant, where the individual model was built with his/her one fold data for training only. Our calibration-based approach first constructed 14 individual models from 14 other people, measured the prediction accuracy of these models on the one fold data for training of the participant, and then selected a model obtaining a highest accuracy.

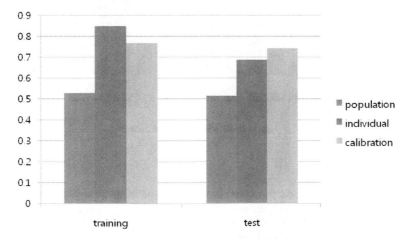

Fig. 6. Recognition accuracy

Fig. 6 shows the recognition accuracy of the three approaches for 15 participants. Due to individual variation, population models failed to achieve high accuracy not only for the test data but also for the training data. Individual models could fit to the training data by achieving an accuracy of 85% where they only obtained an accuracy of 69% on the test data because of the lack of training data. However, our calibration-based approach could get the highest accuracy of 74% on the test data among the three approaches without any additional training data. This result signifies that our approach can be applied to new users without collecting much training data from themselves to build new activity models but only relying on a small amount of data for calibration.

Fig. 7 shows a comparison of three approaches in terms of individual performance. For most participants, our approach could find a good activity model from the pool of activity models learned from other people, but sometimes it was worse than individual models since it failed to find a suitable one out of 14 other activity models. In order to get a better performance with our approach, it is required to train various models from a larger population. On this matter, we need a further investigation on each individual to understand the variation of activities across the population.

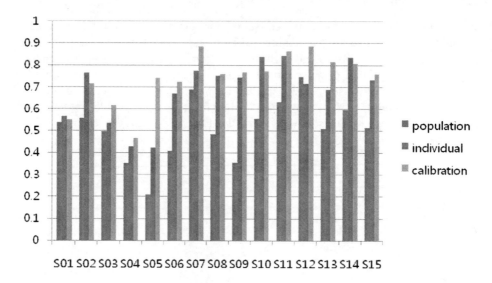

Fig. 7. Individual performance

5.3   Discussion

In our experimental result, we presented the comparison of three approaches in terms of model construction where our calibration-based approach was the best in accuracy. As shown in Table 2, however, some activities were hard to classify due to their similarity in terms of chest movement, such as standing vs. walking (8.7% errors in total), and standing vs. sitting (3.4% errors in total). Especially, many activities were confused by walking (8.9% errors in total), and bending was also misclassified by other activities many times (45.8% errors in bending). Many of the errors were occurred due to the limitation of one modality of chest movement, which could be addressed by applying the refining modules based on two types of information from the localization system and Android smartphone (see the section 4.2). For example, standing and sitting could be discriminated from each other by considering the 3D acceleration information of the smartphone. The walking activity should show a speed by the localization system, otherwise a user activity could be hard to be regarded as walking.

Table 2. Confusion matrix (st: standing, wa: walking, si: sitting, be: bending, bi: bicycling, fa: falling, ly: lying).

		Predicted						
		st	wa	si	be	bi	fa	ly
Targeted	st	73.7%	18.1%	2.9%	2.8%	1.1%	1.0%	0.4%
	wa	14.4%	77.2%	2.9%	1.5%	0.8%	1.5%	1.7%
	si	12.2%	8.8%	70.1%	1.2%	1.6%	0.7%	5.3%
	be	9.0%	18.3%	2.6%	54.2%	6.1%	5.2%	4.7%
	bi	7.7%	12.6%	1.0%	6.7%	69.6%	1.9%	0.5%
	fa	4.1%	23.1%	3.6%	6.5%	3.5%	51.4%	8.0%
	ly	1.1%	3.1%	0.6%	1.2%	1.3%	1.3%	91.5%

Our activity recognition system has been submitted to the EVAAL competition 2012 (http://evaal.aaloa.org/), and it produced an accuracy of 72% for a unknown actor who performed 7 activities in the The CIAmI Living Lab (http://www.ciami.es/valencia/), which is the highest accuracy obtained among the participating teams. On the competition, our system was only performed with the Bioharness and Android smartphone, and the localization system was excluded from the evaluation because of its malfunction by some wireless interference from the environment.

6   Conclusion

In recent, ambient assisted living facilities provide assistance and care for the elderly, where activity recognition is one of key components of the facilities. In order to address several challenging issues in activity recognition, in this paper, we presented an activity recognition system working with multiple sensors to correctly recognize 7 types of activities, where we obtained an accuracy of 74% with the hybrid model of our activity recognition system. For the easy setup of the system for new users, we proposed a calibration approach that only requires a small amount of calibration data. Besides the bioharness, we also included a localization system and an Android smartphone as other modality to address the limitation of modeling activities based on chest movement. Through an experiment and the participation of the EVAAL competition, we have shown the superiority of the proposed activity recognition system.

Acknowledgement. This material is based upon work supported by the National Science Foundation under Grant Numbers: CNS-0910878 and CNS-1035152, funded under the American Recovery and Reinstatement Act of 2009 (Public Law 111-5).

References

[1] Matthew, L., Dey, A.K.: Reflecting on pills and phone use: supporting awareness of functional abilities for older adults. In: Proc. of the 2011 Annual Conf. on Human Factors in Computing Systems, pp. 2095–2104 (2011)

[2] ACSM 2009 Guidelines for exercise testing and prescription

[3] Bao, L., Intille, S.S.: Activity Recognition from User-Annotated Acceleration Data. In: Ferscha, A., Mattern, F. (eds.) PERVASIVE 2004. LNCS, vol. 3001, pp. 1–17. Springer, Heidelberg (2004)

[4] Maurer, U., Smailagic, A., Siewiorek, D.P., Deisher, M.: Activity recognition and monitoring using multiple sensors on different body positions. In: Int. Workshop on Wearable and Implantable Body Sensor Networks, pp. 113–116 (2006)

[5] Ravi, N., Dandekar, N., Mysore, P.: Activity recognition from accelerometer data. In: Proc. of the National, pp. 1541–1546 (2005)

[6] Li, M., Rozgic, V., Thatte, G., Lee, S.: Multimodal physical activity recognition by fusing temporal and cepstral information. IEEE Transaction on Neural Systems and Rehabilitation Engineering 18(4), 369–380 (2010)

[7] Lisetti, C.L.: Using Noninvasive wearable computers to recognize human emotions from physiological signals. EURASIP Journal on Applied Signal Processing, 1672–1687 (2004)

[8] Wilson, J., Patwari, N.: Radio tomographic imaging with wireless networks. IEEE Transactions on Mobile Computing 9(5), 621–632 (2010)

[9] Zhao, Y., Patwari, N.: Noise reduction for variance-based device-free localization and tracking. In: 2011 8th Annual IEEE Communications Society Conference on Sensor, Mesh and Ad Hoc Communications and Networks, pp. 179–187 (2011)

[10] Wilson, J., Patwari, N.: See-through walls: motion tracking using variance-based radio tomography networks. IEEE Transactions on Mobile Computing 10(5), 612–621 (2011)

[11] Guyon, I.: An Introduction to Variable and Feature Selection. Journal of Machine Learning Research 3, 1157–1182 (2003)

[12] Hong, J.-H., Ramos, J., Dey, A.: Understanding physiological responses to stressors during physical activity. In: Proc. of the 14th Int. Conf. on Ubiquitous Computing (2012)

[13] Brooks, R.: A robust layered control system for a mobile robot. IEEE Journal of Robotics and Automation I, 14–23 (1986)

[14] Hong, J.-H., Min, J.-K., Cho, U.-K., Cho, S.-B.: Fingerprint classification using one-vs-all support vector machines dynamically ordered with naive Bayes classifiers. Pattern Recognition 41(2), 662–671 (2008)

[15] Hong, J.-H., Cho, S.-B.: A probabilistic multi-class strategy of one-versus-rest support vector machines for cancer classification. Neurocomputing 71(16-18), 3275–3281 (2008)

Human Behavior Recognition
by a Mobile Robot Following Human Subjects

Myagmarbayar Nergui[1], Nevrez Imamoglu[1], Yuki Yoshida[1], Jose Gonzalez[2],
Masashi Sekine[2], Kazuya Kawamura[1], and Wenwei Yu[1]

[1] Medical System Engineering Department, Graduate School of Engineering, Chiba
University, 1-33 Yayoi-cho, Inage-ku, Chiba 263-8522 Japan
[2] Research Center for Frontier Medical Engineering, Chiba University,
1-33 Yayoi-cho, Inage-ku, Chiba 263-8522 Japan
myagaa@graduate.chiba-u.jp

Abstract. Our research is focused on the home healthcare support system for
motor function impaired persons (MIPs) whose motor function should be
closely monitored during either in-hospital or at-home training therapy process.
Especially, for the at-home monitoring, the demand of which is increasing, not
only close observation, but also accurate behavior recognition of daily living
activity, as well as motor function evaluation, are necessary. In this study, such
a system was established by developing a cost-effective, safe and easy to use
mobile robot. With such a robotic monitoring system, the in-hospital time for
most MIPs and the burden to therapists can be significantly decreased. In order
to realize the robotic monitoring system, we proposed several algorithms to
solve the difficulties arising from the mobile sensing for moving MIPs, and
recognize several frequent daily living activities, including impaired walking.
Concretely, algorithms to use both color images and depth images was
proposed to improve the accuracy of MIPs measurement, and a Hidden Markov
Model (HMM) was implemented to deal with the uncertainty on time sequence
data and relate the state transitions over time for daily living activity
recognition. Experiments have demonstrated promising results on joint
trajectory measurement, and recognition of daily living activities.

Keywords: Mobile robot, home healthcare, human behavior recognition.

1   Introduction

Recently, the number of people with motor function impairments has been increasing,
due to high incidence of stroke, other diseases and increasing elderly population.
Demographic survey shows that Japanese population with aged over 65 is expected to
double between 2000 and 2050 [1]. Also, there has been a shortage of healthcare
professionals due to declining young populations, and placing demand on home
health care services. So, due to the increasing demand on home health care,
researches on home healthcare systems also have been attracting more and more
attention than before. The reasons to the emergence of home healthcare services are to

S. Chessa and S. Knauth (Eds.): EvAAL 2012, CCIS 362, pp. 159–172, 2013.

improve medical treatment and prevent lifestyle diseases. In addition, home healthcare aims to reduce hospital admissions and make it possible for people to remain at home rather than use residential, long-term, or institutional-based nursing care.

Our research basically focuses on at-home bio-monitoring for motor function impaired persons (MIPs) that should provide a home healthcare support both for patients and professional therapists. To be able to achieve this support, MIPs need to be monitored during their training and daily living activities. Monitoring MIPs is to tend for basically observing their gait motions and recognizing their behavior or activity. Human gait motion measurements based on human joints are usually obtained by using motion capture systems and wearable sensors [2]. However, motion capture systems are costly and only effective in limited areas, thus not suitable for at-home monitoring. Wearable sensors are not convenient for patients due to the fact that they can restrict the patient's movement. And also, wearable sensors are easy to broken, when patients fall down. Except the smart house or wearable sensors, one other solution for monitoring MIPs can be a mobile robot, which can closely monitor MIP, observe their motion, and recognize their behavior.

In this study, we propose a new system for monitoring MIPs using a mobile robot. This system can observe and measure MIPs' motion, recognize their daily activities. In order to achieve this goal, we have divided our studies by following parts.

1)   To observe MIPs' motion, and measure joints trajectory of their lower limb joints
2)   To recognize their behavior from the measured trajectory data.

Our proposed system should be able to bring cost effective, safe, easier monitoring both at home and in hospital.

Current mobile robot based person tracking and following applications are using various sensors, such as vision and infrared cameras, LiDAR (laser range finder), audio sensors, and integration of them. But these systems are generally equipped with expensive products, or as far as to our knowledge, they don't consider MIPs tracking with their behavior analysis. In order to bring a cost effective system, a Kinect sensor, a product of Microsoft Corporation®, is used as a vision sensor of our robot system in this study. The Kinect sensor is becoming more popular nowadays in robotics applications due to its reasonable price and 2D depth data output along with the RGB camera support.

For observing and measuring MIPs' motion, we need to develop the human motion tracking and following algorithm from suitable viewpoints. In this study, tracking and following with gait recognition have been developed from three different viewpoints, such as front/ back, side and middle angle that is between front and side viewpoints.

For measuring joint trajectories, first, we have used the skeleton points extracted from the Kinect SDK, but, inaccurate skeleton points are observed when we utilized the Kinect SDK during measurement experiments. Then we have developed a new compensation algorithm to deal with the Kinect SDK's inaccuracy of skeleton points extraction. The compensation model is using color markers attached to several joint points for easy, fast and accurate feature extraction, in order to bring accurate joint trajectory system.

Regarding human behavior recognition, there have been many research works for image sequential features [7-10]. Basically, in contrary to this study, most of the behavior recognition systems are detecting foreground objects using static cameras. In this study, human behavior recognition has been achieved by a Hidden Markov Model (HMM) [6] which takes advantage of the lower limb joint angles and body angle as the feature space for recognition system. HMMs are selected for our application as being capable of handling uncertainty and modeling time series data since the statistical nature of HMM could render overall robustness to gait representation and recognition. In human behavior recognition experiments, we have conducted several important common human daily activities.

The paper is organized as follows: In section 2, we explain about mechanical structure of our system. Section 3 presents our mobile robot based human motion tracking and measurement system Section 4 presents experiments of measurement and human behavior. Section V describes human behavior recognition procedure. Section 6 demonstrates the results of our system. In section 7, we conclude our work.

2   The Mobile Robot System Used

2.1   Mobile Robot and Kinect Sensor

In this study, a pioneer-3dx robot of Adept Technology Inc, is used, and equipped with 8 ultrasound sensors in front of the mobile robot, a Kinect sensor, a controller of the Kinect sensor movement in horizontal direction using a rotating table, and a notebook computer. Fig.1 shows our mobile robot and its components. We used a hold-up tool to put the Kinect camera at high position, in order to capture the whole body of subject in near distance.

Due the advantages mentioned in the introduction, the Kinect sensor is used in this study. It has two cameras, such as color camera, and depth camera which can output 2D depth data. The Kinect sensor has its own SDK, which can extract 20 skeleton points from a detected human subject. In this study, we have used the Kinect sensor data for human motion tracking and following, and also for joint trajectory measurement.

2.2   Kinect Camera Movement Controller

In order to track and follow the subject from different viewpoints, we have put the Kinect on a rotating table structure, which is installed at the hold-up tool (Fig1.b) in order to control the movement of the Kinect camera in a horizontal direction. The Kinect sensor itself has a vertical tilt between -27 to 27 degrees (Fig1.a). Thus, the Kinect sensor is able to rotate in vertical and horizontal plane. Controller program of the rotating table has been implemented by a PID controller. Addition of the rotating table also helps to avoiding obstacles while constantly tracking and following the subject and keeping a certain distance between the subject and the robot. Fig.1.b shows the mobile robot with different faced Kinect sensor, where the Kinect sensor observes the environment with different angle on x axis (Fig.1.a).

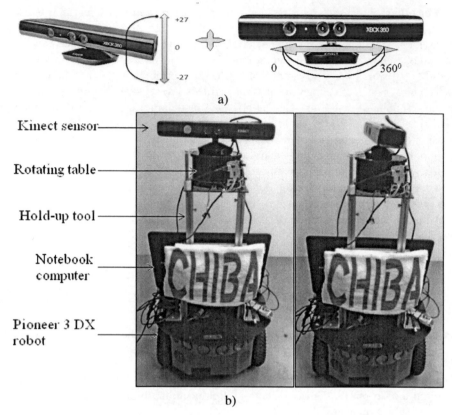

Fig. 1. a) The Kinect sensor movement, b) The mobile robot with different faced Kinect sensor

3   Human Motion Following and Joint Trajectory System

3.1   Human Motion Following

In real mobile sensing environment, human tracking and following by the mobile robot from different viewpoints is a challenging task. Because, there have been many difficulties, such as obstacles on the way of robot, keeping a certain distance between target human and the robot, and keeping the human at center of the robot vision. In this study, we developed our human motion following program using several data of the skeleton points extracted from the Kinect SDK function. Kinect sensor is capable of tracking the human within 1.2-3.5m distance. In order to get good source data, our program is developed to keep 1m distance between the mobile robot and target human. Three different types of human tracking and following by the mobile robot were developed, such as, side viewpoint, front/back viewpoint and middle angle viewpoint which is at between side viewpoint tracking and front viewpoint tracking. Our robot speed is controlled by the distance data extracted from the infrared camera of the Kinect sensor.

3.2   Joint Trajectory System

A joint trajectory measurement system based on the skeleton points is demonstrated by using Kinect SDK and color markers for body and lower limb joint angles. In order to verify the results of joint trajectory measurement system, several experiments have been done with different motion capture systems as shown in our previous work [3, 4, 5]. During measurement experiment, we have realized that the skeleton points extracted from the Kinect SDK function are not accurate regarding their position on spatial domain during the subject and the robot motion. Therefore, a new compensation algorithm has been built by using color markers attached to several joint points as in Fig.2 [3, 4]. Comparison results of color marker based algorithm with the skeleton points extracted from the Kinect SDK function are given in Fig 3 [4, 5].

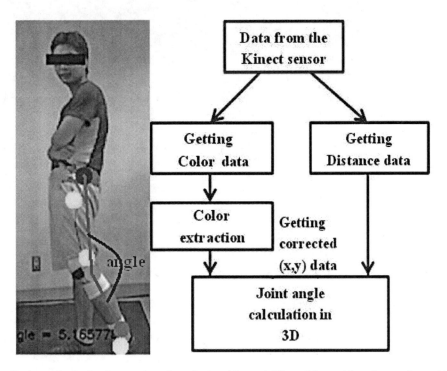

Fig. 2. A method of color markers based algorithm. a) The subject with color markers, b) Algorithm of joints angle calculation using color markers [3, 4].

In Fig.3a, red points are skeleton points extracted from the Kinect SDK function from side point tracking. In this figure, it is obvious that the skeleton points are not at correct points on the human body. Joint trajectory measurement comparison between the skeleton points extracted from the Kinect SDK function and Optitrack motion

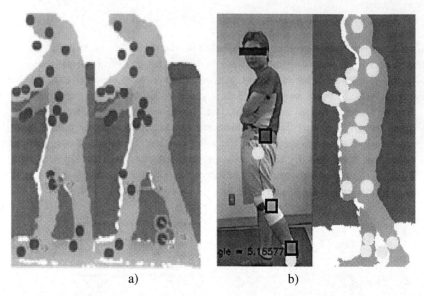

a)   b)

Fig. 3. Comparison results of color marker based algorithm with the skeleton points extracted from the Kinect SDK function [4,5]

capture system can be seen in the results section. In Fig.3a, yellow points are skeleton points from the Kinect, and blue, green, and red rectangular ones are skeleton points extracted from color markers based algorithm.

4   Experiments

In this study, two kinds of experiments have been established that were joint trajectory measurement and human behavior recognition experiment.

For measurement experiment, the performance of our joint trajectory system has been verified by joint trajectory measurements of Optitrack motion capture system, a product of NaturalPoint, Inc. the results of this experiment has revealed that our system and Optitrack motion capture system are synchronized by each other, which expresses the reliability of the extracted body and joint angles by the proposed model.

For human behavior experiment, three subjects were conducted; the objective and procedure were explained, with informed consent signed, before the experiment. The subjects were asked to do the following activities: stand, sit on the chair, walk, and impaired walking, which is artificial impairment wearing simulated hemiplegic gait in Fig.4. For impaired walking, each subject was asked to wear simulated hemiplegic gait, which gives constraints to ankle joint, on their left side leg. Table 1 shows the experimental activities and its durations. Experiments were conducted with and without treadmill.

Fig. 4. Simulated hemiplegic gait

Table 1. Experiment activities and its duration

Activities	Standing	Sitting	Walking	Impaired Walking
Trial duration for each	5 seconds	5 seconds	30 seconds	40 seconds
Number of trials	3 trials	3 trials	3 trials	2 trials

5   Human Behavior Recognition Procedure

Recently, there have been many researchers paying attention on human behavior monitoring and recognition for home healthcare. Human behavior analysis is not based on static process (not depending on only one situation), but it needs dynamic time sequences data. Hidden Markov models are especially known in temporal pattern recognition such as speech, handwriting, gesture recognition [6]. So, in this study, Hidden Markov Model (HMM) is applied for human behavior recognition based on the joint angle and body angle data.

5.1   Hidden Markov Models

Hidden Markov Model is a statistical model. In a HMM, the system being processed is considered as a Markov process, which has unknown parameters. The application of Hidden Markov Model is to discover the sequence of states using observable sequence/sequences. Our work consists of 4 different gait gesture states (S1-Standing, S2-Sitting, S3-Walking, S4-Impaired Walking) which is symbolized in Fig.5. We have selected two activities to represent static behavior as sitting and standing that are common daily activities at home. As dynamic behaviors, walking and impaired cases are selected to show they can be classified by HMM.

In order to characterize an HMM completely, following elements are necessary [6]:

➤ The number of states of the model, N=7
➤ The number of distinct observation symbols per state, M=22, both side knee and hip angle quantization data, and body angle quantization data
➤ The state transition probability distribution A={a$_{ij}$}

$$a_{ij} = P(q_t = S_j \mid q_{t-1} = S_i)$$

➤ The observation symbol probability distribution ins state j:

$$b_j(k) = P(V_k \, at \, t \mid q_t = S_j)$$

➤ The initial state distribution: $\pi_i = P(q_1 = S_i)$
➤ The model parameters notation: $\lambda = (A, B, \pi)$

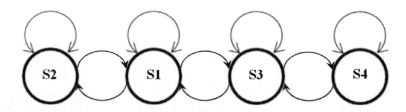

S1- Standing, S2-Sitting, S3-Walking, S4-Impaired Walking

Fig. 5. Coded gait gesture states

5.2   Calculation of Joint Angles

Calculation of joint angles has been done by color markers based algorithm (Fig.3b). In here, equations of calculating joint angles are given in three dimensional coordinates. Five different joints angles have been derived, such as both hip angles, both knee angles of the right and left sides, and body angle. Following equations are to depict the calculation of knee angle data as being one of the examples for joint angle feature extraction. Calculating the distance data between 2 certain points in 3D can be obtained as below:

$$ax = x_{hip} - x_{knee} \; ;$$

$$ay = y_{hip} - y_{knee} \; ;$$

$$az = z_{hip} - z_{knee} \; ; \tag{1}$$

$$bx = x_{knee} - x_{ankle} \; ;$$

$$by = y_{knee} - y_{ankle} \; ;$$

$$bz = z_{knee} - z_{ankle} \; ;$$

A cross product (2) and a dot product (3) functions can be employed to get the joint angle from 3 skeleton points or 2 lines data from above calculated distance data (1) in 3D dimension.

$$i = (ax*bx) + (ay*by) + (az*bz) \tag{2}$$

$$j = ((ax*ax) + (ay*ay) + (az*az))* \\ *((bx*bx) + (by*by) + (bz*bz)) \tag{3}$$

Then, the knee angle can be obtains as in (4) by using equations (2) and (3):

$$Knee\_angle = a\cos(i/\sqrt{j}) \tag{4}$$

Hip angle is calculated based on shoulder center, hip and knee joints data. In order to recognize fallen down, body angle was calculated based on shoulder center, hip center point and virtual ground points. Virtual ground point is assumed as x and z axis data same as x and z axis data of hip center and y axis data same as average y axis data of both ankle points.

5.3   Preprocessing Data

Before applying for HMM, the joint angle data were quantized by several levels. This quantization helps to recognize person pattern and make sparse representation of feature space for HMM. Every subject has their own quantization data based on their walking pattern. Table 2 shows one example of quantization of angle data with threshold value and quantization level.

Table 2. Quantization of angle data

	Threshold value	Quantization level
Knee angle	>170	1
	160-17	2
	150-160	3
	140-150	4
	120-140	5
	<120	6
Hip angle	>165	7
	125-165	8
	<125	9
Body angle	>160	10
	142-160	11
	100-142	12
	<100	13

6   Results

We developed human following algorithm, while avoiding obstacles and constantly tracking the target human in indoor environment. Human following algorithm is tracking and following from different viewpoints, such as side, front/back and middle angle viewpoints. Then, joint trajectory measurement system was done using the skeleton points extracted from the Kinect SDK function. But during measurement experiment, the skeleton points extracted are inaccurate, and not at correct position of the joints. That is why; color markers based algorithm was implemented to deal with inaccurate skeleton points. We also did experiments including color markers based algorithm, using the skeleton points extracted, and Optitrack motion capture system (10 V100:R2 cameras). Comparison results of experiments are shown in Fig.6 [3, 4].

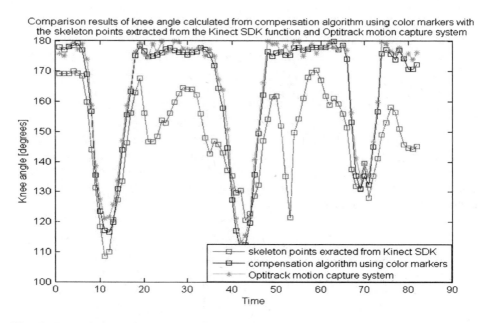

Fig. 6. Comparison results of knee angle calculated from compensation algorithm using color markers with skeleton points extracted from the Kinect SDK function and Optitrack motion capture system [3, 4]

Our compensation algorithm's result shows similar to reference motion capture system.

After implementing compensation algorithms of motion measurement system, we developed human behavior recognition process by using Hidden Markov Models based on preprocessed calculated lower limb joint and body angle data measured and recorded from side viewpoint tracking. In every subject measurement data, we selected one sequential data include all states data as training data, estimated model parameters which are the state transition probability distribution, the observation symbol probability distribution and the initial state distribution from training data.

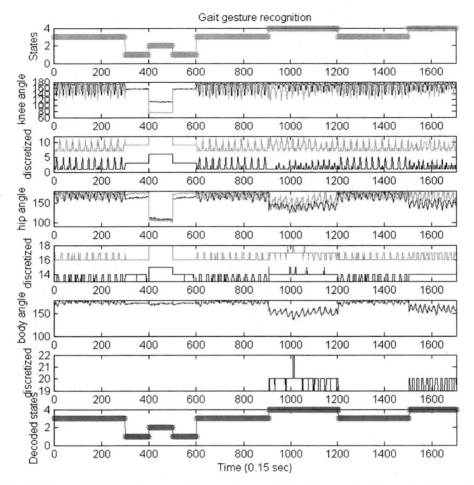

Fig. 7. Human Gait behavior recognition results. y axis is: a) knee angle b) quantized data of knee angle c) hip angle d) quantized data of hip angle e) body angle f) quantized data of body angle g) recognized states/most likely decoded states (Viterbi paths), x axis is time.

HMMs of each subject were built from one series data. Different series of joint and body angle data were performed to recognize the gait gesture using HMM and to find the most likely decoded paths (Viterbi paths).

Experiment series data of human behavior recognition process (Walking-sitting-standing-sitting-walking-impaired walking-walking) is shown in Fig 7.

In Fig.7, y axis is: a) knee angle of both legs b) quantized data of knee angle c) hip angle of both legs d) quantized data of hip angle e) body angle (calculated based on shoulder center, hip center and virtual ground points) f) quantized data of body angle g) recognized states/most likely decoded states (Viterbi paths), x axis is time. From Fig.7, we can see that recognized states are 3-1-2-1-3-4-3-4, this means walking (S3)-standing (S1)- sitting (S2)- standing (S1) - walking (S3) - impaired walking (S4)-walking (S3) states from coded gait gesture states in Fig.7. Table 3 shows the summarized results of corrected rate of gait gesture states of all subjects' data.

Table 3. Correct rate of all subjects

Subjects/ Activities	Standing	Sitting	Walking	Impaired walking
Subject-1	100.00	100.00	99.00	97.01
Subject-2	100.00	100.00	98.27	97.11
Subject-3	100.00	100.00	99.47	97.31

In table 3, human behaviour recognition is using their own HMM for their testing data sets. From here, the recognition rate is almost 97%. We can conclude from this result that HMM based human behaviour recognition, which is personalized, shows promising results.

In this paper, we want to make cross validation analysis of human behavior recognition using different subjects' HMM extracted from their training dataset, and applying for other subjects' testing datasets. Basically, static cases of activities, such as standing and sitting, were recognized by 100%, because its five joint angles were almost constant and have less variance.

But, in dynamic cases of other activities, such as walking and impaired walking, recognition rate was reduced a lot, due to that every subject has their own biometric data for their activities. Cross recognition results of dynamic activities are shown in Table 4.

Table 4. Correct rate of cross recognition

Subject for training data set	Walking	Impaired walking	Walking	Impaired walking
	For testing data set			
	Subject-2		Subject-3	
Subject-1	78.79	25.86	73.89	28.11
	Subject-1		Subject-3	
Subject-2	85.4	43.14	96.01	67.01
	Subject-1		Subject-2	
Subject-3	84.38	66.98	80.11	25.91

From here, we can see that every subject has their own patterns of walking.

This result proves that rehabilitation process and human behaviour recognition for each subject should be focused on their own data recorded and measured.

We have participated to "Evaluating Ambient Assisted Living (AAL) Systems through Competitive Benchmarking" competition in Valencia, Spain in order to test our system. Results in the competition were not so good such as in our controlled experiments. Following several factors were influenced to the results in the competition. Because we did not have training datasets of the actor and this means that we did not have actual HMM model of the actor motion. And also, there are some other things, such as the speed of the actor, actor's clothes, light conditions, and the two Kinect cameras used. Our system was aimed to develop for the impaired walking person, in actual competition; the actor was healthy young person, and moving very fast. The environment and its light conditions were different than our lab. It is influenced to our results, because our system was used color information extracted from the captured images of the Kinect camera. During competition, we did not bring our real robot, Pioneer-3DX to there, due to its transportation. We used an iRobot Create robot, a product of iRobot Corporation®, as our platform with two the Kinect cameras, of which, one was used for the subject tracking, and another was used for avoiding obstacles. Due to interference between two infrared cameras of the Kinect sensors, the distance data between the actor and the robot had some errors. It also influenced to our results in the competition.

7   Conclusion

We have developed control programs for a mobile robot to track and follow human by three different viewpoints; side viewpoint, front viewpoint and from a middle angle between side viewpoint and front viewpoint. Joint trajectory measurement system through the mobile robots in real time is proposed and implemented. And also its accuracy is investigated by comparing different motion captures system. Finally, we proposed a method of human behavior recognition from side viewpoint tracking by applying HMM based on preprocessed lower limb joint angles and body angle without any attached sensors to human body. Method of applying HMM for five joint angle motion data has high recognition rate when training data set and testing data sets are of same subjects. We did also cross recognition using different subjects' testing data sets. Cross recognition rates were low due to every subject has their own walking pattern. Behavior recognition method brings the high rate of recognition of human walking behavior using its own HMM and is effective in indoor environment.

References

[1] United Nations. World Population Prospects: The 2006 Revision population ageing. United Nations, New York (2006)
[2] Scanaill, C., Carewa, S., et al.: Review of Approaches to Mobility Telemonitoring of the Elderly in Their Living Environment. Annals of Biomedical Engineering 34(4), 547–563 (2006)
[3] Nergui, M., Yoshida, Y., Gonzalez, J., Koike, Y., Sekine, M., Yu, W.: Human Motion Tracking and Measurement by a Mobile Robot. In: ICIUS, Chiba, Japan (2011)

[4] Nergui, M., Yoshida, Y., Yu, W.: Human gait behavior interpretation by a mobile home healthcare robot. Journal of Mechanics in Medicine and Biology 12(04) (2012), doi:10.1142/S0219519412400210

[5] Nergui, M., Imamoglu, N., Yoshida, Y., Yu, W.: Human Gait Behavior Classification using HMM based on Lower Body Triangular Joint Features. In: The 14th IASTED International Conference on Signal and Image Processing, pp. 212–219. ACTA Press, Honolulu (2012)

[6] Rabiner, L.R.: A Tutorial on Hidden Markov Models and Selected Applications in Speech Recognition. Proceedings of the IEEE 77(2) (February 1989)

[7] Wang, L., Tan, T., et al.: Silhouette Analysis-Based Gait Recognition for Human Identification. IEEE Transactions on Pattern Analysis and Machine Intelligence 25(12) (December 2003)

[8] Uddin, M.Z., Kim, T.S., et al.: Video-based Human Gait Recognition Using Depth Imaging and Hidden Markov Model: A Smart System for Smart Home. In: 3rd International Symposium on Sustainable Healthy Buildings, SHB 2010, Seoul, Korea, May, 27 (2010)

[9] Rohila, N., et al.: Abnormal Gait Recognition. International Journal on Computer Science and Engineering 02(05), 1544–1551 (2010)

[10] Pushpa Rani, M., et al.: An efficient gait recognition system for human identification using modified ICA. International Journal of Computer Science & Information Technology 2(1) (February 2010)

Visual Experience for Recognising Human Activities

Na Li, Martin Crane, and Heather J. Ruskin

Centre for Scientific Computing & Complex Systems Modelling,
School of Computing, Dublin City University, Ireland
na.li@dcu.ie, {mcrane,hruskin}@computing.dcu.ie

Abstract. Technologies for Ambient Assisted Living (AAL) combine new Information and Communication Technologies (ICT) to improve and increase the quality of life of the elderly. The SenseCam visual lifelogging device is now used not only to support memory recall, but also by research groups in other fields in order to investigate human lifestyle. Recent and continuing work in Dublin City University's SCI-SYM centre has been an application and evaluation of a novel approach, namely use of the cross correlation matrix and Maximum Overlap Discrete Wavelet Transform (MODWT) to analyse SenseCam lifelog data streams. By examination of the eigenspectrum, we show that these approaches enable detection of key sources or major events in the time SenseCam recording, with MODWT also providing useful insight on details of major events. In this paper, we analyse the data collected from the EvAAL (Evaluating AAL System Through Competitive Benchmarking) competition. The results confirmed our previous findings [1, 2]. We believe that highlighting key episodes to identify event boundaries can be used to develop automatic classifiers for visual lifelogs, helping to infer different lifestyle characteristics.

Keywords: Ambient Assisted Living, SenseCam, time series methods, EvAAL competition.

1 Introduction

Recently, the numbers of elderly people in developed counties has been increasing dramatically. Ambient Assisted Living (AAL) combines new Information and Communication Technologies (ICT) with the aim of improving the quality of life and health of the older population. EvAAL is an international competition aimed at the evaluation and assessment of Ambient Assisted Living systems, components, services and platforms[1]. In order to evaluate each competing system, the EvAAL competition applies a set of evaluation criteria such as performance, user acceptance, recognition delay, installation complexity and integrability to AAL systems in order to evaluate and rank AAL applications [3]. In EvAAL 2012, Dublin City University (SCI-SYM) centre used the SenseCam lifelog device to

---

[1] http://evaal.aaloa.org

S. Chessa and S. Knauth (Eds.): EvAAL 2012, CCIS 362, pp. 173–185, 2013.

track activity and recognition in the competition scenario. In this paper, we introduce a time series approach to analyse and evaluate the SenseCam lifelog data, collected for the EvAAL competition.

Developed by Microsoft Research in Cambridge, UK, SenseCam [4] is a small, wearable camera that, along with other sensor data recorded, takes images automatically, in order to document the events of the user's day. It can be periodically reviewed by the user to refresh and strengthen memory of an event. Besides a camera, the SenseCam also contains several electronic sensors. including those which record light-intensity and light-colour, a passive infrared (body heat) detector, a temperature sensor, and a multiple-axis accelerometer for monitoring changes in movement in the X, Y, Z directions of the user's environment. The device takes pictures at VGA resolution, (480x640 pixels), and stores these as compressed JPEG files on internal flash memory (1Gb). It can collect a large amount of data, even over a short period of time. Since SenseCam typically takes a picture every 30 seconds, thousands of images are captured per day. Experience shows that the SenseCam can be an effective memory-aid device [5, 6], as it helps users to improve retention of an experience. SenseCam is now used to support not only memory recall, but also by research groups [7] in other fields to investigate human lifestyle. The challenge is to manage, organize and analyse these large image collections in order to automatically highlight *key episodes* in the wearer's life.

In terms of this analysis, we note that in recent years, the role of the largest Eigenvalue of a cross-correlation matrix over small windows of time, has been studied extensively, e.g. for financial series [8–11], electroencephalographic (EEG) recordings [12, 13], magnetoencephalographic (MEG) recordings [14] and a variety of other multivariate data. In this paper, we apply the same approach to analyse SenseCam lifelog data streams. We aim to apply the multiscaled cross-correlation matrix technique to study the dynamics of the SenseCam images, where this time series should exhibit *atypical* or *non-stationary* characteristics, symptomatic of "Distinct Significant Events" in the data. We can use such highlighted *key episodes* to identify the boundaries between different daily events. These might include the wearer working in the office, walking outside, shopping etc. We found that different distinct events or activities can be detected at different scales [1, 2]. In this context, we expected analysis of data collected from EvAAL to confirm previous findings.

This paper is organized as follow: in Section 2, we review the methods to be used in the paper, in Section 3 we describe the data used, while Section 4 details the results obtained. Finally the conclusion is followed by details of future work to be preformed.

2   Methods

Our previous research [1] has shown that SenseCam image time series reflect strong *long-range correlation*, indicating that the time series is not a random walk[2], but is cyclical, with continuous low levels of background information

---

[2] A random walk is a mathematical formalization of a path that consists of a succession of random steps.

picked up constantly by the device. In this section, we first use equal-time cross-Correlation Matrices to characterise dynamical changes in non-stationary multivariate SenseCam time-series. The Maximum Overlap Discrete Wavelet Transform (MODWT) is then used to calculate equal-time Correlation Matrices over different time scales. This enables exploration of details of the Eigenvalue spectrum and in particular, examination of whether specific events show evidence of distinct *signatures* at different time scales.

2.1   Correlation Dynamics

The equal-time cross-correlation matrix can be used to characterise dynamical changes in non-stationary multivariate time series.

Given pixels $G_i(t)$, of a collection of images, we normalize G_i within each window in order to standardize the different pixels for the images as follows:

$$g_i(t) = \frac{G_i(t) - \overline{G_i(t)}}{\sigma_{(i)}} \tag{1}$$

where $\sigma_{(i)}$ is the standard deviation of G_i for image numbers $i=1,...,N$, and $\overline{G_i}$ is the time average of G_i over a time window of size T. Then the equal-time cross-correlation matrix may be expressed in terms of $g_i(t)$

$$C_{ij} \equiv \langle g_i(t)g_j(t) \rangle \tag{2}$$

The elements of C_{ij} are limited to the domain $-1 \leq C_{ij} \leq 1$, where $C_{ij} = 1$ defines perfect positive correlation, $C_{ij} = -1$ corresponds to perfect negative correlation and $C_{ij} = 0$ corresponds to no correlation. In matrix notation, the correlation matrix is expressed as $C = \frac{1}{T}GG^t$, where G is an $N \times T$ matrix with elements g_{it}.

The Eigenvalues λ_i and eigenvectors $\overline{v}_i$ of the correlation matrix C are found from the Eigenvalue equation $C\overline{v}_i = \lambda_i\overline{v}_i$ and then ordered according to size, such that $\lambda_1 \leq \lambda_2 \leq ... \leq \lambda_N$. Given that the sum of the diagonal elements of a matrix (the Trace) remains constant under linear transformation, $\sum_i \lambda_i$ must always equal the trace of the original correlation matrix. Hence, if some eigenvalues increase then others must decrease, to compensate, and vice versa (*Eigenvalue Repulsion*).

2.2   Wavelet Multiscale Analysis

The Maximum Overlap Discrete Wavelet Transform (MODWT) [15–18], is a linear filter that transforms a series into coefficients related to variations over a set of scales. It produces a set of time-dependent wavelet and scaling coefficients with basis vectors associated with a location t and a unitless scale $\tau_j = 2^{j-1}$ for each decomposition level $j=1,...,J_0$. Unlike the DWT, the MODWT, has a high level of redundancy. However, it is *non-orthogonal* and can handle any sample size N, whereas the DWT restricts the sample size to a multiple of 2^j. MODWT retains downsampled[3] values at each level of the decomposition that would be discarded by the DWT. This reduces the tendency for larger errors at lower frequencies when calculating frequency dependent variance and correlations, as more data are available.

Decomposing a signal, using the MODWT to J levels, theoretically involves the application of J pairs of filters. The filtering operation at the jth level consists of applying a rescaled father wavelet to yield a set of detail coefficients

$$\tilde{D}_{j,t} = \sum_{l=0}^{L_j-1} \tilde{\varphi}_{j,l} f_{t-l} \tag{3}$$

and a rescaled mother wavelet to yield a set of scaling coefficients

$$\tilde{S}_{j,t} = \sum_{l=0}^{L_j-1} \tilde{\phi}_{j,l} f_{t-l} \tag{4}$$

for all times $t = ..., -1, 0, 1, ...$, where f is the function to be decomposed [19]. The rescaled mother, $\tilde{\varphi}_{j,t} = \frac{\varphi_{j,t}}{2^j}$, and father, $\tilde{\phi}_{j,t} = \frac{\varphi_{j,t}}{2^j}$, wavelets for the jth level are a set of scale-dependent localized differencing and averaging operators and can be regarded as rescaled versions of the originals.

The wavelet variance $\nu_f^2(\tau_j)$ is defined as the expected value of $\tilde{D}_{j,t}^2$ if we consider only the non-boundary coefficients. An unbiased estimator of the wavelet variance is formed by removing all coefficients that are affected by boundary conditions and is given by

$$\nu_f^2(\tau_j) = \frac{1}{M_j} \sum_{t=L_j-1}^{N-1} \tilde{D}_{j,l}^2 \tag{5}$$

where $\tilde{D}_{j,l}$ is a rescaled father wavelet, which yields a set of scaling coefficients, $M_j = N - L_j + 1$ is the number of non-boundary coefficients at the jth level.

The wavelet covariance between functions $f(t)$ and $g(t)$ is similarly defined to be the covariance of the wavelet coefficients at a given scale. The unbiased estimator of the wavelet covariance at the jth scale is given by

$$\nu_{fg}(\tau_j) = \frac{1}{M_j} \sum_{t=L_j-1}^{N-1} \tilde{D}_{j,l}^{f(t)} \tilde{D}_{j,l}^{g(t)} \tag{6}$$

The MODWT estimate of the wavelet cross-correlation between functions $f(t)$ and $g(t)$ may be calculated using the wavelet covariance and the square root of the wavelet variance of the functions at each scale j. The MODWT estimator, of the wavelet correlation is thus given by

$$\rho_{fg}(\tau_j) = \frac{\nu_{fg}(\tau_j)}{\nu_f(\tau_j)\nu_g(\tau_j)} \tag{7}$$

---

[3] Downsampling or decimation of the wavelet coefficients retains half of the number of coefficients that were retained at the previous scale. Downsampling is applied in the Discrete Wavelet Transform.

where $\nu_{fg}(\tau_j)$ is the covariance between $f(t)$ and $g(t)$ at scale j, $\nu_f(\tau_j)$ is the variance of $f(t)$ at scale j and $\nu_g(\tau_j)$ is the variance of $g(t)$ at scale j.

The multiscaled cross-correlation matrix technique is adopted in order to help highlight non-stationary events at various different granularities (in SenseCam lifelog data streams), which could be of importance.

3   Data

In this study, the data were generated from the EvAAL competition. In 2012 EvAAL, the activity recognition track took place in CIAmI Living Lab located on the industrial park, Valencia, Spain. The CIAmI Living Lab is an approximately $90\ m^2$ infrastructure that simulates the real environment of a citizen's home combined with provision of Information and Communication Technologies (ICT) massively distributed across the physical space, but as invisible as possible to the people occupying it as shown (Figure 1). In this work, the data are collected by one user (the actor), wearing the SenseCam over two experiments. Total duration of collection was approximately 13 minutes, forming a total lifelog collection of 66 images, with average capture time of 5 images per minute. As the data capture time was limited, the SenseCam camera capture rate was changed in order to generate as many images as possible during the competition. Figure 2 shows some examples of SenseCam images.

4   Results

4.1   Eigenvalue Dynamics

From our previous studies [1, 2], we selected the least asymmetric (LA) wavelet, (known as the Symmlet, [19]), which exhibits near symmetry about the filter midpoint. LA filters are defined in even widths and the optimal filter width is dependent on the characteristics of the signal and the length of the data series. The jth level equivalent filter coefficients have a width $L_j = (2^j - 1)(L - 1) + 1$, where L is the width of the $j = 1$ base filter. In practice the filters for $j > 1$ are not explicitly constructed because the detail and scaling coefficients can be calculated, using an algorithm that involves the $j = 1$ filters operating recurrently on the jth level scaling coefficients, to generate the $j + 1$ level scaling and detail coefficients [20]. The filter width chosen for this study was the Haar[4], since this enables accurate calculation of wavelet correlations to the 5th scale, which is appropriate given the length of data series available. Although the MODWT can accommodate any level, J_0, the largest level, is chosen in practice, so as to prevent decomposition at scales longer than the total length of the data series, hence the choice of the 5th[20], while still containing enough detail to capture subtle changes in the signal.

---

[4] The jth level equivalent filter coefficients have a width 2^j.

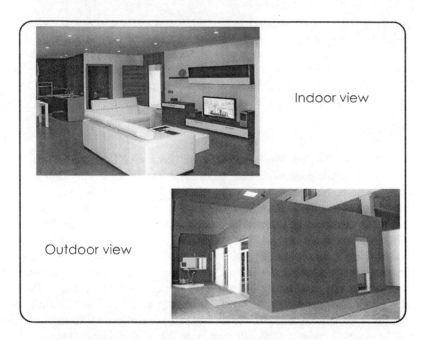

Fig. 1. Indoor and outdoor views of the CIAmI Living Lab

Fig. 2. Example of SenseCam Images

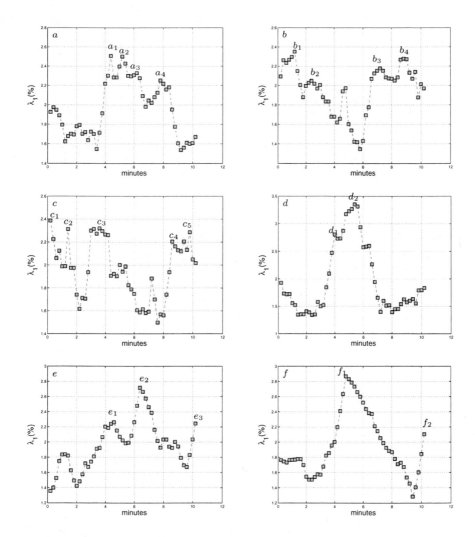

Fig. 3. (a) The Largest Eigenvalue λ_1 dynamics for original data, (b) 30 seconds scale, (c) 1 minute scale, (d) 1.5 minutes, (e) 3 minutes and (f) 6.5 minutes

Table 1. Activity Trait Analysis

Activities	Wavelet Scales
From Outdoor to Indoor	$a_1 \& e_1 \& f_1$
From Standing to Lying	$a_2 \& d_2$
From Bending to Walking	$a_3 \& e_2$
From Walking to Sitting	$b_1 \& c_2$
From Indoor to Outdoor	$b_4 \& c_4$
From Falling to Standing up	$c_3 \& d_1$

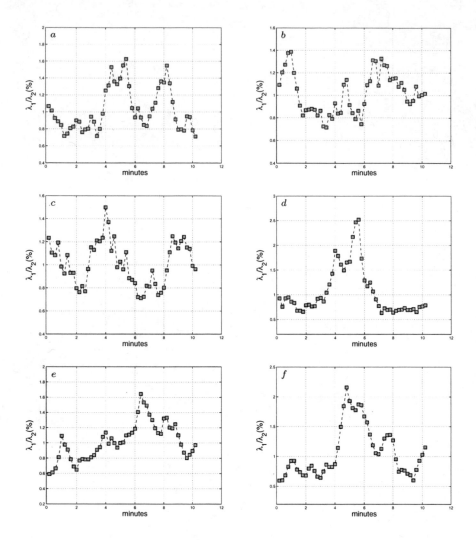

Fig. 4. (a) The ratio of λ_1/λ_2 dynamics for original data, (b) 30 seconds scale, (c) 1 minute scale, (d) 1.5 minutes, (e) 3 minutes and (f) 6.5 minutes

Before examining the image time series in detail, it is important to introduce the *gray scale pixel values* concept. In a gray scale image, a pixel with a value of 0 is completely black and a pixel with a value of 255 is completely white. The images captured from SenseCam are coloured and in order to simplify the calculation, the images are converted to gray-scale images.

To reduce the size of the calculation, we first adopted an averaging method to decrease image size from 480x640 pixels to 3x4 pixels. We analysed the equal-time cross-correlation dynamics between each images pixels using a sliding window of 12 images. This window was chosen such that $Q = \frac{T}{N} = 1.25$, thus

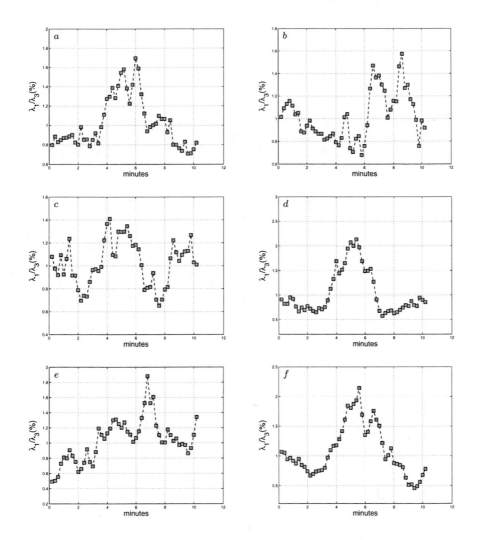

Fig. 5. (a) The ratio of λ_1/λ_3 dynamics for original data, (b) 30 seconds scale, (c) 1 minute scale, (d) 1.5 minutes, (e) 3 minutes and (f) 6.5 minutes

ensuring that the data would be close to non-stationary in each sliding wind: (different values of Q were examined, with little variation in the results). First, the MODWT of each image's pixels was calculated within each window and the correlation matrix between pixels at each scale found. The eigenvalues of the correlation matrix in each window were determined, and eigenvalue time series were normalised in time. During the experiment, SenseCam captured five images every minute, so we can measure wavelet eigenvalue dynamics in time (minutes). These results are shown in Figure 3 and discussed below.

Eigenvalue Dynamics at Various Wavelet Scales. In financial data, it has been known for some time that the largest eigenvalue (λ_1) contains information on risk associated with the particular assets of which the covariance matrix is comprised, (i.e. the 'market' factor) [20, 21]. Similarly we would expect the largest eigenvalue here to present information from the image that reflects the largest change in the SenseCam recording. We also wish to ascertain whether the sub-dominant eigenvalues λ_2, λ_3, etc hold further information on the key sources or major events and what information these contribute in addition λ_1 to the images. The dynamics of the largest eigenvalue and changes of ratio eigenvalues were examined by the MODWT analysis.

We have studied the largest eigenvalue λ_1 time series for a window size of 12 images to try to identify the position and nature of peak sources or major events from the real images generated from SenseCam.

In Figure 3, the dynamics of the series for the largest eigenvalue were examined from the MODWT analysis. The technique gives a clear picture of the movements in the image time series by reconstructing them using each wavelet component. The MODWT captured the particular features markedly apparent at specified scales. A number of features from the image are reproduced and can be examined by studying these eigenvalue series. Table 1 shows the different features found at various scales, suggesting that the correlation matrix captured different major events with different time horizons. For example, the user moving from walking to sitting in the living room. When the user is sitting at the table, the camera captures the light on the ceiling. Thus, the lights and unchanged 'seated position' contribute higher pixel values in these sequences of images. These changes are captured by wavelet scale 1, 2 (peaks b_1 & c_2) and correspond to a 30 seconds and 1 minute period. These peaks at different (representative) timescale(s) should help us to identify major events or activities in the data. By examining the dynamics of the largest eigenvalue, we can see that changes in lights, strong sunshine and the subject seating position unchanged over an extended period, contribute to high pixel values in a sequence of images. This confirmed our previous findings. This typical case was always marked by a peak in the SenseCam signal. Similarly it can be seen that the other major events in Table 1 correspond to eigenvalue signal fluctuations visible elsewhere in Figure 3, for example the subject moving from indoors to outdoors, changing light levels, the subject changing position from sitting to moving, movement increase etc.

Above, we have shown that the largest eigenvalue λ_1 contains information on major events captured by the SenseCam. Here, we wish to ascertain whether the subdominant eigenvalues (λ_2, λ_3) hold further information on the key sources or major events and this information contributes additionally to the images. For Figure 4 and 5, we see the λ_2 and λ_3 have some variations compared with Figure 3. This would seem to imply that the second and third largest eigenvalue carry additional information to describe the images, but both eigenvalues do not contribute in large part to the major events for SenseCam, but do appear to carry information for events surrounding the major ones, e.g. possible lead-in, lead-out [2].

5   Conclusions and Future Work

In this paper, we employed initially a time series method in order to highlight *key episodes* in identification of the boundaries on classification of event type in Sense-Cam data streams. The Maximum Overlap Discrete Wavelet Transform (MODWT), involving calculation of equal-time correlation matrices over different time scales, was used to investigate the largest eigenvalue and the changes in the sub-dominant eigenvalue ratio spectrums, (Figure 3, with the different features, found at various scales, shown in Table 1). This suggests that the correlation matrix for different information captured by the SenseCam can be filtered by different time horizons. These consistently occurring peaks should help us to identify major events captured by the SenseCam. By examining the behaviour of the largest eigenvalue and the change in the eigenvalue ratios over time, the eigenvalue ratio analysis confirmed that the largest eigenvalue carries most of the major event information, whereas subsequent eigenvalues could carry information on supporting or lead in/ lead out events. On analysing major events, (with a sliding window set to 12 images), we identified light level as an important event delineator during static periods of image sequence. It is possible to identify the time series fluctuation caused by single type change, e.g. with the environment mostly constant, but with the subject movement increased. It is also possible to confirm that the largest time series effects are due to 'grouped' or combined changes, e.g. when the subject's environment is totally changed including light level, introduction of other people and so on. The change in eigenvalue ratios obtained using MODWT provides results in good agreement with those found for the largest eigenvalues. This indicates that the MODWT method may prove a powerful tool for examination of the layered nature of the captured SenseCam data at different time scales. Although the data sets, generated from EvAAL competition were quite limited, some confirmation of our initial findings was obtained, only with a far more challenging dataset; over all the length of the datastream collected during the EvAAL competition did not permit the extent of multiresolution analysis possible for our earlier work [1, 2] was obtained.

In future, investigation of the value of other data sources towards activity recognition would be indicated. The accelerometer could be as an important option in this respect, as has been shown in [22, 23]. Motion of the SenseCam is calculated using the 3-axis accelerometer data captured by the device. By analysing acceleration data, we can easily combine contributions from the three different axes by using standard algebra ($\sqrt{X^2 + Y^2 + Z^2}$). Inference of contextual information about common daily activities such as sitting, walking, driving and lying should then be possible from these data also. The combination of the accelerometer and image sensor datastreams together may enable more accurate event boundary identification for life logging data. Larger values for movement indicate that the associated image is quite likely to represent a boundary between different events or activities such as walking from home to work, walking from the office to lunch, walking from home to the shops, etc. So that combining sensor information may help to classify

SenseCam images into more meaningful activities. Possible methods include employing such different algorithms as SVM (Support Vector Machines) for example. Activity recognition is a core requirement for Ambient Assisted Living systems.

Acknowledgements. NL would like to acknowledge generous support from the Sci-Sym Centre Small Scale Research Fund.

References

1. Li, N., Crane, M., Ruskin, H.J.: Automatically detecting "significant events" on sensecam. ERCIM News 87 (2011)
2. Li, N., Crane, M., Ruskin, H.J., Gurrin, C.: Multiscaled Cross-Correlation Dynamics on SenseCam Lifelogged Images. In: Li, S., El Saddik, A., Wang, M., Mei, T., Sebe, N., Yan, S., Hong, R., Gurrin, C. (eds.) MMM 2013, Part I. LNCS, vol. 7732, pp. 490–501. Springer, Heidelberg (2013)
3. Chessa, S., Furfari, F., Potorti, F., Barsocchi, P., Tazari, M.-R., Wichert, R.: Evaluating AAL System Through competitive Benchmarking (EvAAL) - Technical Aspects of The First Competition Partnerships for Social Innovation in Europe, Proceedings of the AAL Forum, 617-623 (2011)
4. Hodges, S., Williams, L., Berry, E., Izadi, S., Srinivasan, J., Butler, A., Smyth, G., Kapur, N., Wood, K.: SenseCam: A Retrospective Memory Aid. In: Dourish, P., Friday, A. (eds.) UbiComp 2006. LNCS, vol. 4206, pp. 177–193. Springer, Heidelberg (2006)
5. Harper, R., Randall, D., Smyth, N., Evans, C., Heledd, L., Moore, R.: Thanks for the Memory. In: HCI 2007- Proceedings of the 21st BCS HCI Group Conference, Lancaster, U.K., pp. 39–42 (2007)
6. Harper, R., Randall, D., Smyth, N., Evans, C., Heledd, L., Moore, R.: The Past is a Different Place: They Do Things Differently There. In: Designing Interactive Systems, Cape Town, South Africa, pp. 271–280 (2008)
7. Doherty, A.R., Smeaton, A.F.: Automatically segmenting lifelog data into events. In: WIAMIS: 9th International Workshop on Images Analysis for Multimedia Interactive Services, pp. 20–23. IEEE Computer Society, Washington, DC (2008)
8. Plerou, V., Gopikrishnan, P., Rosenow, B., Nunes Amaral, L.A., Stanley, H.E.: Universal and non-uiversal properties of cross-correlations in financial time series. Phys. Rev. Lett. 83(7), 1471–1474 (1999)
9. Sharifi, S., Crane, M., Shamie, A., Ruskin, H.J.: Random matrix theory for portfolio optimization: A stability approach. Physica A 335(3-4), 629–643 (2004)
10. Conlon, T., Ruskin, H.J., Crane, M.: Random matrix theory and fund of funds portfolio optimisation. Physica A 382(2), 565–576 (2007)
11. Conlon, T., Ruskin, H.J., Crane, M.: Wavelet multiscale analysis for Hedge Funds: Scaling and Strategies. Physica A, 5197–5204 (2008)
12. Schindler, K., Leung, H., Elger, C.E., Lehnertz, K.: Assessing seizure dynamics by analysing the correlation structure of multichannel intracranial EEG. Brain 130, 65–77 (2007)
13. Schindler, K., Elger, C.E., Lehnertz, K.: Increasing synchronization may promote seizure termination: Evidence from status epilepticus. Clin., Neurophysiol. 118(9), 1955–1968 (2007)

14. Kwapien, J., Drozda, S., Ionannides, A.A.: Temporal correlations versus noise in the correlation matrix formalism: An example of the brain auditory response. Phys. Rev. E 62, 5557–5564 (2000)
15. Peng, C.-K., Buldyrev, S.V., Havlin, S., Simons, M., Stanley, H.E., Golderberger, A.L.: On the mosaic organization of DNA sequences. Phys. Rev. E 49, 1685–1689 (1994)
16. Matos, J.A.O., Gama, S.M.A., Ruskin, H.J., Sharkasi, A.A., Crane, M.: An econophysics approach to the Portuguese Stock Index-PSI-20. Physica A 342, 665–676 (2004)
17. Buldyrev, S.V., Goldberger, A.L., Havlin, S., Mantegna, R.N., Matsa, M.E., Peng, C.-K., Simons, M., Stanley, H.E.: Long-range correlation properties of coding and noncoding DNA sequences: GenBank analysis. Phys. Rev. E 51, 5084–5091 (1995)
18. Heneghan, C., McDarby, G.: Establishing the relation between detrended fluctuation analysis and power spectral density analysis for stochastic processes. Phys. Rev. E 62, 6103–6110 (2000)
19. Burrus, C.S., Gopinath, R.A., Gao, H.: Introduction to wavelets and wavelets transforms. Prentice Hall (1997)
20. Percival, D.B., Walden, A.T.: Wavelet methods for time series analysis. Cambridge University press (2000)
21. Sharkasi, A., Crane, M., Ruskin, H.J., Matos, J.A.: The reaction of stock markets to crashes and events: A comparison study between emerging and mature markets using wavelet transforms. Physica A 368, 511–521 (2006)
22. O Conaire, C., O'Connor, N., Smeaton, A.F., Jones, G.J.F.: Organising a Daily Visual Diary Using Multi-Feature Clustering. In: SPIE Electronic Imaging- Multimedia Content Access: Algorithms and Systems, San Jose, California, USA (2007)
23. Doherty, A.R., Smeaton, A.F., Keansub, L., Daniel, E.: Multimodal segmentation of lifelog data. In: RIAO 2007 - Large-Scale Semantic Access to Content (Text, Image, Video and Sound), Pittsburgh, PA, USA, May, 30-June 1, pp. 21–38 (2007)

Author Index

CPSIA information can be obtained at www.ICGtesting.com
Printed in the USA
LVOW070502170413

329518LV00003B/108/P